BEHIND THE MASK

||||||| **RANDI DRUZIN** |||||||

BEHIND THE MASK

||||||||||||||||||||||||||||||||||||||||||

A Revealing Look at Twelve of the Greatest Goalies in Hockey History

||||||||||||||||||||||||||||||||||||||||||||

GREYSTONE BOOKS

Vancouver/Berkeley/London

Greystone Books Ltd.
greystonebooks.com

Cataloguing data available from Library and Archives Canada
ISBN 978-1-77164-963-6 (cloth)
ISBN 978-1-77164-964-3 (epub)

Editing by Brian Lynch
Copy editing by Derek Fairbridge
Proofreading by Meg Yamamoto
Jacket design by Jessica Sullivan and Fiona Siu
Text design by Fiona Siu
Jacket photograph by Len Redkoles/Getty Images
Printed and bound in Canada on FSC® certified paper at Friesens. The FSC® label means that materials used for the product have been responsibly sourced.

Greystone Books thanks the Canada Council for the Arts, the British Columbia Arts Council, the Province of British Columbia through the Book Publishing Tax Credit, and the Government of Canada for supporting our publishing activities.

Canadä

Greystone Books gratefully acknowledges the xʷməθkʷəy̓əm (Musqueam), Sḵwx̱wú7mesh (Squamish), and səlilwətaɬ (Tsleil-Waututh) peoples on whose land our Vancouver head office is located.

To my father, Numero Uno now and forever

CONTENTS

||||||||||||||||||||||||||||||||||||||||||||||

Marc-André Fleury heads to his hometown
with his prized possession, in 2017.

AUTHOR'S NOTE

||||||||||||||||||||||||||||||

THE INFORMATION IN *Behind the Mask* is gleaned from dozens of sources, including books, newspapers, magazines, websites and television broadcasts. You will find full citations for quotes from those sources in the endnotes. Other quotes are taken from my own interviews. There are no citations for those quotes or for those taken from public appearances such as press conferences.

A goalie's overall rank in three statistical categories (games, wins, shutouts) is indicated in a table at the end of his chapter. In every case, the ranking is not determined by numbers alone but by how that goalie stacks up against others. For example, Roberto Luongo recorded 77 regular-season shutouts in his career. As of April 2023, that was the seventh-highest total in NHL history. But because three goalies had posted 81 shutouts, eight goalies had more shutouts than Luongo and he was ranked ninth overall.

THE NERVOUS WRECK
ROGER CROZIER

||||||||||||||||||||||||||||||

JUST FOUR YEARS after making his NHL debut, Roger Crozier retired. He left the Detroit Red Wings in November 1967 and retreated to his hometown, in Ontario. He found work as a carpenter and soon wielded, in his own estimation, "the fastest hammer in the north." For the first time in years, he was in good health.[1]

A teammate headed to Bracebridge, located 123 miles north of Toronto, where he found Crozier pounding shingles onto the roof of a house. But he wasn't able to convince the goalie to return to the ice. "If I bend a nail up here, I don't have 12,000 people booing me!" Crozier explained.[2]

He unfastened his tool belt and rejoined the Red Wings six weeks later. But he continued to suffer from ulcers and bouts of pancreatitis, even while making headlines with his acrobatic performances.

By the time he retired for good in 1977, he had established himself as one of the best goalies of his era—a remarkable accomplishment, especially for someone who was a bundle of nerves from his first game to his last.

CROZIER WAS born in March 1942 and raised in a working-class family. He was the fourth of 14 children—yes, you read that right, 14—in a family headed by Lloyd and Mildred Crozier.

Crozier, seen here in December 1963, was fearless on the ice but far from unflappable. **MICHAEL BURNS SR./HOCKEY HALL OF FAME**

No sooner had he learned to walk than he took his first tentative steps on the ice. Crozier started playing goal when he was seven years old, primarily because he was small, but he soon grew to like it.

When Crozier was 13 years old, a coach with a keen eye realized that the young goaltender, unlike most, was more comfortable catching with his right hand than his left, so he bought the boy a catching glove he could actually use—and it worked wonders.

A year later, the head of the town's senior hockey team, the Bracebridge Bears, recognized the nimble goalie as a special talent and added him to their roster. Even though Crozier was just 14 years old, he excelled playing alongside others who were, you know, old enough to shave.

Crozier grew a few inches, though not many, in the next few years and was good enough to play in the Ontario Hockey

Association (OHA), a major junior league that served as a breeding ground for NHL players.

In the fall of 1959, he traveled 175 miles south to join the St. Catharines Teepees, which were sponsored by the Chicago Black Hawks. Crozier was a standout playing with future NHL stars such as Chico Maki and Vic Hadfield, and the fleet-footed young goalie helped the Teepees win the Memorial Cup in his first season.

Crozier also developed an ulcer around this time, but the pain didn't affect his play. He continued to excel and caught the attention of the Buffalo Bisons of the minor-pro American Hockey League (AHL), who needed a goalie to fill in for their injured starter. Crozier played three games for the team in the 1960–61 season, recording two wins, before rejoining the Teepees.

Over the next two seasons, Crozier played a handful of games for the Bisons and the Sault Ste. Marie Thunderbirds of the minor-pro Eastern Professional Hockey League (EPHL). But he spent most of his time with the Teepees and then with the St. Louis Braves of the EPHL.

In June 1963, the Black Hawks traded his rights to the Detroit Red Wings, who sent the goalie to their AHL team, the Pittsburgh Hornets. In the Steel City, Crozier adopted an unconventional playing style. His coaches urged him to face the puck standing up, but he preferred to make saves on his knees with his legs extended like the beating wings of a monarch butterfly—and it worked for him. He emerged as one of the best players in the AHL.

Still, scouts weren't convinced he could play in the NHL; he was only five foot eight and weighed less than 160 pounds. That was uncommon then and is unheard of today—the average NHL goalie is seven inches taller and 40 pounds heavier.

NHL

1963-64

Crozier got a break when the Red Wings' star goalie, Terry Sawchuk, got injured. Crozier made his NHL debut in November at Maple Leaf Gardens. Detroit was leading 1-0 when Toronto forward Frank Mahovlich fired a shot that struck Crozier in the face, shattering his cheekbone. One eloquent sportswriter noted that Crozier's face was "mashed like chicken fricassee." The goalie left the ice for treatment but soon returned wearing a new contraption meant to keep his cheekbones intact and his teeth in his mouth. It was called—wait for it—a *mask*. He made 23 saves in that game, which ended in a 1–1 tie.[3]

Sawchuk soon returned to the ice, but Crozier was back in net for a game against Chicago in December. He played well in the contest, which Detroit won 5–4, but he felt he would have played better had he not been wearing a mask early in the game. "That was a bad move on my part," he said, explaining that he had worn it, despite his misgivings, because his doctor had said another shot to the cheek would sideline him for the season.[4]

By the time the season ended, Crozier had played in 15 regular games and three playoff games for the Red Wings, including the seventh and deciding game of a semifinal against the Black Hawks. In that contest, he took over from Sawchuk, who was nursing a sore shoulder, in the third period. He stopped all seven shots he faced. Detroit won 4–2 and advanced to the final against the Leafs, who won the Stanley Cup.

When he wasn't with the Red Wings that season, Crozier was honing his skills in the AHL. He played 44 games for the Hornets, winning 30 of them. That spring, he won the Hap Holmes Memorial Award, given to the goalie with the league's lowest goals-against average, and was named the AHL's best rookie.

The Red Wings managed to look beyond his diminutive size—literally and figuratively—and decided the 22-year-old would be their starter. They left Sawchuk, who was 12 years older and nearing the end of his legendary career, unprotected in the intra-league draft in June. The Leafs claimed him.

"It was a big boost for me to know the job in Detroit was mine and all mine," Crozier said years later. "If Terry had still been on the team, I would have been on the spot every game. The fans would just have been waiting for me to make a mistake and demanding his return."[5]

1964-65

Detroit's decision baffled some people in hockey circles. Critics looked at Crozier flopping on the ice like a smallmouth bass on a dock in Lake Muskoka and predicted disaster for the Red Wings. Jacques Plante, the high priest of goaltending, said Crozier would never make it in the NHL.

"One look at pale, self-conscious Roger Crozier when he is not in the nets would convince almost anybody that Plante was right," one journalist wrote. "He is small and wispy, filled with doubts about his ability, and he even has an ulcer. He is the despair of coaches who try in vain to cure him of the habit of flopping and falling all over the ice, often in attempts to stop shots that would probably never reach the goal anyway."

The journalist noted that criticism upset Crozier and that his eyes "seemed almost to brim with tears" when discussing it. "People are sitting around, waiting for the big collapse," he quoted Crozier as saying. "They're waiting to say, 'I told you so.'"[6]

Popular sports columnist Dick Beddoes described Crozier as "a splinter of bone and shred of gristle who resembles a dissipated jockey," and said he played "like a frenzied acrobat plagued with itch." Huh?[7]

But Red Wings coach Sid Abel was confident the franchise had made the right choice, and he praised Crozier for having "the fastest hands of any goalie I have ever seen."[8]

Abel was rewarded for his faith in Crozier. By mid-November, the goalie had the best goals-against average (1.75) in the NHL. Thanks to his performance and that of star forward Gordie Howe, who poked fun at the pint-sized goalie by calling him "Muscles," the Red Wings sat atop the standings. "I'm glad we got off to such a good start," Crozier said. "If we hadn't, everybody would be on my back."[9]

But the good times didn't last. Two months later, the team was in a slump and sitting fourth in the six-team league. Abel decided that Crozier needed a break and dispatched him to Florida. He and his wife, Arlene, stayed in Miami, where they lounged on beach chairs, went swimming and played shuffle-board. "I just put on the sun tan oil and relaxed," he said. "I felt as though I didn't have a care in the world." He returned to Detroit for the team's next game, to find sun lamps and a beach umbrella set up in the dressing room, compliments of his teammates.[10]

In the following months, the Red Wings got their groove back and climbed up the standings. They ended the regular season in first place with 87 points. Much of the credit went to three hotshots: Norm Ullman finished second in league scoring (83 points), while Howe finished third (76 points) and Alex Delvecchio placed fifth (67 points). But Crozier was the toast of Motown.

He started in all 70 of his team's games that season—the last NHL goalie to accomplish that feat—and led the league in wins (40) and shutouts (6). He also had the second-best goals-against average (2.42), behind the Leafs' Johnny Bower. To no one's surprise, Crozier won the Calder Trophy as the NHL's top rookie.

Sportswriters marveled at his abilities that season—one stated that "his acrobatic movements were a thing of pure delight. On many plays around his goal crease, Crozier would be flat on the ice, his legs and arms flapping to reach the puck or cover as much space as possible."[11]

He was riding high when the team opened the playoffs against Chicago. The Black Hawks' roster included two of the NHL's top offensive threats: Stan Mikita, who led the league in scoring (87 points), and Bobby Hull, who placed fourth (71 points). Known as the Golden Jet, Hull took flight in the seven-game series, scoring eight goals and adding five assists to lead his team to victory. Crozier posted a 3.29 goals-against average in that semifinal.

The season was over for him, but his health woes weren't. A few months later, he suffered a bout of pancreatitis, which is inflammation of—you guessed it—the pancreas. The chronic ailment worsened until he had to be hospitalized. He was fed intravenously and lost almost 20 pounds.

1965-66

Crozier's health forced him to spend some time on the sidelines in this season, but he eventually played 64 games and led the NHL in shutouts (6) once again. He also had the third-most wins (27).

The Red Wings had been on a fast track to success early in the season and were tied with the Black Hawks for most points (52) by the end of January. But the wheels fell off in February, and they won just six of their final 20 games. Still, they managed to squeak into the playoffs by finishing fourth in the league (74 points). They took on the Black Hawks (82 points) in the semifinals.

Howe had placed fifth in league scoring (75 points) during the regular season, but the NHL's top two scorers, Hull (97 points) and Mikita (78 points), were in the Windy City. The Black Hawks, a powerhouse that often fell short of expectations in the playoffs, also had a star in net. Glenn Hall had led the league in wins (34) and had a sparkling goals-against average (2.63) and save percentage (.916). The Red Wings were in tough.

They suffered a 2-1 loss in the opening game at Chicago Stadium, but bounced back to win four of the next five games and advance to the Stanley Cup final. Crozier was a big factor in his team's success against the Black Hawks; he allowed just 10 goals, a dozen fewer than Hall.

But the series hadn't been all sunshine and lollipops for Crozier. He'd been rushed to the hospital with abdominal pain after one game and stayed there until just hours before the next one. He had suffered another bout of pancreatitis and had, in the opinion of many people at the time, no one to blame but a hot dog. Not even the Maalox he drank by the gallon could counter the harmful effects of the concession stand delicacy.

Five days after eliminating Chicago, Detroit players took the ice at the Montreal Forum to face the Canadiens, a well-balanced team that had won the Stanley Cup the previous season and had also finished the regular season at the top of the standings (90 points). Forward Bobby Rousseau had tied Mikita for points, and "Gentleman Jean" Béliveau had finished fourth (77 points). The munchkin standing in the crease opposite Crozier was an inch shorter but more than 20 pounds heavier. Gump Worsley had finished second in wins (28) and also had an excellent goals-against average (2.36) and save percentage (.917).

The Red Wings managed to silence raucous Habs fans by winning the first two games, thanks in large part to Crozier's fast glove hand. "The hottest man on the ice in those games was Roger Crozier, the Detroit goaltender," one reporter commented. "A little fellow, Crozier looks vastly more like an amiable clerk than a hard-nosed goalie, but his deftness and courage as he stood up to and deflected 100-mile-an-hour slap shots had Montreal fans gasping and Montreal players dismayed."[12]

Some optimistic Detroit supporters started preparing for a Stanley Cup parade, but fate soon rapped them on the knuckles—hard. The Habs won the next two games at Olympia Stadium in Detroit, and in the second of those contests, Crozier got injured while attempting to block a shot. He had to be helped off the ice. One newspaper speculated that the injury to the "gutsy little guy could be the kiss of death for the hungry Red Wings."[13] It was.

Crozier was in net for the next two games, but with a sprained left knee and a twisted ankle, he couldn't stop the Canadiens—they won both contests and their second consecutive Cup. Henri Richard's overtime goal in Game 6 remains controversial to this day: many fans and players insist that he pushed the puck into the net with his hand.

Despite the outcome, Crozier became the first goalie and the first player on a losing team to win the Conn Smythe Trophy as the most valuable player in the postseason. He found out while he was removing tape from his injured leg in the dressing room. He changed into his street clothes to accept the trophy. If the MVP award didn't take the sting out of losing, the prize might have. He won $1,000 and a gold Mustang convertible, which he drove around Bracebridge that summer with the wind blowing through his close-cropped hair but failing to budge even a strand. Residents of his hometown held a parade in his honor.

1966-70

Detroit fans who thought their team was on track for a Stanley Cup victory were sorely mistaken. The Red Wings' next few years were mediocre at best. Despite having Howe and two other high-scoring forwards in Alex Delvecchio and Frank Mahovlich, who joined the Red Wings in March 1968, the Red Wings finished near the bottom of the standings and missed the playoffs in three straight seasons. They made the playoffs in the 1969–70 season but were eliminated in the first round.

Crozier managed to post the second-most wins (22) and shutouts (4) in the NHL in the 1966–67 season, but other than that, his statistics were middling. Fans fretted as he fell apart as dramatically as the Ford Pinto would four years later.

He suffered several more bouts of pancreatitis during that span, but that wasn't the worst pain he endured. In the first game of the 1967–68 season, Boston Bruins star Bobby Orr fired a shot that struck Crozier in the temple and flattened him.

The goalie was back in action by November, but when he allowed 18 goals over three straight losses, Abel decided Crozier would benefit from time on Detroit's farm team in the Central Professional Hockey League (CPHL). He summoned the goalie to his office, but before he could inform him he was being sent to the minors, Crozier delivered some bad news of his own: he was retiring. "My confidence was gone," Crozier explained later. "I would have been a nut in a month if I had continued to play."[14]

"Roger has taken this thing worse than anyone," Abel said, referring to the Wings' losing streak. "He needs a rest very badly in order to keep his health and I hope that after a few weeks he will feel better and begin to think about playing hockey again."[15]

The dressing room door had barely swung shut behind Crozier when he was back in cottage country, working as a carpenter. He was far more relaxed playing Mr. Fixit in the Muskokas than he was playing goal in Detroit. "It was a different world and I was a different person," Crozier later recalled.[16]

The stress of playing for the Red Wings was too much for him, says his daughter Katie. "That stress is what caused all his health problems. He left the game at that point because, in Detroit, he was thinking, 'Oh my God, this is just crazy. I don't know if I can do this anymore.'"

Within six weeks, the mercury had plummeted and working indoors must have seemed like an attractive option. Crozier returned to active duty in the NHL.

"My father realized there was no job he could take on that would give him as much money as playing professional hockey," says Katie. "Also, there was nothing else that would keep him as busy and feeling as successful."

Unfortunately, the Red Wings continued to struggle for the rest of that season and the next two. Sawchuk returned to the team in October 1968 and played in 13 games, but even he couldn't make the team a contender. The Red Wings traded him away in June.

One year later, they did the same to Crozier, dispatching him to the not-so-sunny climes of Buffalo, New York. The Sabres and the Vancouver Canucks expanded the NHL ranks in 1970, bringing the league's team count to 14. (Six other teams had joined the league in 1967.)

"Punch told me, 'Look, we're going to be awful. Your job is to keep us from getting embarrassed. Can you handle that?'" Crozier said, recalling a conversation with Sabres general manager and coach Punch Imlach. "What a sales pitch that was!"[17]

In the off-season, Crozier landed in the hospital with yet another bout of pancreatitis. "The affliction is just something I have to live with," he said. "I just have to remember to stick to my diet. A plain, bland diet and no alcohol at all."[18] But Crozier might have been tempted to drink nonetheless; the Sabres were bad enough in their first few seasons to lead even the most dedicated teetotaler to crawl under the covers clutching a bottle of vodka.

1970-77

Buffalo was so weak in its first season that Crozier often faced 50 shots a game. He was applauded for withstanding the onslaught instead of leaving the team's dressing room with his hands raised in a sign of surrender. The Sabres missed the post-season in three of their first six seasons. They were eliminated in the first round of the playoffs in 1973 and the second round in 1976.

One of Crozier's saving graces was a teammate. Gilbert Perreault was the first overall pick in the 1970 Amateur Draft and lived up to the hype in his rookie season. He was among the 20 highest scorers in the NHL and won the Calder Trophy. No one valued his contribution to the team more than Crozier. "I remember, at the beginning, none of our defencemen were capable of skating the puck out of our end," Crozier said later. "I finally got so tired of it. I told him, 'Gil, every game you keep me out of trouble by carrying the puck yourself, I'll buy you dinner.' So, he began wheeling around the net and making those great end-to-end rushes that he became famous for. It made him an all-star and I kept him fed for months."[19]

Starting in the 1972–73 season, Perreault played on a line with Rick Martin and René Robert. It proved to be a high-scoring trio and was dubbed "the French Connection," not only because the linemates were francophones but also because they were as badass as the detectives in the 1971 movie of the same name.

The three forwards were among the NHL's top scorers in the 1974–75 season. They led the Sabres to the top of the Prince of Wales Conference standings with the same number of points (113) as both the Canadiens, who had won two fewer games and placed second in the conference, and the Philadelphia Flyers, who finished first in the Clarence Campbell Conference.

In the playoffs, the Sabres beat the Black Hawks (82 points) and the Habs, en route to the Stanley Cup final against the talented but brutish Flyers. The Sabres were down by two games when the teams met for Game 3 at Buffalo Memorial Auditorium. The Sabres' objective was clear—gaining traction in the series—but little else was. In fact, the ice was covered in fog for much of the game, thanks to the hot, humid weather conditions outside and the absence of air conditioning inside. Play was suspended repeatedly in regulation time, which ended in a 4-4 tie, and in the first overtime period. Robert brought the sordid affair to an end when he scored with less than two minutes remaining.

Buffalo fans were elated, but the party didn't last long. The Flyers—led by star goalie Bernie Parent and the dynamic trio of Bobby Clarke, Reggie Leach and Bill Barber—won two of the next three games to clinch their second straight Cup.

Sabres goalie Gerry Desjardins was in net for most of the series, but after he allowed three goals in the fog, Crozier took over and allowed just one. "You couldn't see the puck through the fog until it was three feet away," he later recalled.[20] The veteran also played in the deciding game, which the Flyers won 2-0.

No one who played with Crozier was surprised by his feat. "He was amazing in the sense that he managed to cover the entire net," says former forward Gerry Meehan, whom the Sabres had traded away earlier that season. "He was small given the dimensions of the net. Today, goalies are too big given those dimensions." Meehan adds that Crozier was humble despite his heroics. "He was a quiet family man who came to the rink, did his job and went home."

Crozier showed flashes of brilliance in that series, but his best days were behind him. During his six full seasons in Buffalo, his statistics were mostly uninspiring. His health woes contributed to his decline. In addition to dealing with bouts of pancreatitis, Crozier suffered from a groin tear and more ulcers. As if that weren't enough, he also had to have his gall bladder removed.

In March 1977, the Sabres traded him to the Washington Capitals for cash. But there were no hard feelings. In fact, despite the many challenges he faced in Buffalo, he always regarded his years there as some of the best of his playing career. "Great city, great people," he said more than a decade later. "You know, I think that going to Buffalo added years to my career. It made me enjoy playing again."[21]

In his second outing with the Capitals, they beat the Colorado Rockies 5–0. "The little 35-year-old goalie with the nervous, 85-year-old stomach stopped 14 shots in two periods before giving way to Ron Low, who preserved the shutout," a wire service reported.[22] Still, Crozier was running out of gas. He retired after his third game with the team.

RETIREMENT

Even after leaving the ice, Crozier remained close to it. He was the Capitals' interim general manager for the 1981–82 season and even served as head coach for one game.

Not long after, he left hockey and started working for a Delaware-based bank that was later acquired by Bank of America. He rose from salesman to director of facilities management. More than 200 people worked for him at one point.

He also started the Roger Crozier Foundation, which went on to raise hundreds of thousands of dollars for initiatives such as buying hockey equipment for underprivileged kids and providing college scholarships for promising students.

In January 1996, Crozier died of cancer at the age of 53. He was survived by daughters Katie and Brooke, and his second wife, Janice, a nurse whom he had met at a Toronto hospital while being treated for one of his many bouts of pancreatitis.

Despite his success, including two individual awards, Crozier isn't in the Hockey Hall of Fame. Many people feel he should be. "It's hard to understand why he hasn't been inducted, given his success," says Katie. "It irritates me.

"People often tell me how entertaining he was to watch," she continues. "He was such an acrobat. He threw his body at every puck. It exhausted him, but he gave it his all."

||||||||||||||||||||||||||||||||||||||||||||||||||||||||||||||||||||||||||||||||||||||||||||||||||||||||

ROGER CROZIER • ALL-TIME RANKING

REGULAR SEASON			PLAYOFFS		
GAMES + RANK	WINS + RANK	SO + RANK	GAMES + RANK	WINS + RANK	SO + RANK
515 [73RD]	206 [91ST]	29 [73RD]	32 [103RD]	14 [101ST]	1 [133RD]

+ NHL ALL-STAR TEAM (1ST) 1964–65

IIIIIII 2 IIIIIII

THE CASTAWAY
ROGIE VACHON

IIIIIIIIIIIIIIIIIIIIIIIIIIIIII

ROGIE VACHON ONCE joined two of his Los Angeles Kings teammates on *Sports Challenge*, a 1970s television quiz show. They squared off against Mickey Mantle and two other retired baseball players. Watching from the sidelines, former Milwaukee Braves pitcher Lew Burdette was confused. "What are the hockey guys doing here?" he asked. "What's hockey?" He was joking—or maybe not.[1]

In the hierarchy of professional sports in California, hockey was ranked below all others, with the possible exception of cricket. When the NHL established a new franchise in Los Angeles in 1967, the response from most local sports fans was "Huh?" Hockey fans on the East Coast had a similar reaction. An arena just miles from the sand and surf of Venice Beach? That seemed preposterous. Skeptics let out a collective guffaw and turned away.

Today, hockey fans remember Vachon's solid performance in the Montreal Canadiens' net during three championship seasons and his heroics at the 1976 Canada Cup, but they recall little else about his career because he spent much of it in Los Angeles. Still, he views his seven years there as the best of his career. His only regret is having been scored on by a chimpanzee, the star of an ice-skating show, during a photo shoot.

Rogie Vachon, looking poised in a game in December 1977, was humiliated on the ice only once—when a great ape scored on him during practice.
LEWIS PORTNOY/HOCKEY HALL OF FAME

THREE DECADES before that humbling experience, in September 1945, Vachon was born in Palmarolle, a tiny farming community in northern Quebec, an eight-hour drive from Montreal. He grew up on a dairy farm with his parents, Joseph and Lucia, and seven brothers and sisters.

Joseph built a rink in the barnyard, giving the cows and chickens a front-row seat for spirited games of shinny. He strung up lights around the ice so the kids could play at night.

Vachon suffered the same fate as other small kids of that era: he was banished to the wilds of the goal crease. As he worked on his game, he drew inspiration from the legendary Terry Sawchuk, not, as one would expect with a French-Canadian kid in those days, from Jacques Plante.

When Vachon was 14 years old, before he could even consider growing the awesome mustache that would later become his trademark, he was playing on a senior team with men who were twice his age. He often spent hours alone in a car after games while his teammates enjoyed some drinks in a bar.

But the little goalie never took a back seat to them. He was so good that he landed a tryout with the Montreal Junior Canadiens, a team in the OHA, in 1961. He didn't win a spot on the roster, but all was not lost. He made the cut two years later and, between 1963 and 1966, sharpened his skills with that team along with the Montreal NDG Monarchs of the Montreal Metropolitan Junior A Hockey League and the Thetford Mines Canadiens of the Quebec Provincial Junior A Hockey League.

In the 1965–66 season, he played 39 games for Thetford and won 25 of them. That was enough to earn him an all-star designation and to convince the Montreal Canadiens to send him to their AHL affiliate, the Quebec Aces. (The Canadiens had secured sole negotiating rights to Vachon when he signed a C form with the franchise.)

He was stocky—at five foot seven, he was barely tall enough to reach the top shelf of his kitchen cupboard—but he played 10 games with the Aces and won six of them. Coach Bernie "Boom Boom" Geoffrion, who had starred for the Montreal Canadiens, was impressed with Vachon's quick reflexes and glove hand, and his ability to cut down angles.

NHL

1966-67

Through a combination of skill and the benevolence of the hockey gods, Vachon was invited to the Montreal Canadiens' training camp in the fall of 1966. He played well, but he doubted he would ever don the iconic Habs jersey; there were two big roadblocks on his path to the NHL—Habs goalies Gump Worsley and Charlie Hodge.

"Gumper" had helped the Habs win the Stanley Cup in the previous two seasons, and had just won his first Vezina Trophy. Until 1982, it was awarded to the goalie(s) on the team allowing the fewest goals during the regular season. He shared the award with Hodge, who had also been part of the 1965 Habs championship team.

Sure enough, the club sent Vachon to the Lone Star State—about as far from northern Quebec as a little goalie could travel—to play for the Houston Apollos of the minor-pro CPHL.

Vachon spent the first part of the season twiddling his thumbs on the bench—decades too early to play *Candy Crush* on a smartphone—while Gerry Desjardins tended net. But when Desjardins suffered an injury, Vachon took over. He played 34 games, posting 17 wins and 5 ties.

He got his big break in February, when a New York Rangers fan hurled an egg at Worsley and hit him in the head during a game at Madison Square Garden. The egg scrambled Gumper's brain and sent him to the sidelines with a concussion. The Canadiens recruited Vachon to be their backup goaltender, but when Hodge floundered, Vachon headed to the net.

He made his NHL debut against the Detroit Red Wings in Montreal. Gordie Howe welcomed him to the league in the first minute of play, breaking in alone on the young goalie and firing a low shot at the net. Vachon stopped him cold. "I didn't have time to be nervous, or to think about the fact it was Howe who was coming in on me," Vachon said later about his brush with greatness. "Good thing, eh?"[2]

The Red Wings had nine more shots than the Habs, but Montreal won the game 3–2, thanks mostly to Vachon, who made 41 saves. He was named the first star of the game, much to the delight of the thousands of Habs fans, including his mother, who packed the Forum.

Vachon ended up winning 11 of his 19 games that season, as the Canadiens finished second in the six-team league with 77 points. But his big coming-out party occurred in the playoffs, when he allowed just eight goals on 117 shots in a four-game sweep of the Rangers (72 points) in the semifinals. His performance impressed everyone in the NHL—everyone, that is, except the Toronto Maple Leafs' general manager and coach.

Acting like the meanest mean girl in junior high school, Punch Imlach rolled his eyes and dismissed Vachon as a "Junior B" goalie, insisting he wasn't at all concerned about the Leafs' chances against the Canadiens in the final. Toronto had 75 points.

When the teams took to the ice in Montreal for Game 1, Vachon faced two of the best goalies in hockey—Johnny Bower and Sawchuk. But if he was nervous about meeting his childhood hero, he didn't show it. He made 24 saves in the game, including a brilliant stop on Tim Horton. Montreal won the contest 6–2.

After the game, a journalist asked Vachon if he knew what Imlach had said. "Tell me," he responded. "What did Horton say about me?"[3] Lifting a fork full of humble pie to his mouth, Imlach conceded that Vachon was "the best damn Junior B in the country."[4]

The series was squared at two games apiece when the teams met at the Forum for Game 5. Vachon allowed four goals in the first two periods, so Worsley replaced him in the third. The Leafs won the game, 4–1. Many observers felt the heavy workload was a factor in Vachon's performance; up to that point, he had played in every postseason game.

Worsley was back in the net for the next game, which turned out to be the Canadiens' last of the season. Toronto won 3–1 to clinch their fourth Stanley Cup in six seasons.

Henri Richard and Jean Béliveau had led the Habs by scoring 13 points combined, but Vachon was feted in Montreal for winning six playoff games, more than any other goalie that season.

1967–69

When the NHL doubled in size in the summer of 1967, and the new Oakland Seals claimed Charlie Hodge in the expansion draft, Vachon became Gumper's goaltending partner. They split the regular-season games and notched the same number of wins (21), the third-highest total in the NHL. The Habs allowed fewer goals than any other team, securing the Vezina for both goalies.

But coach Toe Blake leaned on Worsley in the playoffs, forcing Vachon to watch from the sidelines in all but two games as the Habs (94 points), who had finished first in the East Division, blew past the Boston Bruins (84 points) and the Chicago Black Hawks (80 points), then won the Cup by sweeping aside the St. Louis Blues (70 points), a new expansion team that had placed third in the West Division and was overmatched.

VACHON WAS in top form in the 1968–69 season. Despite suffering a fracture in his right hand in November, he played in 36 games and lost only nine of them. Along with two high scorers, Yvan Cournoyer and Béliveau, Vachon helped the Canadiens finish atop the NHL standings with 103 points. But when the playoffs started, he was sent to the bench again. He didn't spend much time there, though.

The Canadiens had beaten the Rangers (91 points) in three straight games when the puck dropped for the fourth game of the first round in the Garden. A bench-clearing brawl broke out four minutes into the game. All four goalies, starters and backups, put up their dukes. At one point in the festivities, Rangers goalie Ed Giacomin, who had notched more wins (38) than all his counterparts in the regular season, sat on Worsley, leaving Gumper looking like a deflated air mattress. He left the game soon after. Vachon took over and helped the Habs win the game, 4–3, and the series.

"He really showed us his mettle," Rangers coach Emile Francis said about Vachon. "He played his angles well, he's agile, he keeps his cool under pressure and he's got a great glove hand, which is 60 percent of goalkeeping."[5]

Worsley started the semifinals against the Bruins (100 points), an emerging powerhouse led by prolific goal scorers Phil Esposito, who had finished first in NHL scoring in the regular season (126 points), and Ken Hodge, who had placed fifth (90 points). Goalie Gerry Cheevers had the third-most wins (27) in the league.

The Habs won the first two games but lost the third, 5–0. Worsley suffered a dislocated finger in his glove hand in that game, so he retreated to the bench and stayed there for the rest of the series.

The Bruins won the fourth game 3–2, but that was their last hurrah of the season. Vachon allowed two goals on 42 shots in the fifth game and was even better in the sixth. Bruins fans watched in disbelief as he allowed just one goal on 51 shots through regulation time and 31 minutes of overtime.

The Bruins had a two-man advantage for more than a minute in the second period, but Vachon kept them at bay by "lashing and plunging like an enraged animal," according to one sportswriter, who added that Vachon showed "some of the finest and toughest goaltending seen in playoff hockey." Montreal won the game 2–1 to eliminate the Bruins, leaving Boston fans crying in their clam chowder.[6]

The Habs moved on to play the Blues, who had finished first in the West Division with 88 points, in the final.

Blues forward Red Berenson was one of the league's top scorers, but the team's greatest strength was in net. Jacques Plante, now 40 years old, had led the league's starters in save percentage (.940) and goals-against average (1.96) and placed third in shutouts (5). Glenn Hall, another star of the Original Six era, had finished just behind his teammate in save percentage (.928) and goals-against average (2.17) and had recorded more shutouts (8) than every other goalie in the league.

But Montreal's young netminder outshone both stars in the final. The veterans played two games each, allowing 11 goals combined. Vachon, who often inhaled smelling salts before stepping on the ice, played in four games and allowed three goals. He posted a shutout in Game 3. With help from Cournoyer, Béliveau and Dick Duff, Vachon and the Habs swept the Blues to win another Cup.

As Habs fans danced on St. Catherine Street, their heroes celebrated in a St. Louis Arena dressing room. One of the reporters took note of Vachon's dapper dress while poking fun at his broken English. "As Rogie stood sipping Moet et Chandon champagne from the Stanley Cup after it was all over, he was almost 15 pounds lighter in his striped chartreuse suit and very, very tired," he wrote. "'The playoffs are like another season, you know,' the dark-haired, mod goalie stated. 'They're really something else because every people are listening and watching games. It's tough.'"[7]

Vachon looks back on that season fondly, not just because of the Habs' success, but also because of some of his teammates' antics. "On every team, there are one or two guys who are jokesters, playing pranks in the dressing room or on the plane," he says today. "In Montreal, I recall skate laces being cut before practices, telephone receivers being covered in Vaseline, and other incidents." It's not clear who the culprits were, because Vachon is no snitch. But, under interrogation, he would admit to Serge Savard and Guy Lapointe being high-spirited teammates.

Vachon might not have been the most mischievous player on the team, but many observers felt he was the most stylish when it came to facial hair. One reporter took note of his "luxurious pair of sideburns" and said the goalie planned to cover them with a mask the following season.[8]

1969-71

Sure enough, he dialed down the glamor by donning a plain white mask, making him one of many NHL goaltenders who started wearing face protection in the 1960s. "After a couple of good shots in the mask [during practice], I saw that I didn't get cut, or break a nose or jaw," he explained. "Then I realized how stupid I had been for not wearing a mask before."[9]

By February 1970, it was clear that Vachon had replaced Worsley as the team's top goalie. "At 23, Vachon has his future in front of him. At 40, Worsley has his stomach in front of him," a tactful reporter noted. Few were surprised when the Habs sent Worsley to the Minnesota North Stars for cash.[10]

Vachon had a good season, placing third in the NHL in wins (31), but the Habs struggled. They finished in the middle of the pack in the East Division (92 points) and missed the playoffs for the first time since 1948. Fairly or not, Vachon took a lot of heat for that failure.

THE TEAM made the playoffs the next year but faced a formidable foe in the opening round. The Bruins, the defending Stanley Cup champions, had finished first in the standings with a whopping 121 points, 24 more than the fourth-place Habs, and had six of the NHL's top 10 scorers. Esposito (152 points), Bobby Orr (139) and John Bucyk (116) led the way.

Montreal had just one player on the list of top 10 scorers; Béliveau had placed ninth with 76 points. Even worse for the Habs, the Bruins had beaten them in all but one of their six showdowns that season. Rookie Phil Myre had been in net for the lone Habs victory.

Concerned by Vachon's inability to beat the Bruins and impressed by Ken Dryden, a newcomer who had played six games for the Habs and won all of them, Habs coach Al MacNeil chose to start Dryden in Game 1, in Boston.

Although Vachon had placed third in wins (27) that season, he sat on the sidelines while Dryden and the Habs realized they could make beautiful music together. Dryden allowed just 25 goals on 285 shots as the Canadiens stunned the hockey world by defeating the Big Bad Bruins in a seven-game series.

Vachon continued to look on while Montreal eliminated the Minnesota North Stars (4-2) and the Chicago Black Hawks (4-3) to win their fifth Cup in seven seasons.

DRYDEN'S REMARKABLE playoff performance made him a hero to Montreal fans. But from where Vachon was sitting—on the bench—the big goaltender must have seemed more like a flesh-eating zombie from *Night of the Living Dead*. He was killing Vachon's career.

When Dryden allowed four goals on 33 shots in a game against the Rangers early in the 1971-72 season, Vachon replaced him and suffered a worse fate. He allowed four goals on 17 shots, and the Rangers won 8-4. The zombie apocalypse was drawing near.

In a meeting with Canadiens general manager Sam Pollock, Vachon said that if the franchise wouldn't guarantee him at least

25 games that season, he wanted out. The Habs responded by trading him to the Los Angeles Kings in a five-player deal.

1971-74

In the hockey world of that era, Los Angeles was to Montreal what the moon is to the Earth—a dazzling orb that is far, far away. The Kings had joined the NHL four years before and made it an annual tradition to finish at or near the bottom of the standings. Their home games rarely drew more than 10,000 spectators.

But after riding the pine in Montreal for more than a month, Vachon was California dreamin'. He sold his fur coat and, to ensure he would fit in with the locals that winter, bought some sport shirts and light sweaters.

He also grew his hair long and started sporting a Fu Manchu mustache. His new teammates called him Bono because his mustache was like the one worn by Cher's husband. Did Vachon's new wife dig it? That's unclear, but like her husband, Nicole Blanchard grew to love life in LA. Rogie wasn't bothered by the fact that the Kings were barely a blip on the radar for sports fans in the City of Angels at the time. In fact, he was delighted.

"In Montreal, the whole crowd gets on the goalie when he has a bad night. In LA you have an off-game you might hear a few catcalls. You can relax. You don't tighten up. In Montreal, it is always pressure. Now I just go to the games and play."[11]

After his first victory with the Kings, a 3-1 decision over the Red Wings, some of the team's few fans stood outside the Fabulous Forum chanting Vachon's name—and that put a spring in his step.

Despite his plan to boldly go where no man had gone before in a Kings jersey—deep into the playoffs—Vachon's quest was interrupted in February, when he tore a knee ligament so badly it had to be surgically repaired. He was done for the season.

He also had to stay off the tennis court for several months, which was another disappointment. Vachon had played the sport for years and had even joined some former teammates to play a few matches in front of, not with, prison inmates.

When Vachon finally returned to the ice in mid-February the following year, he made a big contribution, helping the Kings develop into a respectable team. Their point total climbed from 49 to 78 over Vachon's first three seasons in LA. In the last of those seasons, Los Angeles finished third in the West Division and advanced to the playoffs. The Black Hawks (105 points) beat them four games to one in the opening round, but Kings fans, whose numbers were steadily growing, had a good feeling about the team and their star goalie, who had posted a stellar 1.77 goals-against average in the series.

1974-78

The Kings soared to new heights in the 1974-75 season. They finished third in the Prince of Wales Conference and fourth in the NHL with 105 points—a total the franchise has never surpassed.

Observers attributed the team's success to their emphasis on defense under coach Bob Pulford, and to Vachon, who led the NHL in save percentage (.927) and placed second in goals-against average (2.24) and shutouts (6).

His teammates were impressed. Forward Mike Murphy marveled at Vachon's ability to read the play. "The great players seem to know where the puck is going before it gets there. Rogie had that skill," he says today. Another factor in Vachon's success, says Murphy, was his competitive zeal. "He really hated to lose on and off the ice. When we played golf, Rogie would bust his hump to win, even [if] there were only five bucks at stake."

Vachon stood out off the ice too. "Rogie loved fine dining. He would sometimes go to nice restaurants by himself and order a very expensive bottle of wine," Murphy recalls. Teammates sometimes joined him for dinner. "Rogie once ordered a bottle of wine and, after tasting it, sent it back. He knew it wasn't good," Murphy says. "I was floored, because I had no idea what a good bottle of wine was."

Vachon was getting comfortable in his new home. "I love Los Angeles," he said at the time. "The organization is great, they

MONKEY BUSINESS

DURING A Los Angeles Kings practice at the Fabulous Forum in January 1975, the star of the *Holiday on Ice* show posed for photographs with Rogie Vachon. Charlie the Chimp, perhaps the only one on the ice with more facial hair than the goalie, took a shot on net using a sawed-off stick, while his handlers recorded the moment. Vachon blocked the first shot but not the second. "Get him outta here," Vachon shouted after Charlie scored, "and burn the film!"[12]

treat me well, my wife and I love the weather out here and the entire situation is fantastic."[13]

But few hockey fans east of the Colorado River took notice; most Kings games ended after midnight eastern time, so most fans saw Vachon's exploits only in short highlight reels that played on nightly newscasts.

"Rogie Vachon had to be content with being a legend in his own time zone," sportswriters Kevin Allen and Bob Duff wrote in their book *Without Fear: Hockey's 50 Greatest Goaltenders.* "Having spent the prime of his career laboring for the Los Angeles Kings in a pre-cable and pre-ESPN world undoubtedly would cost Vachon some richly deserved notice."[14]

Still, his statistics were too good to be ignored by sportswriters. In 1975, members of the Professional Hockey Writers Association looked at the West Coast, possibly for the first time, and made Vachon a finalist in voting for the Hart Trophy, awarded to the NHL's most valuable player.

Vachon was solid in the opening round of the playoffs against Toronto (78 points), allowing seven goals on 99 shots, but the Kings couldn't generate enough offense to top the Leafs. Toronto won the series, two games to one.

That summer, Vachon almost drowned when he was thrown overboard while fishing with his brother and friends in Quebec.

"We laughed about it later," he recounted, "but first I nearly had a heart attack."[15]

Cardiac arrest would have been just one of his health scares that summer. He also came down with a high fever and spent weeks convalescing at his home. He suffered a long, difficult separation from his gold Mercedes-Benz.

The next three seasons didn't go according to plan for the Kings. They never notched more than 85 points or finished higher than fourth in the conference. They managed to make the playoffs in all those seasons but failed to advance past the second round.

Vachon placed third in the NHL in shutouts (5) in the 1975–76 season and was even better the following year, when he was third in wins (33), second in shutouts (8) and a Hart Trophy finalist. But he couldn't lead his team to the top.

TODAY, MANY hockey fans remember Vachon not for what he accomplished in a Kings jersey, but for his exploits at the 1976 Canada Cup. With injuries to Ken Dryden and Philadelphia Flyers great Bernie Parent, Vachon won the top job on the Canadian roster for the international tournament, which featured games in five Canadian cities and Philadelphia.

Before the tournament, Pollock, who was also general manager of Team Canada, said Vachon was good, but not in the same class as Dryden and Parent. That lit a fire under Vachon, and he proceeded to put on a brilliant display of goaltending.

He played in all seven games, winning six and recording a 1.39 goals-against average. He also posted two shutouts.

One of them was in the first game of the best-of-three final. Team Canada won that contest, 6–0. The atmosphere was electric two days later, when players from Canada and Czechoslovakia stepped onto the ice at the Montreal Forum for the second game. Players spotted several prominent people in the stands, including Canadian prime minister Pierre Trudeau and tennis star Bobby Riggs, who was still smarting from his humiliating defeat to Billie Jean King—a woman, of all things—in the Battle of the Sexes.

Vachon brought spectators to their feet with acrobatic saves, and he whipped them into a frenzy early in overtime. With the game tied 4–4, Czech forward Vladimír Martinec fired a blistering shot from point-blank range. Vachon stopped him cold with a glove save. Sports columnist Frank Orr described it as "one of the great stops in hockey history."[16]

Canada's Darryl Sittler scored the winning goal soon after, sending spectators into a frenzy. They jumped into each other's arms and cheered so loudly they nearly blew the roof off the building.

Vachon was named the tournament's top goalie and Team Canada's MVP. No one was more excited than the PA announcer. "From Team Canada," he bellowed, "I think you know who it is… *Roga-tien Vachon!*" In addition to the adoration of millions of Canadians, Vachon won a vehicle worthy of his greatness: a station wagon. It wasn't a Lamborghini, but, hey, it wasn't a harvest-gold dishwasher or a lava lamp either.

Canadian players later celebrated their victory in the dressing room, where Bobby Orr sipped beer while chatting—not singing—with acclaimed singer and songwriter Gordon Lightfoot. A trainer poured champagne over Vachon, who may or may not have been making a mental list of grocery items he could cram into his new station wagon.

"Team Canada's biggest star was its littlest player, Rogie Vachon, a long-haired man with a drooping mustache, a small man built like a barrel on skates," one reporter wrote.[17]

Vachon has always regarded the tournament as two of the most exciting weeks of his life. "This series was like a Stanley Cup final. The publicity, the packed arenas, the roaring crowds, the hard games really got to me. Mostly, it made me not nervous, but enthusiastic, inspired."[18]

He had another memorable experience a year later, in a regular-season game on Long Island. "They had an incredible team," he says about the New York Islanders, who won the first of four consecutive Cups in 1980. Vachon faced 41 shots that night and stopped all of them. He was so dialed-in that he saw exactly how a play would unfold in advance and made the save without a problem. "That only happened to me once in my career," he says now, recalling the scoreless tie. "That was probably the best game I ever played in the NHL."

1978-82

In August 1978, Vachon became a free agent and signed a five-year deal with Detroit that made him the highest-paid goalie in the NHL. The deal was worth $1.9 million.

The Red Wings shared Vachon's enthusiasm at the outset, but the relationship, like many that start with great promise, deteriorated. His time in the Motor City proved to be nothing short of disastrous.

In his debut, Vachon allowed five goals on 14 shots against the sad-sack Blues in a 5–4 loss. Detroit fans booed loudly and threw garbage at him. One reporter felt that Vachon played "more like the Ancient Mariner, who stoppeth one of three, than the highest-paid goaltender in hockey."[19]

Vachon notched four shutouts in the 1979–80 season, the second-highest total in the NHL, but his performance was weak overall. He led the NHL in losses (30) and goals allowed (209).

The Red Wings didn't fare much better. Detroit finished at the bottom of the Prince of Wales Conference (62 points) in Vachon's first season with the team and second from the bottom (63 points) the next year. The franchise had buyer's remorse.

Vachon had problems with his vision, thanks to a concussion, but he later admitted his problem in Detroit was "mostly mental. I signed for a big salary and everyone in town saw that. All of a sudden, I was supposed to be God. Just because I was making more money, I was supposed to become a better goalie. I had a bad start and everybody in town was down on me."[20] Not even the hypnotist Vachon saw could help him break out of his funk.

The Red Wings put him on waivers in 1980, and the Bruins picked him up, sending goalie Gilles Gilbert to Detroit. "We didn't stop to figure out why he went sour in Detroit," Bruins general manager Harry Sinden explained. "We just felt it was because he went to Detroit as Moses and the fans and the management would never let him forget it."[21]

In Boston, Vachon failed to match his sparkling numbers of the 1974–75 season, but his statistics were better than they had been in Detroit. Also, he now sported a new cage mask, which he had worn around the house to get used to. The Bruins made the playoffs in the first two seasons after his arrival—but didn't advance past the second round. In the second season, his protégé, Marco Baron, replaced him as starter. Vachon played just 20 minutes in the postseason, allowing one goal on three shots against the Quebec Nordiques. With his future in the Bruins' net looking far from bright, the aging goaltender announced his retirement.

RETIREMENT

Vachon headed back to the West Coast, where he had made a great life with Nicole and their children, Nicholas, Jade and Marie-Joie.

The Kings welcomed him with open arms, and for more than two decades, he worked for the franchise in many capacities, including that of general manager. He was in that role when the Kings traded with the Edmonton Oilers for Wayne Gretzky.

The Kings retired Vachon's jersey in 1985, but the ultimate honor, induction into the Hockey Hall of Fame, eluded him for decades. Finally, in 2016, the moment arrived. By then, he had resigned himself to being overlooked—again. "I thought if it was going to happen it would have happened by now," he said at the time. "And then, bang! Surprise!"[22]

Bill Barber, one of Vachon's teammates in the Canada Cup, was not at all surprised it had taken so long for Vachon to be recognized for his excellence. "I think a player is recognized through the success of his team," Barber says, noting that the Kings were never contenders when Vachon was a star there. "When two teams compete in the finals, you'll remember the winner years later but forget the loser." Also, says Barber, the significance of geography can't be overlooked. "If Rogie had been playing in Montreal in the 1970s, do you really think he would not have won more recognition?"

Mike Murphy agrees. "If he had stayed in Montreal, his record would have been much better than it was in Los Angeles and Detroit," he says, looking back. "He probably would have been much more recognized and admired, and he probably would have been inducted much sooner."

In 2021, four years after Nicole died of cancer, Vachon moved to Montana to live with his son, daughter-in-law and grandchild on a spacious property. "It feels great to be here," he said at the time. "I can go out and smoke my cigar, cut the grass, work in the garden and breathe fresh air all the time."

These days, when his family members are away, Vachon enjoys watching *Jeopardy!* to keep his mind sharp. He also takes care of six chickens, none of whom are related to the domesticated birds that once watched him play shinny on his parents' farm.

He also plays a lot of golf—but not well. "The best club in my bag is my putter," he said. "The worst would be the other 13 clubs."[23]

Vachon's name still comes up when hockey fans and pundits talk about great goaltenders—but not as often as it should. "Perhaps it's because he toiled outside the spotlight for most of his career that it's easy to forget Rogie Vachon's brilliance," Ken Campbell wrote in the *Hockey News*. "The kids might not be able to fathom this now, but there was a time when playing in Los Angeles was the NHL's version of being dispatched to Siberia."[24]

||||||||||||||||||||||||||||||||||||||||||||||||||||||||||||||||||||||||||||||||||||||||||||||||||||||

ROGIE VACHON • ALL-TIME RANKING

REGULAR SEASON			PLAYOFFS		
GAMES + RANK	WINS + RANK	SO + RANK	GAMES + RANK	WINS + RANK	SO + RANK
795 [19TH]	353 [24TH]	51 [28TH]	48 [66TH]	23 [65TH]	2 [92ND]

+ NHL ALL-STAR TEAM (2ND) 1974-75, 1976-77

|||||||| **3** ||||||||

THE CHARACTER
GERRY CHEEVERS

||||||||||||||||||||||||||||

WHEN THE BOSTON Bruins invited Gerry Cheevers to their training camp in 1967, the young goaltender knew he had to slim down, so he slipped into something comfortable, a giant plastic bag, and slid behind the wheel of his car. He drove around for hours with the heat blasting, the windows rolled up and beads of sweat dripping onto his seat.

It isn't clear how much weight he lost, if he lost any, but one thing is certain: Cheevers went on to play a pivotal role in two Stanley Cup victories and earn a reputation as a clutch goaltender. He's remembered as much for his hijinks and sharp wit as for his success between the pipes.

IN DECEMBER 1940, decades before he adopted the plastic bag as outerwear, Cheevers was born in St. Catharines, Ontario, a small community on the southern shore of Lake Ontario, about 35 miles from Toronto.

His father, Joe, had been an elite lacrosse player in his youth, a forward who had played goal for a few glorious minutes in the final game of the 1941 national box lacrosse championship. He managed to keep the ball out of the net and later described his "shutout" as the highlight of his playing career. His team, the St. Catharines Athletics, won the title that season, and he was later inducted into the Canadian Lacrosse Hall of Fame.

Gerry Cheevers keeps his eye on the puck from behind his iconic mask. If he hadn't introduced it, he once said, goalies would still be wearing plain white masks. No fun! **JACK MECCA/HOCKEY HALL OF FAME**

Joe put a lacrosse stick in Gerry's hands as soon as they were big enough to hold one. Gerry excelled in the sport and was so competitive he once stomped on the foot of a loathsome opponent—his brother, Patrick. The incident didn't cause ill will between the boys—no purple nurples on the walk home from school—but it did raise the ire of their mother, Bette, who gave Gerry the cold shoulder for days.

But hockey was Gerry's first love, and he sat glued to the radio every Saturday night, listening to *Hockey Night in*

Canada. He hung on every word of announcer Foster Hewitt, who detailed the exploits of Toronto Maple Leafs goaltender Turk Broda.

Cheevers fancied himself a clone of Broda even though he was still more than a foot shorter and 100 pounds lighter than the NHL star, whom a sportswriter once described as "the fattest, baldest and best goalkeeper in professional hockey."[1]

Within a few years, Cheevers was tending goal for one of the top bantam teams in Ontario, the St. Catharines Conroys. It won the Ontario Minor Hockey Association title in 1954 and 1955. Cheevers and Stan Mikita, another future NHL star, were given much of the credit for the team's success.

Cheevers was dedicated to hockey, but it wasn't his only interest. There was a racetrack near his home, and, as a sportswriter with a flair for the dramatic once wrote, "the smell of the stables attracted Cheevers with the magnetism of a dope sheet to a two-dollar bettor." Cheevers spent hours cleaning out stalls and bedding horses down, as the intoxicating scent of manure filled his nostrils and tickled his limbic system. Horse racing became a lifelong obsession.[2]

Cheevers's success on the ice helped him win a scholarship to St. Michael's College, a storied Toronto high school that had already produced NHL stars such as Dave Keon and Frank Mahovlich. The school had one of two OHA teams affiliated with the Toronto Maple Leafs. Cheevers joined the school's Junior A squad in the 1959–60 season. The team lost to the St. Catharines Teepees in the final.

Despite that setback, Cheevers's star was on the rise. He developed a reputation as an acrobatic goalie who often wandered out of his net to play the puck. He was so good at skating and stickhandling that his teammates viewed him as a third defenseman capable of making perfect clearing passes. None of them balked when, in the 1960–61 season, the team's coach, a priest named David Bauer, had Cheevers play forward in several games.

"Bauer told me that if I wanted to play in the NHL, I would have to improve my skating, so I worked hard at that," says

Cheevers. "There is a belief that goaltenders don't have to be good skaters, but that is totally false."

Cheevers's greatest accomplishment as a forward was a breakaway on Roger Crozier, a Teepees goalie who would soon be tending goal in the NHL. "You would think if anyone knew how to beat a goalie, it would be another goalie, but I drew a blank," Cheevers said after shooting the puck directly at Crozier's pads. "I only wish everyone played forward the way I did. I would never be scored on."[3]

That season, St. Michael's finished second in the OHA standings and won the championship. Cheevers and his teammates went on to win the national championship—the school's first Memorial Cup victory since 1947.

As a student at St. Michael's, Cheevers made an impression off the ice as well, playing cards with his buddies and spending time in pool halls playing snooker. Cheevers once covered bets on the Kentucky Derby. His "clients" were other students.

Even while pursuing his dreams on the ice, he continued to devote time to horse racing. In the summers, he worked at the Fort Erie Race Track, helping to cool down horses after workouts. He later worked in the mutuel department, selling and cashing wagers from bettors, then worked in public relations at the track.

CHEEVERS ATTENDED the Leafs training camp in 1961, and played two games for the team that season, but with Johnny Bower as their starter and veteran Don Simmons as a backup, the Leafs had little use for Cheevers. He spent the next four seasons playing in the EPHL for the Sault Ste. Marie Greyhounds and the Sudbury Wolves, and in the AHL, where he laced up for the Rochester Americans.

He continued to improve, and in the 1963–64 season, he became the Americans' starting goalie. In Rochester, he impressed teammates with his competitive zeal. A rugged defenseman named Don Cherry would sing his praises for years. "I remember one game 'Cheesy' was hit right on the mouth with a shot," Cherry said, referring to the goalie by his nickname. "He lost, I don't know, about a half-dozen teeth. Spit 'em right out on the ice. But he went off for stitches and came right back to the win the game."[4]

Cheevers was developing into an elite goaltender, but the Leafs still had no use for him. In June 1964, the club claimed Terry Sawchuk in the intra-league draft and left Cheevers unprotected. No other club claimed him, but he didn't mope like a spurned tween at a middle school dance. He was more determined than ever to succeed.

He played in all 72 games in the 1964–65 season, a first for an AHL goalie, and won 48 of them—a league record that stands to this day. Cheevers led the Americans to their first league title. In addition to winning the Calder Cup, he won the Hap Holmes Memorial Award.

His exploits impressed Leafs general manager and coach Punch Imlach. He had two great goalies in Bower and Sawchuk, who shared the Vezina Trophy in 1965, but he wanted to keep Cheevers in the Leafs organization. He was prohibited from protecting more than two goalies in the intra-league draft, so he listed Cheevers as a forward. But he wasn't fooling anyone, least of all NHL president Clarence Campbell. Cheevers ended up being listed as a goalie, and the Boston Bruins, who had finished dead last in the previous five seasons, claimed him.

Cheevers found out when he was at Woodbine Racetrack in Toronto and picked up a newspaper to look at the next day's race entries. When he saw the headline about the draft, recounted jockey agent Al Dunn, "he threw the paper in the air and kicked at it. He missed and said 'one-nothing already.'"[5]

NHL

1965-67

In October 1965, Cheevers made his debut with the Bruins in a game against the Leafs at the Boston Garden, where the ice surface was nine feet shorter and two feet narrower than in other arenas because it had been built four decades earlier, when the size of NHL rinks wasn't yet standardized. The architect had designed the arena with boxing in mind, so spectators were much closer to the action than in other rinks.

Cheevers made 33 saves in the game, a 2–1 loss, but gave Leafs forward Ron Ellis an early Christmas present. On one play in the first period, the rookie left a gap on his short side. That allowed Ellis to score Toronto's first goal of the season—and he skated away without so much as a thank-you.

Cheevers ended up playing 29 games for the Bruins over the next two seasons. He was far from dazzling—his goals-against average never dipped below 3.33—but he *was* entertaining. After one lopsided loss, Boston's general manager, Hap Emms, demanded an explanation. "Roses are red. Violets are blue," the young goalie responded. "They got nine. We got two."

Eddie Johnston kept his position as the team's starting goaltender, so Cheevers spent most of his time with the Oklahoma City Blazers in the CPHL.

During his stint there, he lived with fellow goalie Doug Favell, who has fond memories of their time together. "We were driving home from a road game one night and the car caught on fire," recalls Favell, who later played in the NHL. "We jumped out and ran. We were both fast runners, but Gerry left me in his dust."

In one game with the Blazers, three players fell on top of Cheevers while he was smothering the puck. He suffered a dislocated shoulder, which put him on the sidelines for weeks and became a chronic condition. But even with the wonky joint, he helped lead the Blazers to league titles in 1966 and 1967. Cheevers was named the best goaltender in the CPHL in both seasons.

That persuaded the Bruins to protect him in the expansion draft, which was held in June 1967 to fill out the rosters of six new NHL teams. Boston also protected Johnston while leaving Bernie Parent—yes, *that* Bernie Parent—and Favell unprotected. The brand-new Philadelphia Flyers picked up both men.

1967-68

Cheevers considered staying in Oklahoma City to raise his young family, which included his wife, Betty, and two kids, Craig and Sherril. (Another son, Rob, would come along later.) But the Bruins had other plans for the 26-year-old goaltender and invited him to their training camp.

He started camp along with budding superstar Bobby Orr and newcomers Phil Esposito, Ken Hodge and Fred Stanfield. Four months earlier, the Chicago Black Hawks had given up those three players in exchange for Gilles Marotte, Pit Martin and Jack Norris. That trade is now viewed as one of the most lopsided in NHL history for obvious reasons.

In his first season with the Bruins, Esposito finished second in league scoring (84 points). Veteran Johnny Bucyk was also among the NHL's top scorers. With those two forwards, Orr and rookie sensation Derek Sanderson leading the charge, and Cheevers playing well in net, Boston was no longer the laughingstock of the league.

The Bruins' firepower was impressive and their chemistry was undeniable. "You could see the difference in this team as soon as training camp started," Orr told a sportswriter who visited the Bruins dressing room in December, when they sat atop the league standings. "After one practice a few of us went out for a beer, and the whole team ended up in the same place," the teenager continued, not mentioning that he was still under the legal drinking age. "It's been that way all year. We go to the same places, we hang together as a group."[6]

Orr told the sportswriter that none of the players took themselves too seriously. As a case in point, he motioned toward Cheevers, who had posted a sign over the stall of teammate Gary Doak that declared him one of the stars of the previous night's game. The defenseman had played less than three minutes. All the players were having a good laugh at Doak's expense, with the possible exception of Stanfield, who was catching some rays under a sunlamp.

Orr didn't mention Cheevers's response to Esposito's request not to allow sticks to cross each other in the dressing room. Cheesy irritated the superstitious star by doing the exact opposite, creating a pile of oversized pick-up sticks on the dressing room floor.

"I felt that you had to have some fun in the game," Cheevers says. "If players are uptight, it's not a healthy dressing room or a healthy team. I enjoyed the game and I wanted my teammates to enjoy the game and have fun."

"We would always get together after games in those days, and nine times out of 10, Gerry was the life of the party," Johnston recalls, adding that there was no tension between the two goalies. "We were both there for one reason—to win. We would often exchange notes to help each other out. Gerry and I got along extremely well."

That season, the Bruins finished third in the East Division and in the league, with 84 points. Four days after the regular season ended, they stepped onto the ice in the Montreal Forum to start their postseason—and they were in tough.

The Habs had finished first in the league, with 94 points. Forwards Jean Béliveau and Bobby Rousseau were prolific goal scorers, but the Habs' goalies deserved much of the credit for Montreal's success. Gump Worsley and Rogie Vachon were two of the NHL's best goaltenders.

In the second period of Game 1, a goalmouth collision left Cheevers on the ice, grimacing in pain. His shoulder was injured again, but he told the trainer he was just winded, and he finished the game. He managed to rob Habs forward Yvan Cournoyer on a breakaway but couldn't lift his team to victory. The Habs won the game 2–1 and went on to sweep the Bruins aside in four straight. Cheevers allowed 15 goals over four games.

1968-69

Montreal and Boston dominated the following season and finished one-two in the league standings with 103 and 100 points, respectively. The next best team, the New York Rangers, finished nine points back of the Bruins.

Esposito's performance that season was a tour de force. He led the league in total points (126), and Hodge, who played on his line, was also one of the top scorers in the NHL. Cheevers turned heads with his statistics too, placing third in wins (27).

Bruins coach Harry Sinden was impressed. "He may be unorthodox but he stops the puck," Sinden said. "He sprawls, kicks and swings, but he keeps the puck out of the net, and that is what we want."[7]

Cheevers sometimes used his stick "the way a jungle fighter uses a knife," according to one media report. "I'm not dirty, just aggressive," Cheevers explained. "Actually, I'm the worst fighter in the world. There is no way I could win a fight. So, I have to get my licks in before the fight starts."[8]

Cheevers had a notable season off the ice, too. During one practice, a puck hit his mask. The shot wasn't hard enough to break an egg, but Cheevers pretended to be injured and left the ice. Sinden was aware that Cheevers enjoyed practicing as much as kids love eating Brussels sprouts, so he headed to the Bruins dressing room, where he found Cheevers stretched out, reading a horse-racing form. Sinden ordered the goalie to return to the ice.

Before Cheevers rejoined his teammates, Bruins trainer John "Frosty" Forristall painted eight stitches on the goalie's mask. Back on the ice, the goalie skated toward Sinden, pointed at the paint on his mask and exclaimed, "See how bad the cut is?" From that day on, Forristall painted a stitch on Cheevers's mask every time a puck hit it—and the mask became one of the most iconic in hockey history.

"At times, I feel I was somewhat of a pioneer in hockey because I actually did something to my mask," he later told the video-streaming service Dailymotion. "If you know goalies the way I do, you know that none of them would be smart enough to put designs on their masks. So, if I hadn't done it, goalies would be wearing plain white masks today, and what good would that be?"

Cheevers was wearing his mask when the puck dropped in the Boston Garden to start the playoffs against a familiar foe, the

Leafs. Toronto had finished fourth in the division with 85 points and boasted talented players in forward Norm Ullman, one of the NHL's top goal scorers, and netminder Bruce Gamble, who had the second-most wins (28) in the league.

The Bruins trounced the Leafs in Game 1 of the opening round, scoring 10 unanswered goals. But by the time the siren sounded to end the game, the score was an afterthought. In the second period, Leafs defenseman Pat Quinn stepped into Orr and knocked him out cold. In an instant, it was so quiet in the Boston Garden you could have heard a kernel of popcorn land on the floor after tumbling from the open mouth of a Bruins fan. Spectators breathed a collective sigh of relief when Orr regained consciousness, and they went back to eating their concession stand treats.

Orr left the ice and Quinn did too—to serve a five-minute major penalty for elbowing. But Bruins fans were determined to mete out their own justice. They laid siege to the penalty box. Men pounded their fists on the glass and women swung their purses like machetes. Quinn tussled with the police officer guarding the gate, shattering a pane of glass. Quinn was escorted to the Leafs dressing room but later returned to the ice, where Boston fans hurled an assortment of objects at him. "Something hard hit me, and I looked down to see one of those metal change holders that bus drivers carried," Quinn recalled years later. "Unfortunately, there wasn't any money in it."[9]

One period and four Boston goals later, Imlach tapped the shoulder of Forbes Kennedy, a scrappy player who was known for bowling over opposing players. When the Leafs forward stepped onto the ice, chaos ensued. He and Cheevers exchanged blows by the Bruins net and knocked over a linesman. Boston fans were soon treated to a bench-clearing brawl. Kennedy set a host of penalty records that night and was suspended for four games.

Orr suffered a concussion but returned to the ice the next day and helped his team win the next three games. After sweeping aside the Leafs, the Bruins headed back to Montreal to play the Canadiens in the semifinals.

Béliveau, then in his 18th season, and Cournoyer were among the top scorers in the NHL that season. Worsley was in his 16th season but was still formidable in the Habs net.

The series turned out to be a dogfight. With the exception of Game 3, which the Bruins won 5–0, every game was close, and three of them went into overtime. That included the sixth and deciding game, which the Habs won 2–1 in double overtime at the Garden.

After Béliveau scored the series-winning goal, Hodge drew his stick back like a hatchet and brought it down on the crossbar. Cheevers slammed his own stick into the boards. Later, in the dressing room, Sanderson struggled to make sense of the loss. "How do you explain it?" he said. "They don't have the team, the defense, the talent or the guts. But they get the goals."[10]

Béliveau was called "Gentleman Jean" because he was a class act on and off the ice. Cheevers remembers the late Habs captain as a "great man," but he says, with tongue planted firmly in cheek, "He was no gentleman to us."

1969-70

Boston was strong again the next season, finishing second in the division and in the NHL with 99 points. Esposito and Orr were so dominant, a casual fan could have been forgiven for assuming they scored all the league's goals and assists. Orr was first in scoring (120 points), one spot ahead of Esposito (99 points).

In the first round of the playoffs, the Bruins took on the New York Rangers, who had emerged as one of the NHL's best teams after almost two decades of mediocrity. The Rangers had placed fourth in the division and the NHL with 92 points, and had three high scorers in Walt Tkaczuk, Jean Ratelle and Dave Balon, and one of the few goalies who could hold a candle to Cheevers.

Ed Giacomin had played in a league-leading 70 games that season and finished second in wins (35). His backup was no slouch either. Terry Sawchuk, who had landed in New York in June 1969, was past his prime, and had played in only a handful of games for the Rangers that season, but he was still capable of making spectacular saves, and his scowl was as fierce as ever.

In the dressing room the day before the first game, Cheevers assured reporters he was putting on his game face. "Now it's gotta be 100 percent hockey, 24 hours a day," he said earnestly. Without skipping a beat, he told them he was heading to Suffolk Downs, a racetrack in Boston, for the afternoon.[11]

Cheevers appeared to benefit from playing the ponies. The next day, he made 36 saves, and Esposito and Orr combined for five goals as the Bruins walloped the Rangers 8–2. The teams split the next four games. In Game 6, Rangers fans tried to tip the scales in their team's favor by pelting the visiting Bruins with items from each of the five food groups, but it was no use. Boston beat New York 4–1 to win the series. When the game ended, the Bruins left the ice, taking great care to skate around the eggs and apple cores.

In the semifinals, they took on the Black Hawks, whose roster included high scorers such as Bobby Hull and Stan Mikita, and the best young goalie the NHL had seen in years. Tony Esposito won the Calder Trophy and the Vezina Trophy that season, and was a finalist for the Hart Trophy. But the Bruins were too hot to handle. They swept the series, and Phil put his younger brother in his place by notching nine points over four games—increasing the odds of a food fight erupting at the Esposito dinner table that Christmas. Cheevers posted better numbers than his rival.

That victory sent the Bruins to the Stanley Cup final for the first time since 1958. They squared off against the St. Louis Blues, who had finished first in the West Division, which included only expansion teams, with 86 points. The Blues boasted a few high scorers in Red Berenson, Phil Goyette and Frank St. Marseille, and the team had thrived under the guidance of coach Scotty Bowman. They also had three good goalies.

Ernie Wakely had notched the best goals-against average among starters that season (2.11) and finished second in save percentage (.930). Glenn Hall and Jacques Plante were also on the roster. Both men were nearing the end of their legendary careers but were still capable of keeping the puck out of the net.

Plante, who was 41 years old, had placed third in goals-against (2.19).

He was between the pipes when the puck dropped in St. Louis to start the series. Early in the second period, Stanfield fired a slap shot that struck Plante's fiberglass mask. The goalie dropped to the ice like a sack of potatoes and was unconscious for two minutes. He eventually left the ice and didn't return until the following season.

The Bruins trounced the Blues in that game and in the next two. St. Louis regrouped in Game 4, pushing it into overtime. For a brief, shining moment, it looked like they stood a chance of taking a game from the Big Bad Bruins, but Orr wasn't feeling charitable toward the new team.

In the first minute of overtime, he took a pass from Sanderson and tucked the puck behind Hall. Orr was tripped by Blues defenseman Noel Picard a split second later and soared through the air with his arms extended in jubilation, looking a little like a bird or a plane and a lot like Superman. A photographer snapped a shot, creating one of the most iconic images in sports history.

Boston players made a beeline to their own net to celebrate with Cheevers, who had thrown his stick in the air only to see it get caught on the glass surrounding the boards and dangle there for a few tenuous moments before falling to the ice.

The roar from the crowd was deafening. Fans leaped into each other's arms and threw crepe paper streamers on the ice to celebrate the Bruins' first Cup victory since 1941. Some of them made their way into the Bruins dressing room and ended up filling every square inch of space. Orr was spotted holding court in a terry cloth robe, artfully dodging kisses proffered by ecstatic female fans. Cheevers and two of his teammates sneaked into the stick room to drink beer. His father, who joined the team's celebration, was exuberant—perhaps a little too much so. Later that night, he suffered a heart attack and ended up spending more than a week in hospital.

Fans are still talking about Orr's goal decades later, and Cheevers is still taking credit for it. The final game was his weakest outing of the series. He gave up two soft goals in the Bruins' 4–3 win. If he hadn't, he often says with a wink, the game wouldn't have gone into overtime, and Orr wouldn't have scored that dramatic goal.

That summer, Cheevers was master of ceremonies at a promotional event at the Fort Erie Race Track, where he interviewed star jockey Sandy Hawley. He told a sportswriter he was interested in purchasing a Canadian-bred yearling, but balked at the prospect of using the bonus he had been given for winning the Stanley Cup. "Use my Stanley Cup money? Hardly. I spent that before we won the Cup."[12]

1970-71

The Bruins gained momentum the following season, setting a points record (121) that catapulted them to the top of the standings. The team set dozens of records overall and had seven of the league's 10 highest scorers—a feat never accomplished before or since.

Esposito led the way, placing first in overall scoring (152 points), while Orr finished second (139). Bucyk was in his 16th NHL season, but there was still gas in his tank: he placed third in overall scoring (116 points). Cheevers had a good season too, placing third in wins (27).

Cheevers couldn't have been more relaxed. He would often stretch out and nap in the Bruins dressing room after the morning skate on game days. On one occasion, when the Bruins were in New York, he skipped the shut-eye and went to a movie with teammates instead. On that day, as on most game days, he showed up in the dressing room just 45 minutes before puck-drop.

"I know old Johnny Bower when he was with Toronto used to like to get into the dressing room at six but I don't want to be thinking too deeply about the game a full hour and a half before," he once explained. "That's the kind of tension than can drive you nuts."[13]

The Bruins were favored to repeat as champions, but, as it turned out, they ran into a roadblock in the first round of the playoffs—namely, a goalie who was as imposing as Sasquatch, but much more articulate.

Ken Dryden, who had studied at Cornell University and would later earn a law degree, had played six games for the Habs that season. He had won every one, convincing Habs coach Al MacNeil to choose him to start the playoffs. When Dryden skated to his crease in the Garden for Game 1, fans did a double take. He was six foot four, at least half a foot taller than most of his peers.

Dryden looked down at his teammates in the literal sense, but he held them in high regard. Cournoyer, defenseman J.C. Tremblay and the legendary Béliveau had posted solid numbers that season—good enough to occupy the few spots near the top of the scoring ladder that weren't taken by Boston players.

The Bruins won the first game and carved out a 5–2 lead by the end of the second period of the next tilt. But the Habs scored five unanswered goals on Johnston in the third period and won Game 2, 7–5.

Cheevers, who kept a diary that season that would later be published as a book called *Goaltender*, noted that sales of neckties bearing the Bruins' insignia flattened the day after the loss. Cheevers quoted a clothing store salesman as saying the loss "absolutely killed business."[14]

The Bruins managed to win two more games but couldn't clinch the series. The Habs won Game 7 by a score of 4–2, thanks in large part to Dryden, who made 46 saves to hold off the Bruins' onslaught—16 more than Cheevers, who had been in goal for every game of that series aside from the second one.

During the first intermission of that final game, Cheevers had taken stock of his rival's play. "I find I'm thinking of that bastard Dryden, how he lies down across the goal-mouth when we're pressing, all six-feet-four of him sprawled out on his side, filling half the net with sheer bulk, an amazingly cool kid under the conditions," Cheevers wrote in *Goaltender*. "The long-legged son of a bitch has been taking money out of my pocket."[15]

Cheesy didn't spend much time in mourning. The next day, he showed up at Suffolk Downs to watch his new horse, Falls Church, race. Unlike his hockey team, his horse proved to be a winner that week.

1971-72

Boston was dominant again the next season, finishing at the top of the standings with 119 points. In keeping with tradition, Esposito and Orr finished first and second in overall scoring with 133 and 117 points, respectively. Bucyk and Stanfield were also among the league's most prolific scorers.

Cheevers's season was one for the ages. He went undefeated in 32 consecutive starts, an NHL record that still stands, and finished with 27 wins. Only two of his rivals finished with more wins: Tony Esposito and—you guessed it—Dryden. "We have everything," Cheevers said about the Bruins. "Sometimes we even have adequate goaltending."[16]

The Bruins brushed aside the Leafs (80 points) in a five-game opening round, then squared off against the Blues (67 points), who had finished third in the West Division, in the semifinals.

Johnston and Cheevers split goaltending duties in the first three games, which the Bruins won handily. Tom Johnson, who had replaced Sinden as coach two years earlier, chose Cheevers to start the critical fourth game, in St. Louis. The Bruins posted a 5–3 victory and advanced to the Stanley Cup final for the second time in three seasons.

They squared off against the Rangers, who had placed second in the East Division and the NHL with 109 points. New York was led by one of the top lines in the league. All three men—Vic Hadfield, Jean Ratelle and Rod Gilbert—were high scorers. Ratelle was third in points (109).

But the Bruins were unfazed. Preparing for the opening game in Boston, they were "looser than one of Ted Williams' ties," according to a sportswriter, who also said the dressing room "resembled an airport terminal at rush hour." He spotted Esposito leaning against a wall, complaining that a photographer

BONDING BRUINS

T HE BIG Bad Bruins had fun together and so did their wives. They sang their hearts out, karaoke-style, to celebrate one Stanley Cup victory and even hit the ice for a game of shinny, with each woman playing her husband's position. Ed Johnston's wife, Diane, and Betty Cheevers played in net while Cheesy served as play-by-play announcer. "It was absolutely hysterical," says Diane.

had confused him with his brother, Tony. "That's all I had to hear," the star forward said. "I told him to buzz off." The sportswriter then glanced at Cheevers, who was sitting in the corner reading the daily racing form. "Is Riva Ridge for real?" the incredulous goalie asked, referring to a horse that won the Kentucky Derby and Belmont Stakes that year.[17]

The Bruins won the first two games, then traveled to New York for Game 3. Cheevers anticipated the welcome at Madison Square Garden to be less than congenial. "I'm scared playing there," he confessed. "It's the apples they throw. You get an apple thrown from near the top of the building, it can knock you out. Then they throw coins, naturally. I remember from our series in 1970. And apples and oranges, occasionally lighters, which could kill you."[18]

The Rangers won two of the next three games even though two of their best players, Ratelle and Giacomin, were nursing injuries, but the Bruins weren't about to roll over. In Game 6, Boston forward Wayne Cashman, once described as "the meanest Bruin," scored two goals and Cheevers made some spectacular saves to record a shutout. The Bruins posted a 3–0 victory to win the Cup.

Boston players celebrated on the ice as Rangers fans—including President Richard Nixon's national security advisor, Henry Kissinger—filed out of Madison Square Garden, some pausing to hiss at the Bruins. "Eat your hearts out!" Cheevers shouted at the fans, who had hurled a bag of nuts at his head in Game 3. The goalie was named the first star of the game.[19]

"I know I probably shouldn't say this, but I knew damn well they wouldn't beat me tonight. I felt like Riva Ridge out there," Cheevers said as he and his teammates sipped beer out of the Cup. (No one had brought champagne.)[20]

After the victory, the Bruins gathered at Orr's restaurant, the Branding Iron, which had casseroles and other party treats prepared several days earlier.

Today, Cheevers cites his shutout in the final game as one of his most cherished memories. "I'll always remember that game because it is the only one I can recall where the puck went by me so many times without going in," he says. "The puck would hit a stick or a defenseman and bounce past the net. One time, the puck got by me, but it hit a glove someone had dropped on the ice and dribbled wide of the net."

1972-75

Cheevers and the Bruins entered contract negotiations that summer but couldn't reach an agreement, so Cheevers jumped ship. He signed a lucrative seven-year deal with the Cleveland Crusaders of the new World Hockey Association (WHA), a professional league that upended hockey's world order by outbidding stingy NHL executives for marquee players such as Bobby Hull. That contributed to the rise of salaries for NHL players in subsequent years.

The Crusaders' owner, Nick Mileti, declared Cheevers a franchise player and described him as "an intelligent, alert and honest individual." Cheevers corrected his new boss. "I wouldn't have been a goaltender if I was intelligent," he said.[21]

Bruins fans and players were disappointed, but the club's management was incensed. They took Cheevers to court, claiming he had violated the terms of his existing contract, which stipulated the Bruins kept his playing rights after his contract expired. But the court ruled in Cheevers's favor, stating the goalie couldn't be bound to the franchise through the so-called reserve clause. The ruling forever changed labor relations between NHL franchises and their players.

Cheevers resettled on the shore of Lake Erie. In his first season with the Crusaders, he finished with more wins (32) than all rivals except for Bernie Parent, who had left the NHL to suit up for the Philadelphia Blazers. But Cheevers had the best goals-against average (2.84) in the league, and won the Ben Hatskin Trophy as the top goalie. He finished second in wins (30) and goals-against average (3.03) the following season, but his experience in Cleveland was not rewarding. The team was eliminated in the first round of the playoffs in two of its first three seasons.

Cheevers was uninspired, but a tournament in the fall of 1974 got his blood pumping. He joined the WHA's top players, many of whom had defected from the NHL, to play against a team from the Soviet Union. The series featured four games in Moscow and four in Canadian cities. With stars such as Cheevers, Hull, Gordie Howe, Frank Mahovlich and Paul Henderson on the roster, Canadian fans were hopeful the team would at least push the powerful Soviets to the brink, but it was not to be. The Soviets posted four wins, one loss and three ties to come out on top, and Canadian fans were denied the opportunity to celebrate as they had when Henderson scored the winning goal two years earlier, in the historic Summit Series.

Cheevers played in seven of the series' eight games despite suffering a muscle strain that limited his mobility. His father-in-law had a heart attack while watching the second game—a 4–1 Canadian victory—so Cheevers sat out the next one to be with his family. His goals-against average in the tournament was an uninspiring 3.43, but that didn't diminish his stature in the eyes of Vladislav Tretiak. The Russian goalie blushed like a Moscow schoolgirl when Cheevers tapped him on the pads before each game to wish him luck.

1975-76

Back in Cleveland, the Crusaders continued to redefine mediocrity. Cheevers became so disheartened that, when a friend was admitted to hospital, the goalie sent him a message that read, "Cheer up. Things could be worse. You could be playing goal in Cleveland."[22]

The franchise's finances were not in order either. The players' paychecks came late and often bounced. Cheevers responded by lending some of them money.

His gesture didn't endear him to management, though. General manager Jack Vivian grew more frustrated with each second-rate performance and lashed out at his marquee player. After a loss in January, he fined Cheevers and suspended him, insisting that the goalie wasn't playing as well as his salary warranted. Relations between them became so strained that Vivian granted Cheevers's wish to be released from his contract.

The sound of groaning in the Cleveland dressing room was music to the ears of Bruins management, who still owned the goalie's NHL rights and wanted him back in the fold.

The prospect of returning to Boston appealed to Betty Cheevers, who told reporters she missed her many friends in the area. Also, her husband missed his horses. He had sizable investments in several that raced at tracks on the East Coast.

To the delight of Boston fans and maybe even the horses Cheevers so adored, the goalie returned to the Bruins in January 1976. He ended up with a front-row seat to a gruesome sight.

On February 7, Darryl Sittler stepped onto the ice at Maple Leaf Gardens with his sights trained on Boston's rookie goalie, Dave Reece. The Leafs captain set a single-game NHL record by notching six goals and four assists, lessening Reece's will to live with each shot on net. Cheevers looked on in horror with a famous proverb playing in an endless loop in his head: "There but for the grace of God go I." The Leafs won 11–4.

Don Cherry, who had become the Bruins' coach in 1974, didn't end Reece's suffering and pull him from the game; he wanted Cheevers's first appearance with the Bruins in four years to be on home ice. That happened the next night.

With Reece picking up the pieces of his shattered ego, Cheevers made a triumphant return to the Boston Garden. He made 22 saves and didn't allow a single goal in a 7–0 win over the Detroit Red Wings.

Esposito was no longer with the Bruins because he had been traded to the Rangers three months earlier, and Orr was sidelined with a knee injury, so Boston lacked the firepower that had once catapulted the team to the top of the standings. But recent Boston acquisition Gilles Gilbert was a very good goalie—he finished third in wins (33) that season—and Cheevers was no slouch either. They helped the Bruins finish second in the Prince of Wales Conference (113 points).

Boston started the playoffs by taking on the Los Angeles Kings (85 points) and won the series in seven games. The Bruins then met the Flyers, who had won the Cup in the two previous seasons, in the semifinals. Their brutality had earned them legions of fans in the Delaware Valley and just as many enemies everywhere else. The Flyers had bullied, bludgeoned and beaten opponents to finish at the top of the Clarence Campbell Conference standings (118 points). They made quick work of the Bruins in the playoffs, eliminating them in five games.

Cheevers could have spent the entire summer at the racetrack, but he was back on the ice in August to prepare for the 1976 Canada Cup. He was reunited with Orr and Esposito at training camp in Montreal—and it felt so good. Unfortunately, the drive from a hotel to the Forum for an intra-squad game wasn't as pleasant. The cab Cheevers and Esposito were riding in collided with another vehicle. The two players limped away from the accident with bruises, but lived to play another day. As it turned out, Cheevers didn't see ice time in the six-team tournament—Rogie Vachon played in all seven games—but he bore witness to a historic event. Team Canada, which won the tournament, is widely regarded as the most talented Canadian squad ever assembled. Eighteen of its 25 members would end up in the Hall of Fame.

1976-78

Revenge is a dish best served cold—or as cold cuts, according to Tony Soprano—so the Bruins set their sights on another playoff showdown with Philadelphia's Broad Street Bullies, and they got what they wanted.

With Cheevers manning the net in most games and skaters such as Ratelle (who had joined the team in 1975), Terry O'Reilly, Peter McNab and Brad Park racking up the points, Boston finished second in their conference twice (106 points and 113 points, respectively) over the next two seasons, and met the Flyers, who placed first (112 points) and second (105 points) in their conference, in two consecutive semifinals.

The Bruins refused to be cowed by the rough-and-tumble Flyers or by their two biggest stars—captain Bobby Clarke, who was as tenacious as he was talented, and Parent, who had returned to the Flyers from the WHA in 1973 and proceeded to win several individual awards and play a big role in the team's two consecutive championships.

The Bruins held the Flyers to just one win over two semifinal series, and Cheevers deserved much of the credit. He stopped all but eight of 121 shots in the 1977 series, cementing his reputation as a so-called "money goalie," one who played his best when it mattered most. "With Gerry, statistics just don't mean anything," said Cherry. "If we're leading 6–0, he'll let in two, three easy ones. But if we're winning 2–1, look out. There's no goaltender tougher than he is."[23]

In both seasons, Boston met its old nemesis, Montreal, in the final. The Habs were a powerhouse, finishing at the top of league standings in 1977 (132 points) and 1978 (129 points). The defending Stanley Cup champions had depth at every position and one of the NHL's most exciting players—Guy Lafleur. His speed, creamy-smooth skating style and magic touch around the net had vaulted him to the top of the NHL scoring ladder. Habs fans venerated le *Démon Blond* in Quebec's house of hockey worship, the Montreal Forum. Dryden was equally impressive, finishing first or second in most statistical categories.

Still, Cheevers had reason to feel confident playing the Habs. He had been spectacular in a game at the Forum in October 1976, helping the Bruins beat the Canadiens 4–3. It was Montreal's only loss at home that season. Cheevers celebrated by renting a bus and taking his teammates and their wives to see the musical *Grease*. He dressed for the occasion in tails and tennis shoes.[24]

It was clear the Canadiens didn't intimidate him. In Game 2 of the 1977 final, Cheevers charged out of his net and confronted Lafleur after the star fired a shot directly at Bruins defenseman Mike Milbury, with whom he had locked horns earlier in the game. "Hey! You're too good for that sort of thing!" Cheevers shouted at Lafleur, perhaps giving the flying Frenchman something to ponder while hauling on a cigarette between periods.[25]

In Game 2 of the 1978 final, Cheevers seemed superhuman. Manning the net in stifling heat with a battered knee—he had spent much of the regular season on the sidelines with a torn anterior cruciate ligament (ACL)—he made one brilliant save after another, even during a brief stint when he had to play without a stick. The Canadiens swarmed around the Bruins net like angry hornets during overtime, but Cheevers shut them down until Lafleur finally put the puck past him. The Habs won the game 5–4 to take the series lead. "If the Bruins were unable to defeat the champions with the kind of goaltending they got from Cheevers last night," one journalist wrote, "all the confidence in Massachusetts won't help them should Cheesy ever return to earth and play like a mortal."[26]

As it turned out, Cheevers and his teammates were in fact mortal. They lost to the Habs in two straight finals.

Despite being laser-focused on hockey in those years, Cheevers kept an eye on the racetrack. His thoroughbred horse, Royal Ski, was one of the best two-year-olds on the circuit and a favorite to win the 1977 Kentucky Derby. Unfortunately, illness prevented the colt from competing in the race. But that didn't stop journalists from peppering Cheevers with questions about it when the Bruins arrived in Montreal to start the 1977 final, which was held the same day as the derby. "Hey," Cheevers pleaded while puffing on a giant cigar, "doesn't anybody realize we're here to play a hockey game?" The Habs sure did; they trounced the Bruins 7–3 in Game 1.[27]

1978-80

Cheevers remained strong in net in the next two seasons, finishing among the top 10 starters in goals-against average and wins. But as he inched closer to his 40th birthday, the strain on his joints started to take a toll. He underwent several knee surgeries, including one after a knee buckled while he was walking up some stairs, and he spent more time on the sidelines than he would have liked.

His joints faltered but his sense of humor never did. On one occasion, he went missing in action and Betty was concerned enough to call the arena looking for him. When Cherry spotted the goalie in the trainer's room before a practice, he advised him to call his wife, which Cheevers did. Cherry overheard Cheevers on the phone. "Don't pay the ransom," the goalie said to Betty. "I've escaped!"

The Bruins' fortunes didn't improve during that time. They scored fewer goals as a team and none of them finished among the NHL's top scorers. Boston placed second (100 points) and third (105 points) in their conference, but failed to make the final. The Habs (115 points) eliminated them in the semifinals in 1979, and the upstart New York Islanders beat them in the quarterfinals the next season.

When Bruins fans look back on those two seasons, many remember the team's playoff appearances, but many more remember a bizarre incident that involved unruly spectators, furious players and some footwear.

At the end of a game between the Bruins and the Rangers at Madison Square Garden in December 1979, players from both teams engaged in the time-honored but rarely observed tradition of shouting obscenities at each other before leaving the ice. Moved by the spirit of the moment, a spectator leaned down and swatted Bruins forward Stan Jonathan with a rolled-up program. He also grabbed the player's stick for good measure. Several Bruins climbed over the glass panels surrounding the ice in pursuit of the culprit. Their skate blades didn't provide much traction on the concrete, but Milbury managed to catch the fan, forcibly remove one of his shoes and smack him with it. In the weeks that followed, police charged several fans with disorderly conduct and the NHL handed out suspensions and fines like Christmas bonuses.

Cheevers wasn't involved in the altercation at the end of the Bruins' 4–3 win. By the time Milbury grabbed the spectator's shoe—as tenderly as Prince Charming once removed Cinderella's shoe in favor of a glass slipper—Cheevers had clocked out. "I was already on my second beer at the time," he told reporters.[28]

After the season, doctors examined the goalie's knees and told him they wouldn't hold out for another year of hockey. That led Cheevers to make a tough decision: Almost 20 years after his NHL debut, he would retire. "Many mornings I woke up and it's taken me a couple of minutes to straighten out my [left] leg," he told reporters. "My whole decision is based on my legs."[29]

RETIREMENT

On the same day Cheevers announced his retirement, Bruins management introduced him as the team's new head coach. "Coaching the Boston Bruins is a tough position," Cheevers acknowledged a few days later, "but hockey is my life; it's been my whole life. And now this, this could be death after life."[30]

His time behind the bench didn't end his life, but it may have shortened it by a few years. In April 1981, the Minnesota North Stars, who had never before won a game in Boston, swept the Bruins in a preliminary-round playoff series.

However, management had faith in their new coach, and Cheevers rewarded them by leading the Bruins to the top of the conference standings in two of the next three seasons. But he couldn't lead the team back to the promised land; the closest the Bruins came was the 1983 conference final, where they lost to the New York Islanders, hockey's newest dynasty.

Still, Cheevers never lost his sense of fun. Before one game, he instructed the Bruins' video man to record the final episode of the television show M*A*S*H rather than the game. When the opposing team requested a copy of the game tape, Cheevers obtained one from a television station and passed it along. "I couldn't reveal what had really happened," Cheevers says, laughing.

By February 1985, the Bruins had fallen to seventh place in the 11-team conference and Cheevers was no longer feeling the love from Bruins management. That was especially true when they served him his walking papers just before Valentine's Day. Cheevers wasn't heartbroken. "It was great to be coach of the Bruins," he said years later. "Did I like it? No. If I had to do it again, I would probably have played three or four more years rather than switch to coaching."[31]

He wasn't down for long, though. He was inducted into the Hockey Hall of Fame that September. At that point, he was enjoying time in the horse-racing world and working as director of promotions for Rockingham Park racetrack in Salem, New Hampshire. "I'm getting paid for something I'd be doing anyway," said Cheevers.[32]

The following year, he became the color commentator for the Hartford Whalers, a former WHA team that had joined the NHL in 1979, and he stayed in the job for almost a decade. Soon after, he took on the same role for the Bruins. He did that for three years and later joined the team's scouting staff.

Now working on his golf game in Florida, Cheevers focuses on the present. But he has great memories of his NHL career. "How do I want to be remembered? As someone who really enjoyed the game," he says. "I would like to be remembered as someone who had a lot of fun and could, on occasion, win a big game."

III

GERRY CHEEVERS • ALL-TIME RANKING

REGULAR SEASON			PLAYOFFS		
GAMES + RANK	WINS + RANK	SO + RANK	GAMES + RANK	WINS + RANK	SO + RANK
418 [111TH]	227 [77TH]	26 [90TH]	88 [28TH]	53 [20TH]	8 [16TH]

+ **NHL ALL-STAR TEAM (1ST)** 1972-73

+ **NHL ALL-STAR TEAM (2ND)** 1973-74, 1974-75

||||||| 4 |||||||

THE WORKING-
CLASS HERO
ED GIACOMIN

|||||||||||||||||||||||||||||||

AFTER A SKATE blade sliced open his hand in a 1971 play-off game, Ed Giacomin showed up for the New York Rangers morning skate the next day and slipped a catching glove over his swollen, stitched-up paw. Mindful of the goaltender's injury, his teammates left the hot sauce off their shots on net. Giacomin was incensed. "Damn it, you guys! What are you waiting for?" he shouted. "Let's see some real shots!"

Giacomin's famous grit and doggedness helped him become one of the best goalies in hockey and won him legions of fans in New York, where he spent most of his career. From Staten Island to the Bronx, he's still celebrated as a working-class hero.

GIACOMIN'S STORY started more than 725 miles northwest of Gotham, in Sudbury, about 37 miles north of Georgian Bay. He was born in June 1939, 11 years after Falconbridge Nickel Mines opened for business and helped establish Sudbury as a thriving mining town.

He lived in a modest home with his parents, Tony and Cecile, and two older brothers. The boys developed a passion for hockey at an early age and crowded around the radio every Saturday night to listen to Foster Hewitt call NHL games for fans in Canada, the US and that faraway kingdom of Newfoundland.

Ed Giacomin tracks the puck, resisting the urge to wander out of his net and up the ice. **FRANK PRAZAK/HOCKEY HALL OF FAME**

Like countless Canadian kids, Eddie idolized NHL stars such as Maurice "Rocket" Richard and Walter "Turk" Broda, but his true hero was the brother closest to him in age. Rollie Giacomin was a good goaltender whose services were often enlisted by local teams.

Eddie wanted to follow in his brother's footsteps, but the family could afford only one set of goalie equipment, and Rollie wore it most of the time. Eddie spent hours at the rink with his nose pressed up against the glass, waiting for his brother to take a break and hand over the gear.

Eddie was so small he could barely see over the goalie pads he wore, but the little boy had big plans. When his Grade 7 teacher asked students what they wanted to be when they grew up, Eddie announced that he was going to be an NHL goalie. His class-mates snickered at him, but he ended up having the last laugh.

Giacomin was a natural athlete who excelled in baseball and football, but his road to the NHL was rocky.

When he was 16 years old, Giacomin got cut from a local midget team and ended up playing on a team consisting of other players who had suffered the same fate. Two of them, Gary Sabourin and Frank St. Marseille, ended up playing in the NHL.

A Detroit Red Wings scout noticed the scrappy teenager, who had a dexterous, sprawling style of goaltending, and invited him to try out for the club's junior team in the OHA. Giacomin traveled to Canada's steel town to try out for the Hamilton Red Wings—twice. He failed to make the team both times.

Johnny Mitchell, who ran Detroit's farm team in the Eastern Hockey League (EHL), a minor-pro league whose players were paid to play, sized up Giacomin and advised him to pack it in.

Giacomin returned to Sudbury and joined an industrial league. Players had to pay to compete and, to add insult to injury, they were required to help clean the ice. Giacomin spent his days at a chemical plant, where he worked as a mechanic's helper. But he held on tight to his dreams.

"Hockey had become my goal," he later recalled. "I realized that there were only six guys in the whole world who were NHL goalies at the time and I made it a challenge to myself to become one of them."[1]

Late in the 1958–59 season, Leo Gasparini, the coach of a local hockey team and a well-known figure in sports circles, picked up the phone in his Sudbury home. Andy Branigan, coach of the EHL's Washington Presidents, was on the line. He was looking for a goalie. Gasparini recommended Rollie, who was a practice goalie for a local senior amateur team.

But Rollie had a good job at the chemical plant, which he was reluctant to leave, so he sent his kid brother in his place. When

Eddie showed up at the rink in Washington, DC, Branigan was shocked. Instead of a strapping goalie, he was looking at a teenager built like a rice noodle. Branigan balked at the prospect of Eddie playing in the EHL, but when the Presidents lost a few games, he turned to the skinny kid at the end of the bench who had traveled more than 700 miles to chase a dream.

Giacomin played in the next four games, facing around 60 shots in each one, thanks to the team's porous defense, and the Presidents won all of them.

That impressed scouts for the Providence Reds, a Boston Bruins affiliate in the AHL, who invited him to the team's training camp that fall. Eddie was excited about getting a chance to play professional hockey, but fate almost robbed him of that opportunity.

One night that summer, after Eddie had returned to Sudbury for the off-season, smoke filled the Giacomin home and woke up family members, who soon encountered a kitchen stove in distress. As Eddie and Rollie approached the appliance, it burst into flames. The brothers managed to put out the fire, but not before Eddie suffered severe burns on his legs and feet. He ended up undergoing several skin grafts, which forced him to wear bandages for almost a year. Doctors told him hockey was out of the question. Giacomin nodded politely and ignored their advice.

Concerned that Reds management would send him home if they knew about his injuries, he hid them from coaches and players during training camp. He arrived at the rink early every day to wrap his legs in bandages when no one else was there, and he didn't remove them until the end of the day, when the dressing room was empty. "My legs were still bleeding," he said later. "If they'd seen them I would have been cut."[2]

Giacomin played through the pain, hoping no one would notice the blood soaking through his bandages, and fared well enough to convince the Reds to sign him. He played just one game for the Reds that season, and spent most of it on two EHL farm teams in New York State: the New York Rovers and the Clinton Comets. Al Baron, the Rovers' president at the time, later said the team was so bad, "Giacomin had to learn to play goal not to win, but to merely survive."[3]

Giacomin was improving, but he was still unable to crack the Reds' roster. After training camp for the 1960–61 season, the team made Bruce Gamble, who had already played in two NHL games, their starter. Disappointed, Giacomin rejoined the Rovers in Commack. It was home to a motor inn that a local radio station designated as one of the seven wonders of Long Island. Only a building shaped like a duck was ranked higher.

While Giacomin cooled his heels in Commack, Gamble hit his stride 200 miles up the Eastern Seaboard, in Providence. He played so well that the Bruins called him up and dispatched Don Simmons to Rhode Island. Reds coach Phil Watson wasn't thrilled with Simmons, so he called up Giacomin, saving the goalie from the indignity of competing for attention with a giant waterfowl. Giacomin played 43 games for the Reds that season, and he remained the team's starter for the next four campaigns.

For much of that time, the Reds hovered near the bottom of the AHL standings, and for two seasons, they landed there. Giacomin routinely faced 40 or more shots a game. Fern Flaman, who replaced Watson as coach in the 1961–62 season, encouraged Giacomin to handle the puck, not only because the goalie had an aptitude for it, but also because the team desperately needed a third defenseman on the ice.

Giacomin was soon wandering into corners and venturing as far as the blue line to handle the puck. But that didn't prevent him from tending to matters at home, in the crease. He posted more shutouts (6) in the 1963–64 season than any of his AHL counterparts, including future NHL stars Gump Worsley, Roger Crozier and Gerry Cheevers. His exploits impressed a local clothing retailer, who rewarded him with a pair of dress pants for each shutout. Giacomin gave most of them to teammates, creating a dressing room full of sharp-dressed men.

In the summer of 1964, he injured his back in a car accident, so he started the season wearing a leather-and-steel brace around his torso. But he played well enough to attract the attention of several NHL teams. The Reds were hesitant to let their star goaltender go, but owner Lou Pieri agreed to send him to the New York Rangers if they, in turn, sent his club four players who could stand on skates, handle the puck and cause pandemonium in a beauty parlor with their good looks. Pieri figured he could attract more female fans if the Reds' roster included some handsome players. Rangers general manager Emile Francis scrutinized his players' jawlines, hair and teeth—in those who had some—and sent the four who most resembled Sean Connery to Providence. After traveling a long, bumpy road, Giacomin had finally reached his destination.

NHL

1965-66

Giacomin's excellent reflexes and ability to handle the puck won him the starter's job in New York over two other rookies, Gilles Villemure and Cesare Maniago, in training camp. He was solid in his first two outings of the regular season, but he soon started to founder.

The Montreal Canadiens, the defending Stanley Cup champions, shelled Giacomin en route to a 9–3 victory at the Montreal Forum in mid-November. He was so shaken that Canadiens goalie Gump Worsley, an aging star who watched from the bench that night, approached him at a train station after the game to console him. Worsley had felt the same pain. He had left the Rangers in 1963, after 11 seasons with the team. New York had missed the playoffs in all but four of those seasons.

Despite Gumper's pep talk, Giacomin continued to struggle; he mishandled shots and pucks filled the net when he wandered up the ice. Rangers fans grew impatient with his unorthodox style and urged him to return to the crease, chanting "Get back in there!" When that didn't help, they pelted the 26-year-old rookie with garbage.

In early January, the Rangers sent him to the AHL's Baltimore Clippers, and Maniago took his spot as the Rangers' starter.

But Giacomin seized the opportunity to work on his game. His workmanlike attitude impressed Francis, who called him back after a couple of weeks. "This was when we found out what Giacomin was made of," Francis said later. "He did not sulk about going back for a while and he worked like hell to get his timing and confidence back. When I saw this, I was even more convinced that we could make a good goaltender out of Eddie."[4]

Giacomin spent the rest of the season playing second fiddle to Maniago but continued to refine his skills in practice, urging his teammates to pepper him with shots. Although they were competing for the top spot, Giacomin and Maniago got along well and sometimes drove into Manhattan together from Atlantic Beach, a community off the south shore of Long Island where they both lived. The goalies commiserated over the fact that Francis refused to tell them in advance which one would start in a given game. In fact, it was never clear until the team was heading out for the pregame warm-up and the trainer handed the puck to that night's starter. "I remember Eddie looking at me on one drive and saying, 'There are times where I wish you were starting instead of me because I can't prepare myself for a game when everything is a big question mark,'" says Maniago.

After the first week of April, there were no more drives into the city for the two men. The Rangers missed the playoffs for the fourth straight year.

1966-67

The team continued to struggle and dropped to the bottom of the standings early in the following season. Giacomin was part of the problem. He continued to cost the team goals by wandering up the ice like an emperor penguin on a quest to find a mate. He got caught out of position twice in back-to-back games against the Toronto Maple Leafs in early November, allowing critical goals in a loss and a tie. In the latter game, Dave Keon evened the score for the Leafs while Giacomin was far from his home in the crease. "Goalie Ed Giacomin, who will never be accused of being a home body, may wander right out of the National Hockey League," one reporter wrote.[5]

Francis, who had taken over as coach in 1965, was not amused. In the Rangers dressing room after the second game, he announced that "a forward is a forward, a defenseman is a defenseman and a goalie is a goalie. Each belongs in his appointed place." He didn't mention any names, but it was clear he was talking to Giacomin.[6]

The goalie seemed destined to return to Baltimore, but fate intervened. Three nights after tying the Leafs, the Rangers took on the Bruins at home. Maniago started in net, and in the second period, Bruins forward Johnny McKenzie blasted a shot that ripped into the goalie's face. Maniago headed to the dressing room, and Giacomin took his place. After getting stitched up, Maniago said he was in too much pain to play.

Francis, who had suffered broken noses, torn knee ligaments, separated shoulders and hundreds of stitches during his own days as a professional goaltender, wasn't pleased. If Maniago could skate to the bench, Francis reasoned, he could play.

Francis decided then and there that Giacomin would be the team's starter. He stuck to his guns even after fans pelted Giacomin with apple cores, banana peels and unfinished hero sandwiches when the Bruins tied the score 3–3 late in the game. "The next time they throw anything at you, pick it up and throw it right back," he told Giacomin, who had taken shelter in his net after a bottle shattered a few feet from him.

It was a turning point in Giacomin's career. He began working with Francis, learning to cut down angles, give up fewer rebounds and keep his stick on the ice. "He's a worker," Francis said, "and more important, he has plenty of intestinal fortitude."[7]

That was never clearer than in a game against the Leafs in January. Frank Mahovlich, one of the NHL's hardest shooters, blasted a shot that struck Giacomin on the jaw. Francis ran onto the ice, ready to take the goalie out of the game, but Giacomin refused to leave his post. His dedication won over Rangers fans, who started eating their food at games—a novel idea—rather than hurling it at the goalie.

Giacomin shone the rest of the season and ended up playing more games (68) and notching more wins (30) and shutouts (9) than any of his NHL counterparts. He was a finalist for the Hart Trophy.

He helped the Rangers finish fourth in the six-team league with 72 points and advance to the playoffs for the first time since 1962. High-scoring forwards Rod Gilbert and Phil Goyette chipped in.

The Rangers started the playoffs by taking on the Canadiens (77 points), who had two of the league's top scorers, Bobby Rousseau and Yvan Cournoyer, on the roster. With Jean Béliveau leading the charge, the Habs swept the Rangers aside in four games. Not even the fans' chants of "We're not dead yet!" could spur the team to victory in Game 4 at Madison Square Garden.

Giacomin, who struggled in the series, let in the winning goal in overtime—and it wasn't pretty. He blocked a shot and moved to his right, thinking the puck was tucked securely under his arm. But it dropped to the ice and, with Giacomin out of position, Habs forward John Ferguson batted it into the net to end the Rangers' season.

But Francis had faith in Giacomin and protected him in the NHL expansion draft in June. Sportswriter Norman MacLean saw it as a choice between "the cocky wanderer with the cat like reflexes, 'Go Go' Giacomin," and "the elongated Italian [Maniago], whose schnozzola rates with those of football's Joe Namath and baseball's Joe Pepitone." Maniago—and his apparently noteworthy proboscis—ended up playing for the Minnesota North Stars, one of six new NHL teams.[8]

1967-70

In the late 1960s, NHL teams began dividing goaltending duties between two men to ensure their top goalies weren't overtaxed. But New York was slow to adopt this system and Giacomin played in all but a handful of games in each of the next three seasons. In fact, he played in more games than any of his NHL rivals during that span.

His statistics were impressive, too. He notched the most wins in the league twice, and was second in wins in another season. He also led the league in shutouts in one of these years, and was second in shutouts in two others.

The legendary Terry Sawchuk, whom New York acquired in June 1969, played just 11 games in his one season with the team.

Giacomin's work ethic impressed fans and sportswriters, one of whom considered him dogged enough to confront the Red Menace. "[He] is one of the five or six goalers you would consider if you were recruiting a team to fight Russia at the Battle of Armageddon," Dick Beddoes wrote in the Globe and Mail.[9]

Giacomin was nothing if not scrappy. That was evident in Game 3 of the first round of the 1969 playoffs against the Montreal Canadiens. When a brawl broke out, he jumped into the fray. Worsley made a beeline for his counterpart and grabbed him around the neck. The Habs goalie seemed to have forgotten the tender moment the two men had shared at the Montreal train station four years earlier. Giacomin remembered, though, and refused to retaliate. "I turned around and I was surprised to see the Gump behind me," Giacomin said after the game. "I figured, if I hit him, I would kill him. I just didn't want to hurt the guy." It was all for the best. "I'm not a skater or a fighter," Worsley confessed. "I'm a lover."[10] Thankfully, he didn't elaborate.

Despite Giacomin's eagerness to play every game, many observers thought the Rangers paid a steep price for his heavy workload. They noted that he was far from spectacular in the playoffs and attributed it to fatigue. Without their star goalie in top form, the Rangers struggled. They were eliminated in the first round of the playoffs in each of the three seasons following their early exit in the 1967 postseason.

The losses added even more gray hair to Giacomin's head. "I always kid the other guys on the team and tell them that I'm going to convert to a forward later on when I can't stand the tension [of goaltending] anymore," he said. "You don't get gray for nothing."[11]

Giacomin's work ethic made him such a popular figure in New York that he appeared on *The Tonight Show* in December 1967, along with Rangers teammate Bernie "Boom Boom" Geoffrion. The two men put on a demonstration for the audience. Geoffrion fired the puck at Giacomin, who then allowed Johnny Carson, the show's host, to take his place. Geoffrion sent the first shot wide but it spooked Carson, who placed his catching glove over his crotch to prepare for the next shot. Fans were still talking about the appearance days later, but Giacomin wasn't saying much. One of Geoffrion's shots had hit him in the Adam's apple, leaving him without a voice for days.

1970-71

Francis eventually started relying on two goalies—Giacomin and Villemure, who had spent the better part of three seasons as starter for the Buffalo Bisons of the AHL.

The two men were a study in contrasts. Giacomin liked to handle the puck, making clearing passes and even taking the occasional shot at an opponent's empty net—he hoped to become the first NHL netminder to score a goal. Villemure, on the other hand, preferred to smother loose pucks to draw face-offs.

The differences didn't end there. "You can hear Giacomin all over the ice. He's always yelling at us, telling us where the puck is and who is chasing us," said Rangers defenseman Brad Park, adding that Villemure spoke only occasionally during games, and did so in a quiet voice. "He'll never have a voice like Eddie's," Park said. "Who has?"[12]

Giacomin preferred the one-goalie system—he wanted to go to work every day—but the benefits of the change soon became clear. He played in 45 regular-season games, just 11 more than Villemure. The dynamic duo gave the Rangers a much-needed boost. By New Year's Day, they were closing in on the league-leading Bruins.

"Well, it's almost that time of year again, the time for the New York Rangers to begin their annual collapse," Mark Mulvoy wrote in *Sports Illustrated*. "But, wait, something is wrong. The Rangers do not seem to be collapsing. Right now they're holding fast in a neck-and-neck race with Boston in the front of the East Division, and for 24 hours last week they were even in the lead. What's wrong with these Rangers? Two goalies, that's what's wrong."[13]

By the end of the regular season, the Rangers had allowed the fewest goals (177) in the league, and the team's two goalies shared the Vezina Trophy. Giacomin led the NHL in shutouts (8), and finished second in save percentage (.922) and goals-against average (2.16). Villemure was a finalist for the Calder Trophy.

Despite having just one high-scoring forward on the roster, Dave Balon, the Rangers finished second in the division, and in the league, with 109 points, behind only the Bruins (121 points).

The Rangers, now a team on the rise, opened the playoffs at home against the Leafs (82 points). Toronto was a team in transition that season, with an even mix of veterans and newcomers so young they were barely drinking age. Prolific goal scorers Dave Keon and Norm Ullman led the charge, while two future Hall of Fame goalies tended net—veteran Jacques Plante and a whippersnapper named Bernie Parent.

Toronto won Game 2 at the Garden, 4–1, to tie up the series, but it wasn't the score that made headlines the next day. A couple of brawls broke out in the third period, turning the ice into a battlefield. When Parent jumped into the first fracas, Rangers forward Vic Hadfield ripped off his mask and hurled it into the crowd. It deflected off a police officer and into the hands of a Rangers fan. Within seconds, Parent's mask disappeared into a roiling sea of spectators. When the PA announcer pleaded for its safe return, fans responded by chanting, "Keep it, keep it, keep it!" Leafs vice president Francis "King" Clancy ran around the mezzanine on a holy quest to find the mask, threatening to pummel anyone who stood in his way, but he was led away by security personnel. The mask didn't surface until 2012, when a memorabilia collector sent it to Parent for authentication.

Days after that memorable game, the NHL fined both teams and 28 of their players, including Giacomin. NHL president Clarence Campbell described the game as "one of the most derogatory spectacles which the league has produced in years."[14]

The Rangers eventually beat the Leafs in a six-game series, then headed to Chicago to take on the Black Hawks, who had placed first in the West Division (107 points), in the semifinals. Sensing that his star goalie was feeling anxious, Francis asked veteran defenseman Tim Horton to take Giacomin out the night before the game, to calm his nerves. The men had some drinks—none from the coffee shop Horton had opened seven years before—and stumbled into the hotel at 3:30 AM. Giacomin woke up with a hangover, but would soon endure worse pain.

The Black Hawks roster included Bobby Hull, who was greeted as warmly by NHL goalies as Darth Vader was by the Rebel Alliance. Even now, "The Imperial March" from *Star Wars* plays in their heads when they watch a highlight reel of his career. A sonic boom shook Chicago Stadium whenever the Golden Jet unleashed a slap shot, sending shivers down the spines of his opponents. Goalies tended to flinch when he wound up, which helped make him one of the most feared, and revered, players in the game.

In Game 1, Giacomin made a sprawling save on one of Hull's thunderous shots, thanks to great reflexes and God's tender mercy. Hull darted across the crease, chasing the rebound. He skated over Giacomin's catching glove and sliced his hand open. The goalie felt a burning sensation as blood pooled inside his glove, but he refused to leave the ice. He had a team trainer wrap bandages around his hand and he continued to play. As the minutes passed, a dark red stain spread across the leather.

The sight sickened Park. "The bandage kept coming loose and Eddie's glove was all bloody. The cut must have been a quarter-inch deep and the skin was ripped and hanging loose. Isn't he something? I'll tell you, when you talk about guys with guts you've got to mention his name," the defenseman said afterward.[15]

The wound was stitched up during intermission, and Giacomin was in net when the Rangers won the contest, 2–1, in overtime. "We probably shouldn't have won," said New York forward Jean Ratelle, who scored the Rangers' first goal. "Chicago had more chances than us. But Eddie kept us in the game and when he got hurt and wouldn't quit, it made us all play that much harder. I would have felt ashamed to lose because of what he was doing for us."[16]

"Eddie Giacomin is the most determined man I ever saw," Francis said after the game, while hauling on a Lucky Strike cigarette outside the Rangers dressing room. "He's had to work hard for anything he ever got. He wasn't born with a silver spoon in his mouth. This was his finest hour."[17]

Giacomin and Horton went out for drinks again the next night, but it didn't bring them good luck that time. The Rangers lost Game 2 and ended up losing the series in seven games. Rangers fans were disappointed, but not overly so; their team had advanced to the second round for the first time since 1967, and with fearless "Steady Eddie" in net, the future looked bright.

1971-72

When he stepped onto the ice the following season, Giacomin was still gaunt enough to pass for a mortician. But it was hard to tell because his face was covered by a fiberglass shield. He had decided to follow Plante's lead, as most of his peers already had, and don a rudimentary mask not unlike the one later sported by Jason Voorhees, the mass murderer in *Friday the 13th*. Giacomin had misgivings at first because he felt it impeded his vision, but it soon became clear he had made the right decision.

During a home game against the Black Hawks in February, Dennis Hull, whose shot was almost as feared as his brother's, fired the puck at the net at point-blank range. The puck dented Giacomin's mask and blew him off his feet. He lay spread-eagle on his back, looking like a gunshot victim. The Rangers' trainer rushed to his aid, but not to draw a chalk outline around the victim. He gave Giacomin a whiff of smelling salts and covered the gash on the goalie's nose with a bandage. Giacomin slowly rose to his feet, and spectators did the same, giving him a standing ovation. True to form, Giacomin refused to leave the game. He posted 41 saves that night, lifting the Rangers to a 4–1 win. Afterward, Hadfield marveled at the goalie's grit, telling reporters he deserved the Purple Heart. "My wife didn't like the mask," Giacomin quipped. "She said she could never tell if it was me or Gilles Villemure in goal. Maybe she'll appreciate it now."[18]

For the second straight year, the Rangers ended the regular season with 109 points, trailing only the Bruins (119 points) in the division and in the league. In addition to stellar goaltending, the team's best line consisted of three of the NHL's top scorers. Ratelle had placed third in scoring with 109 points, despite missing the last month of the regular season with a fractured ankle. He finished one spot ahead of Hadfield (106 points) and two spots ahead of Gilbert (97 points).

The Rangers took on the Canadiens in the first round of the playoffs. Superstar Jean Béliveau had retired the previous spring, but the Habs had a promising newcomer in Guy Lafleur and high scorers in Cournoyer, Mahovlich and J.C. Tremblay. But the team's young goalie was the undisputed star of the show in Montreal. Ken Dryden had burst onto the scene like a supernova in the previous playoffs, helping the Canadiens stage an upset over the mighty Bruins in the opening round. In the 1971–72 season, he topped the league in wins (39) and was awarded the Calder Trophy. He was also a Hart Trophy finalist.

The Rangers were in tough, but Giacomin thrived under the pressure. He allowed just 14 goals in the six-game series, posting a better save percentage (.914) than Dryden (.911). When the series ended at the Montreal Forum, Giacomin fell to the ice, rolled on his back and kicked his legs in the air looking like a delighted baby playing tickle-tickle. He had helped the Rangers beat the Habs in a playoff series for the first time since 1950.

The Rangers had precious little time to celebrate. They had to prepare for the semifinals against the Black Hawks. Bobby

Hull wasn't the only star on the team that season. He shared the spotlight with goalie Tony Esposito, who had led the league in goals-against average (1.77) and shutouts (9). Esposito had also won the Vezina Trophy.

Giacomin was up for the challenge but fell down on the job in Game 1, in Chicago. After he made an acrobatic save to protect a one-goal lead late in the game, the Rangers' Ron Stewart fell on top of the goalie, whose knee was pinned against the post. Giacomin struggled to stand, and it looked like he was done for the night. But he managed to finish the game, even making some tough saves in the final seconds. The Rangers skated to a 3–2 victory. After the game, Giacomin was diagnosed with a severely strained knee ligament. He had finally met an injury he couldn't overcome with sheer determination. He had to take a seat on the sidelines. Villemure held the fort in his absence and the Rangers swept the Black Hawks aside in four games.

New York advanced to the Stanley Cup final for the first time since 1950. Excitement reached a fever pitch in Gotham in the days preceding Game 1, but fans were also anxious. They knew the Rangers faced an uphill battle; they would take on the Bruins, who were on a mission to redeem themselves following their shocking loss to Montreal in the previous postseason.

Boston had a lot of firepower. Phil Esposito, Tony's older brother, led the league in scoring with 133 points. Bobby Orr—you've heard of him, right?—finished just behind him with 117 points. The two stars had a strong supporting cast in high scorers Johnny Bucyk and Fred Stanfield.

Boston goalie Gerry Cheevers was no slouch either. He finished second in wins (27) and was near the top of the standings in goals-against average and shutouts. He was also considered a goalie who performed his best when it mattered most.

Before the puck dropped at the Boston Garden for Game 1, the Rangers observed their usual pregame ritual. Giacomin led his teammates out of the dressing room and onto the ice, and once there, they skated counterclockwise until he ordered them to switch direction. The ritual was meant to win the favor of the hockey gods, but it wasn't effective that night. The Bruins won the opening game 6–5.

The Rangers fought hard in the series, but with Giacomin nursing a knee injury—forcing him to split playing time evenly with Villemure—and Ratelle skating on an injured ankle after missing the first two rounds of the playoffs, they couldn't hold off the Bruins and the incomparable Orr.

The Bruins clinched the series with a 3–0 win in Game 6 at Madison Square Garden, where rowdy fans had always given the Bruins a rough ride. Orr said the victory was sweeter than the team's 1970 Stanley Cup win because this one happened in New York. "I have to say this is tops because we won here," he said after the game. "We had a lot of pressure on us. It started way back in training camp and just kept mounting. Now we can relax."[19]

1972-74

The Rangers had their revenge the following season, when they brushed the Bruins aside in the opening round of the playoffs. Giacomin was a big factor in the upset. He posted a shutout in the fourth game and was great in the fifth and deciding game. Sports columnist Rex MacLeod wrote that "Giacomin, often derided by the Bruins as a hot-dog type who folds under pressure, played a magnificent game." He added that the goalie "did most of his own fielding, often skating several feet out of his crease to clear the puck or pass to one of his forwards. He had a shot on the Boston goal." Thousands of fans showed up at the airport in New York to greet their returning heroes.[20]

Having defeated the defending Stanley Cup champions, the Rangers were confident they could beat the Black Hawks in the semifinals, but in the end they fell short. Even without Bobby Hull, who had left for greener (i.e., more lucrative) pastures in the WHA, Chicago was able to eliminate New York in a five-game series. The Rangers outshot the Black Hawks in every game but couldn't overcome the team's defense or Tony Esposito, who "was able to throw a leg, a glove, sometimes his complete body, in front of the best drives." Dennis Hull notched

10 points in the series, proving to be as much of a nuisance as his older brother had been.[21]

The Rangers regrouped, but as it turned out, the 1973–74 season wasn't good to them. Their spirits sagged when Horton, who was playing for the Buffalo Sabres at the time, died in a car crash in February. Giacomin, Hadfield and several other NHL players attended the funeral, which was held on a frigid, sunny day in Toronto.

Six weeks later, the Rangers opened the playoffs in Montreal. The Canadiens were the defending Stanley Cup champions, but the Rangers managed to eliminate them in a six-game series, thanks in large part to Giacomin, who was steady in net, and veteran forward Pete Stemkowski, who recorded nine points.

New York then took on the Philadelphia Flyers, who had joined the league in 1967 and were so rough that sportswriters who covered the team peppered their prose with terms most often used to report on gangland warfare. The team's scrappy captain, Bobby Clarke, led the charge with help from players such as Bob "Mad Dog" Kelly and Dave "the Hammer" Schultz. Their goalie, Parent, had emerged as one of the best in the game while wearing a mask that had replaced the one Hadfield tossed into the crowd in 1971.

The semifinal was a pitched battle. In the first period of the seventh game, a fight broke out between Schultz and the Rangers' Dale Rolfe. Schultz beat Rolfe senseless while the Rangers looked on helplessly. Francis had warned them to be mindful of a new rule stipulating that any player who jumped into a fight already underway would be ejected from the game. Giacomin thought the incident sealed his team's fate—a 4–3 loss. "As far as I'm concerned, we were one punch away from winning the Stanley Cup," he said.[22]

Schultz dismissed the Rangers as sissies for allowing the beating to take place—all the Rangers but one. "If every one of the Rangers had Eddie's guts, no one would have let me beat up on Dale Rolfe in the final game," Schultz said years later. "Eddie would have whacked me with his big stick."[23]

1974-78

As Giacomin moved into his mid-30s, the wear and tear on his joints began to show. Injuries kept him on the sidelines more often. He played in just 37 games in the 1974–75 season, the fewest since his rookie year.

He and Villemure split goaltending duties in a first-round series against the New York Islanders, whose dynamic goalies, Billy Smith and Glenn "Chico" Resch, were a decade younger. The upstart Islanders, then in their third NHL season, upset the Rangers two games to one. (Two new teams joined the NHL this season, bringing the total to 18, and the league was reconfigured. A best-of-three preliminary series was added to the postseason.)

The Rangers acquired a promising young goaltender, John Davidson, from the St. Louis Blues in June, making it clear that Giacomin's days in New York were numbered. When he started the 1975–76 season with one tie and three losses, the club put him on waivers. The Red Wings claimed him on Halloween, starting a scary new chapter in his life.

Francis broke the news to him at the team's practice facility in Long Beach, while his wife, Marge, waited in the car. The couple stopped for a drink on the way home and saw the news on television. "It was the emptiest and probably most heartbreaking moment. The team was in Montreal [to play the Canadiens] and I had nobody to turn to after all those years," Giacomin recalled.[24]

Giacomin's teammates were dismayed. "It was a big shock," Rangers forward Steve Vickers said years later. "He was our emotional leader, our captain without the 'C.'"[25]

When Giacomin reported to the Red Wings two days later, management gave him the option of sitting out that night's game against the Rangers at Madison Square Garden, but Giacomin wanted to play. "That was gutty," coach Alex Delvecchio recalled. "He could have copped out."[26]

Giacomin had been popular in New York because of his grit and frequent interaction with fans—he would wave to those he saw regularly at the Garden—but he knew they were temperamental, and he wasn't sure how they would respond. Concerned that a fusillade of half-eaten fruit and other snacks might force him to shelter in place in the back of his net, he urged Marge and their children, Mark, David and Nancy, to stay away.

He stepped onto the ice that night wearing the iconic jersey of the Red Wings, longtime rivals of the Rangers. The Garden was now enemy territory, but he received a hero's welcome. Spectators rose to their feet en masse and chanted "Ed-die! Eddie! Ed-die!" for more than three minutes. "It was amazing, unbelievable. I couldn't even hear the national anthem," Giacomin recalled decades later. "I was shaking so much, I thought I might faint. There were tears in my eyes. I felt like blessing those people."[27]

The cheering continued periodically throughout the game, and the crowd booed Rangers players who had the audacity to shoot the puck in Giacomin's direction. The players themselves felt badly about doing that. After scoring in the third period, Vickers apologized to Giacomin.

While fans—some of whom had hung up a sign that read, STEADY EDDIE, WE MISS YOU ALREADY!—gave the beloved goalie a rapturous welcome, they all but spat at the man who had put him on the auction block. Chants of "Kill the Cat!" rang out in the Garden, a clear reference to Francis's nickname.

When Giacomin arrived home at 1:30 AM, his former teammates were there to greet him. They shared drinks and laughs until the wee hours of the morning.

The following summer, when Giacomin and his sons attended a baseball game at Yankee Stadium, the message board lit up with the words WELCOME EDDIE GIACOMIN, GOALIE FOR THE NEW YORK RANGERS! Someone had to tell the red-faced operator to change the team name.[28]

Giacomin wasn't the best goalie in the NHL or even Detroit over the next two seasons, and he played just 62 games during that span, but he wasn't about to go gentle into that good night. When a brawl broke out during a home game against Toronto in March 1976, the 36-year-old goalie didn't hesitate to jump over the boards and into the fray.

He grabbed hold of Rod Seiling, who had been a defenseman with the Rangers for 12 seasons. "I wasn't going to hit him and he knew it," Seiling says of his former teammate. "I pleaded with him to let me go so I could pair up with another Detroit player, but he just laughed and hung on to me."

Why wouldn't Seiling give the goalie so much as a love tap? "Eddie always had a good word to say, and he was usually very upbeat," he explains. "He was a lot of fun to be around, and he was a good person."

Giacomin played nine games for the Red Wings in the 1977–78 season before the team put him on waivers, in January 1978. This time, he wasn't picked up by another team. With his 40th birthday little more than a year away, Giacomin retired from the NHL. At the time, he had played in more games (610) and posted more wins (318) than any other active goalie. "I didn't feel bad this morning, not having to go to practice," he confessed the next day.

RETIREMENT

In the following years, Giacomin opened a bar and grill in suburban Detroit—he had promised to stay there until his sons finished high school—and dabbled in sports broadcasting, but he missed being at ice level.

In 1984, he confessed to feeling like an outcast because he hadn't been able to land a long-term job in the NHL. "I'm bitter to the point that I simply don't understand why I'm not in the game," he said. "Things have not worked out and I'm dumbfounded."[29]

Two years later, the man who had once crushed his Stanley Cup dreams rode to the rescue. Phil Esposito, whose playing career ended in 1981, had recently become the Rangers general manager. He hired Giacomin as goaltending coach and special-assignment scout. The former goalie stayed in that position for three years.

In 1987, Giacomin was inducted into the Hockey Hall of Fame. "My biggest thrill would have been winning the Stanley

Cup," he said at the ceremony. "But an individual can get no greater honor than this."

His former teammates were happy for him. "I loved playing with Eddie," says Seiling. "He was a good guy, and good things come to good people. He worked hard to get where he did, and he deserved to be honored."

The Rangers retired his jersey two years later. At the time, Gilbert was the only other Ranger to have received that recognition.

Maniago, for one, felt Giacomin had earned it. "Like me, Eddie was born in a working-class community with a lot of new Canadians," he says. "I'm sure he was raised with a strong work ethic, and was encouraged to do whatever was asked of him to the best of his abilities without complaint."

||||||||||||||||||||||||||||||||||||||||||||||||||||||||||||||||||||||||||||||||||||||||||||||||||||||

ED GIACOMIN • ALL-TIME RANKING

REGULAR SEASON			PLAYOFFS		
GAMES + RANK	WINS + RANK	SO + RANK	GAMES + RANK	WINS + RANK	SO + RANK
610 [49TH]	290 [45TH]	54 [24TH]	65 [48TH]	29 [48TH]	1 [133RD]

+ NHL ALL-STAR TEAM (1ST) 1966-67, 1970-71

+ NHL ALL-STAR TEAM (2ND) 1967-68, 1968-69, 1969-70

THE KID BROTHER
TONY ESPOSITO

||||||||||||||||||||||||||||||

TONY ESPOSITO WAS a university student when his older brother, Phil, started an NHL career with the Chicago Black Hawks. Tony would sometimes visit Phil in Chicago and go out for drinks with his teammates. Tony was an NCAA all-star at the time, but the Black Hawks thought of him first and foremost as Phil's kid brother.

Tony would eventually become an NHL superstar in his own right, but throughout his career, he was inextricably linked to his more celebrated brother. In time, bas-reliefs of the brothers were built outside their hometown of Sault Ste. Marie, Ontario. One journalist described the artwork as "a curious mixture of old-country Neapolitan warmth, sibling rivalry and all-out war."[1]

TONY ESPOSITO was born in Sault Ste. Marie, often referred to as "the Soo," a small steel town on the eastern tip of Lake Superior, in April 1943. He lived with his parents, Patrick and Frances, younger sister Terry, and Phil, who was 14 months older than him.

The brothers were close—so close they shared a bathtub. "They had teddy bears in their cribs when they were little, and when they took a bath they pretended the plastic soap dishes were boats," their mother recalled years later. "They would splish and splash all over the place."[2]

"Tony O" keeps an eye on the puck during a game in St. Louis in February 1972—a task that became easier after the nearsighted goalie got contact lenses. **LEWIS PORTNOY/HOCKEY HALL OF FAME**

Their fun extended to the living room of the family home that Patrick, a steelworker, had built. The boys played cops and robbers, chasing each other up and down the stairs, firing imaginary bullets at each other.

They soon became so passionate about hockey that they played indoors at home, taking shots at each other with a rolled-up sock. The competition was so fierce in one game that they cracked a hole in the wall. To throw off the authorities (i.e., Mom and Dad), they covered the hole with a church calendar and took a solemn oath of silence.

When the temperature dropped and Sault Ste. Marie looked like the inside of a snow globe, the brothers lowered their toy guns into their holsters and headed outside. They often rose before the sun and walked to a local outdoor rink, lugging their equipment on a toboggan, using a flashlight to see. They sometimes darted around the ice with their buddies, but were often alone. "I was a year older, so I did the shooting," Phil later recalled. "Maybe Tony didn't like it, but he didn't have much choice."[3]

Phil was tough on his brother when they played shinny and, later, when they played organized hockey. When Tony got beaten on two long shots in a tournament, Phil berated him until his younger brother burst into tears. Their father took Tony for an eye exam and discovered he was nearsighted and needed glasses. "After he got the glasses nobody could beat him," Phil said years later.

The brothers' bond was unbreakable. "I got in many a fight for Tony and he got in many a one for me, and we had some groovy fights with each other," Phil said in 1971, resisting the urge to pepper his prose with the words "far out" and take his leave by saying, "Catch you on the flip side."[4]

The Esposito brothers worked on their game and started turning heads. When Phil was 18 years old, he traveled 370 miles south to play junior hockey in Sarnia, Ontario. Tony preferred to stay home, and because there was no junior team in town, he gave up hockey and focused on football. But when his father and some local businessmen sponsored a Junior A team, they urged him to return to the ice. He hesitated because he hated the pressure that came with playing goal, but the gravitational pull of hockey was too strong to withstand, and he was soon back between the pipes.

Tony did so well in net for the Sault Ste. Marie Greyhounds of the Northern Ontario Junior Hockey League (NOJHL), he won a scholarship to Michigan Technological University. He liked the idea of being able to get a business degree while playing hockey, so he packed his bags and traveled to Houghton, a community on the Upper Peninsula of Michigan. He ended up being a standout for the Huskies and led the team to an NCAA title in 1965. He was a three-time all-American.

His dedication impressed Huskies teammate Jerry Bumbacco, who had also played minor hockey with him in Sault Ste. Marie. "Tony found [giving up goals] an embarrassment. There was no such thing as a good goal in his mind," said Bumbacco, adding that Esposito's intensity rubbed off on his teammates. "He made every team he played on better. He wouldn't tolerate it if you were slack. He expected a lot of himself and everybody around him."[5]

But Esposito didn't spend all his time on the ice or in the library during his three years at university. He was almost expelled after a brawl in his freshman year. "I hit a sneaky guy on the head with a glass when he jumped one of my buddies from behind," Esposito later said. "It cut the guy wide open and took the dean of men to square the beef with the cops."[6]

The drunken revelry and brush with the law didn't detract from his performance on the ice. In September 1967, the Montreal Canadiens signed him as a free agent, making him just the third college player in history to be selected by an NHL team.

NHL

1967-69

The Habs loaned Esposito to the Vancouver Canucks of the minor-pro Western Hockey League (WHL) for cash. He played in 63 games and won 25 of them. As the team sank to the bottom of the standings, his goals-against average ballooned to 3.20. Despite that number, Montreal management moved Esposito higher in their organizational food chain.

He started the 1968–69 season with the Houston Apollos of the minor-pro CPHL, but the Canadiens came knocking in late November. Veteran goalie Gump Worsley, a nervous flier, refused to board a plane on the team's trip to California, so the Habs needed a backup for Rogie Vachon, who was a rising star. Vachon started the game against the Oakland Seals, but when he got injured, Esposito took his place and promptly allowed two goals on six shots.

His debut was far from inspirational, but he stayed with the Canadiens and made his first NHL start less than six days later in Boston, where his older brother had become a man about town. Phil, who had started his NHL career with Chicago in 1963, had been traded to the Bruins after the 1966–67 season and quickly risen to the top of the NHL scoring ladder. Tony stopped 33 shots, but he allowed two goals in the tie game—both scored by his big, bad brother. The fraternal smackdown didn't bring the young goalie to tears this time, but it did raise the hackles of Frances Esposito.

"I got a call from our parents after the game," Phil later said. "They wanted to know how Tony did. I told them, 'Good, real good. Second star.' Frances, my mother, asked who scored the first goal against him. I told her I did. She said, 'Well, that's OK, you're his brother.' Then she asked, 'Who scored the second goal?' I said, 'Well, I got that one too.' She said, 'How the hell can you do that to your brother?' She didn't talk to me for two weeks."[7]

Instant karma got Phil. When the Habs and Bruins faced off again just before Christmas, Tony was spectacular. He made 41 saves, shutting down his brother and the other Bruins in a scoreless tie. "We could have played all night and not scored a goal," Phil said.[8] *Bah! Humbug!*

Tony, who was as reserved as his older brother was outspoken, ended up playing in 13 games that season and posting a 5–4–4 record. He was excellent at some points and less than okay at others. His style of play left many observers scratching their heads. "The paunchy, curly-haired brother of the Boston Bruins' Phil Esposito was the rookie suddenly shoved into the 4-by-6-foot gap normally filled by Worsley or Vachon, and Tony, well, he has this tendency to roam away from the net," one sportswriter noted, adding that Esposito's performance did nothing to "calm the churning stomach of Claude Ruel, who in his first year as coach of the Canadiens has already lost 25 of the 230 pounds he began the season with."[9]

The Canadiens sent Esposito back to the CPHL when Worsley returned, but when Worsley got injured in the playoffs, Apollos management received a phone call from the Habs. *Houston, we have a problem.* Esposito rejoined the Canadiens and looked on as Vachon helped the team sweep the St. Louis Blues in the final. His name was engraved on the Stanley Cup a year before his brother's.

Esposito showed promise, but the Habs had an embarrassment of riches when it came to goaltending, so they left him
unprotected in the 1969 intra-league draft. When the Black
Hawks picked him up, he and his wife, Marilyn, whom he had
met at a YMCA dance as a teenager, relocated to the Windy
City.

1969-70

In his first season there, Esposito became a star in his own right.
He played 63 of the team's 76 games and led the NHL in wins
(38). He also had the best save percentage (.932) and the second-
best goals-against average (2.17). He posted 15 shutouts, a
modern-day record that earned him the nickname "Tony O."
Chicago allowed just 170 goals overall, securing the Vezina Trophy for the rookie goalie. He also won the Calder Trophy and
was runner-up for the Hart Trophy.

"Many goalies don't get 15 shutouts in their entire career,"
says Dennis Hull, who played for the Black Hawks along with
his famous brother, Bobby. "That record probably won't ever be
broken. We were lucky to have some great goalies in Chicago.
We had [Hall of Fame inductee] Glenn Hall. Then we got Tony,
who was just a bit better."

But Hull concedes that, despite Esposito's brilliance, there
were some chinks in his armor. "Tony was terrible at puck-
handling," he says. "I had the puck in the corner once and I had
nowhere to go with it, so I gave it to him, and he almost fainted.
He just covered it up to get the whistle."

"Of course I'm happy I won the Vezina—and about the $250—
but how can I take credit for it?" the goalie said at the time. "You
can't give credit to only one man for a trophy like the Vezina, or
any other for that matter. Everybody had been working so hard
that it would be tough to pick any particular guy."[10]

Watching Esposito in a game, "you think it is indeed fortunate he has a degree in business from Michigan Tech," one journalist wrote. "The way he flops and dives it's easy to see why
the Canadiens gave up on him. Surely his next game will be his

last—but, of course, it isn't, for Esposito has been the best goal-tender in hockey."

Black Hawks coach Billy Reay agreed, saying the goalie was usually a split second ahead of the play. "He may be awkward, but he's rarely out of position," Reay said. "You know, I get kind of tired of people knocking his style. He keeps the puck out."[11]

None of the Black Hawks made as many headlines as Esposito that season, but the team had some offensive might. Stan Mikita, for example, placed third in league scoring (86 points).

Thanks in large part to Esposito, the Black Hawks rose from the bottom of the East Division, where they had finished the previous season, to the top. They clinched first place in the NHL by clobbering the Habs 10-2 in the last game of the season at Chicago Stadium. It was known as "the Madhouse on Madison" because of the boisterous fans and the huge organ that was played during games. Esposito made 37 saves and later described the game as one of the highlights of his career. "The fans were just wild, screaming 'We're No. 1,'" he recalled. "I can't think of a more satisfying game."[12]

Reay didn't hesitate when asked about the secret to the Black Hawks' success in the final stretch of the season. "If I had to pick a key," he said, "it would be Esposito. He has given us the big save, the save that gives you a lift. So many times you get that big save, and bang! You go right down to their end and put the puck in the net."[13]

The Black Hawks finished with 99 points and opened the playoffs by sweeping aside the Detroit Red Wings (95 points). They then flew back to Chicago to start the semifinals against the Bruins (99 points), who had scored far more goals (277) than any other team that season, thanks to the exploits of two of the most prolific scorers in NHL history—Bobby Orr and the guy who had once shared a teddy bear with Chicago's star goalie.

Early in the first game, a shot hit Tony's white fiberglass mask and the puck deflected into the crowd. The goalie crumpled to the ice and stayed there for three minutes. "Tony went down like a ton of bricks," said Phil, who was on the ice at the time, "and I was scared to death. I just skated around in little circles, fighting this impulse to go help my brother. I could see everybody crowding around him, and him lying there on the ice, out cold. It was awful. Then that fine gentleman Bobby Hull came down the ice and skated past me, and as he did he said, 'Don't worry, Phil, he's O.K.'"[14]

Did Phil hold back after that because he was concerned about his brother or afraid of their mother's wrath? Not a chance. He scored three goals as Boston beat Chicago 6–3. He scored two more goals and notched four assists over the next three games, helping the Bruins sweep aside the Black Hawks.

"It took Boston only four games to send the Chicago team reeling out into the cold like West Madison Street winos," one journalist wrote. "What happened? 'I'm not Alibi Ike,' says the Hawks' taciturn Tony, 'but everybody was writing what a great hockey team we were, and we began believing our press clippings.'"[15]

1970-71

Esposito's numbers weren't as good the next season, but he was still one of the top goalies in the NHL. He posted more wins (35) than any of his counterparts, placed second in shutouts (6) and finished third in goals-against average (2.27). He was so good, he outshone his high-scoring brother—in at least one instance: Phil was listed as "Tony Esposito" in the program for a game between the Bruins and the Golden Seals in February. "Don't call me bleeping Tony!" he shouted at no one in particular. "Ain't that a new high in stupidity?" he continued. "They've made my brother the highest-scoring goalie in hockey history!"[16]

Tony Esposito and Bobby Hull, who ended up fifth in league scoring (96 points), helped the Black Hawks finish the regular season as the top team in the newly formatted West Division (107 points).

Chicago headed into the playoffs with just one goalie because backup Gerry Desjardins was out with a fractured arm. Esposito had the weight of the world on his shoulders, but he stood tall even while dropping into the butterfly, a technique he had borrowed from the legendary Glenn Hall and combined with a traditional stand-up approach. Observers couldn't quite process what they were seeing. One journalist said Esposito's unorthodox style reminded him of a "hulking orangutan defending his lair."[17]

Esposito led his team to four straight wins against the Philadelphia Flyers (73 points). In the semifinals, he slammed the door shut on the New York Rangers, who had placed second in the East Division (109 points), as forcefully as an atheist turning away a door-to-door Bible salesman. He held the Rangers to 14 goals through seven games. "In the deciding game, he had the Rangers—and perhaps a few million television viewers—wondering how he did it," wrote one journalist, who wasn't sure what to make of the butterfly. "Without style, and apparently without much thought of what he's going to do with the rebound, he continued to stop the Rangers."[18]

But media didn't find him dancing a merry jig in Chicago's dressing room at the end of the series. "He's a nice guy," one teammate said, "but he's not a ho-ho-ho guy like Phil." The goaltender agreed. "No, I don't joke around a lot," he admitted. "Goaltending is my business. I don't want to be distracted. There's nothing funny about goaltending."[19]

It was such a serious business that Esposito refused to break his concentration by chatting with other people, including family members, on game days. "I just leave him alone and keep the boys away from him," Marilyn said, referring to their young sons, Jason and Mark. "He likes to be alone."[20]

"I used to sit next to him in the dressing room," recalls J.P. Bordeleau, who was a forward with the Black Hawks at the time. "You couldn't talk to Tony on game days. He had a special way of preparing himself. He was so intense, nobody could go near him. He laid out his equipment on the floor and we all had to walk around it.

"Although he kept to himself on game days, he was fun to be around the rest of the time," Bordeleau continues. "It was nice to be his teammate, really enjoyable. We went out for drinks once in a while. We both enjoyed our beer, like so many people."

Esposito kept up the good work against the Canadiens in the Stanley Cup final, even when his teammates stumbled, and he helped the Black Hawks push the series to seven games. But he fell short in the second period of the deciding game when he allowed Jacques Lemaire, who was known for his consistency and a fearsome slap shot, to score from center ice. Esposito's brother might have wanted to let that pass without comment, but he couldn't because he was working as a TV color commentator for the game. "Letting in Lemaire's shot gives Montreal a chance," Phil said on-air. "I know my brother. He may get nervous now." *Sorry, Mom.* Sure enough, forward Henri Richard scored two goals to give the Habs a 3–2 win and their fifth Stanley Cup in seven seasons.

1971-72

Even though he had allowed a soft goal in a crucial playoff game, fans still had faith in Esposito, as did writers at *Sports Illustrated*, who noted he started the following season "ready to spread out in front of the goal wider than ever." The writers also assured the one or two readers who might care that "the summer's pizza and ravioli and lasagna and fettuccini did not get to him."[21]

The off-season carb-loading seemed to work well for Esposito. He posted the best save percentage (.934) and goals-against average (1.77) in the NHL. In fact, that average turned out to be the best of his career. He also recorded the most shutouts in the NHL (9) and the second-most wins (31).

The Black Hawks gave up 11 fewer goals than in the previous season. Esposito and Gary Smith, who was now the team's top backup goalie, shared the Vezina Trophy. Esposito's success made headlines. The *Hockey News* noted that "although overshadowed by his big brother with Boston, Phil, the super-scorer, the stocky 28 year old ex-collegian of Michigan Tech fame, who got a late start in pro play, has become one of the most valuable performers in his sport."

SUSPICIOUS MINDS

THROUGHOUT HIS playing career, Tony Esposito was notorious for adjusting his equipment to give him an edge. He added stuffing to his pads, wore an oversized sweater and even added webbing between his legs to cover the five-hole—though he got away with that for only a short time. He also piled ice shavings in the crease to slow down the puck. "We were always suspicious of Tony Esposito," said former NHL referee Bryan Lewis in an episode of the A&E show *Biography*. "And he would be the master. He's probably changed the game for goalies over the years."

The magazine also described Smith as a physically imposing "swinger" who watched at least one game in "a gaudy green outfit." No doubt, that shade of green was less frightful than the one in the uniforms of the California Golden Seals, a groovy kind of team that relocated to Cleveland in 1976 after just nine seasons in the NHL.[22]

Esposito and Bobby Hull, who was one of the NHL's top scorers once again, helped the Black Hawks finish at the top of the West Division with 107 points.

The Black Hawks swept aside the Pittsburgh Penguins (66 points) in the first round of the playoffs, then took on the Rangers, who had finished second in the East Division with 109 points, in the semifinals. Esposito didn't have the time of his life in that series. He allowed eight goals in two games, including a memorable one by Rod Gilbert in Game 2. The Rangers forward took a shot from 25 feet out. The puck popped out of Esposito's glove and into the net. It proved to be the game winner in a 5–3 Rangers victory.

Esposito was benched for the next game, which the Rangers won 3–2. He was back in net in Game 4, his 29th birthday, but he gave up six goals on 37 shots. The Rangers won 6–2 and moved on to the next round of the playoffs. The Black Hawks' season was over.

ESPOSITO DIDN'T have much time to reflect on the loss. In August, he joined his brother and 33 other NHL stars in Toronto to prepare for an eight-game series against a team from the Soviet Union. The Summit Series captured the attention of Canadians from coast to coast, and is considered a milestone in Canada's sports history.

On September 2, Esposito watched from the bench as the Soviets, wearing shabby equipment and antiquated skates, beat the cream of Canada's hockey crop in Montreal. The 7–3 loss stunned the Canadian players and their fans; they had expected the eight games to be a cakewalk.

Esposito replaced Canadiens star Ken Dryden between the pipes for the second game, in Toronto. Fans and the players themselves breathed a massive sigh of relief when Esposito stopped 20 shots, helping his team post a 4–1 victory. "They came out hard in that first period and got eight or nine shots on my brother, Tony, and he stopped them all," recalled Phil. "That got us going."[23]

"The saviour of Canadian hockey, pro tem, is a swarthy, curly-headed chap who was 29 last April 23. His name is Anthony James Esposito and he became the redeemer of the national pastime last night by making big goaltending saves, particularly in the first period when the score was 0–0," sports columnist Dick Beddoes wrote before dazzling readers with purple prose. "After Saturday's 7–3 defeat in Montreal, desolation spread across the country like undulant fever. Hereford cows hung their heads. The Canada goose was a dead duck. So [Team Canada coach] Harry Sinden put it up to the younger Esposito in goal and the contractor's son from Sault Ste. Marie spit on his palms and went to work."[24]

When broadcaster Foster Hewitt uttered the now famous words "Henderson has scored for Canada!" in the dying seconds of Game 8, wild celebrations erupted across Canada. It was "a delirious scene," the *Toronto Star* reported, "a screaming, dancing, singing, kissing scene that reminded [one elderly woman] of the end of World War II."[25]

The Canadians won the series, and Esposito had played a big part in his team's success. He played in four games and posted a 2-1-1 record. He also had a lower goals-against average (3.25) than the two other goalies—Dryden, who also played in four games, and Vladislav Tretiak, who played in all eight games for the Soviets.

"I believe it was destined that we were going to win because of the emotion and passion that we displayed. By no means were we the better team," Esposito said, sounding like a heretic. "They were the better team."[26]

1972-73

The NHL season started nine days later, and it felt anticlimactic for at least some of the players who had skated in the historic series. Esposito struggled early on. Reay believed that, because the goalie had spent much of September tracking the Soviets' intricate passing plays, he was waiting for an extra pass in front of his net rather than focusing on the shooters.

"I felt it at the start of the season, sorta tough to get your concentration going, you know. Coming back to the NHL, it felt like starting the exhibition season and being expected to play your best," Esposito recalled. "The only other guy I ever discussed it with was my brother. Phil was a little tired."[27]

But Esposito bounced back from his rocky start and posted good numbers. He finished second among NHL starters in save percentage (.917) and third in goals-against average (2.52) He also notched the second-most wins (32).

The Black Hawks competed without Bobby Hull, who had jumped to the upstart WHA, but they still had ample firepower in Mikita, Jim Pappin, Pit Martin and Dennis Hull. The team finished at the top of their division with 93 points. In the postseason, they eliminated the St. Louis Blues (76 points) in five games, then did the same to the Rangers, who had finished third in the East Division (102 points).

They then squared off—again—against the Canadiens in the final. The Habs had led the league with 120 points, and Dryden, who loomed large that season, literally and otherwise, had finished at the top of the standings in wins (33) as well as save percentage (.926) and goals-against average (2.26) among starters.

Fans were anticipating a goaltenders' duel—minus the flintlock pistols—but the series turned out to be a high-scoring one. Esposito let in enough goals (32) to fill a bucket with pucks. After he gave up eight goals in Game 1, Beddoes, the columnist, noted that Chicago fans might have been unhappy with Reay's decision to start "the dark, pudgy Esposito" who "likes cold beer and a few laughs with his brother, Phil, and plays out of a squat crouch which makes purists wince."[28]

Dryden wasn't a butterfly goalie, but he fared only slightly better, allowing 21 goals in the series. But with help from forwards Yvan Cournoyer and Lemaire, he led the Habs to victory in the six-game series and won the team's sixth Stanley Cup in nine seasons.

1973-74

The Black Hawks battled the Flyers for top spot in their division this season, and the Flyers won out. They finished with 112 points, seven more than the second-place Black Hawks. Each team allowed just 164 goals, the fewest in the NHL, so their goalies, Esposito and Bernie Parent, shared the Vezina Trophy. It was the first time goalies from separate teams shared the award. Esposito placed second, one spot behind Parent, in wins (34), save percentage (.929) and goals-against average (2.05). He also placed second in shutouts (10), behind Parent.

Chicago met the Los Angeles Kings (78 points) in the first round of the playoffs and eliminated them in five games. Esposito notched a shutout in a 1-0 win in the deciding game.

The Black Hawks advanced to meet the Big Bad Bruins, who had led the East Division and the league with 113 points that season, and had on their roster the NHL's top four scorers. Phil Esposito led the way with 145 points, just ahead of teammates Bobby Orr (122 points), Ken Hodge (105 points) and Wayne

Cashman (89 points). Boston goalie Gilles Gilbert had as many wins as Esposito.

"Tony O" stopped 46 shots in the first game of the semifinal, in Boston, lifting his team to a 4–2 victory. He held his brother to just one goal and one assist. *Who's your daddy, Phil?* Ultimately, though, the Bruins proved too hot to handle. They won the series in six games and ended the Black Hawks' season.

1974–84

The Black Hawks struggled for much of the next decade. The team never advanced to the final and only once recorded more than 100 points.

Esposito posted some good numbers between 1974 and 1979, placing second in wins and save percentage one time each. He also finished second in shutouts three times.

But in the decade that followed the semifinal loss to the Bruins in April 1974, Esposito played fewer games and notched fewer wins than in previous years. His save percentage dropped, and his goals-against average ballooned until it reached 4.84 in the 1983–84 season.

However, Esposito did rise to the occasion in two international competitions. In 1977, he joined Team Canada for the world ice hockey championship in Vienna and played in nine of 10 games. Canada defeated Czechoslovakia 8–2 in the final round—the biggest margin by which a first-place team had ever lost at the annual tournament. But that Canadian squad is best remembered for some ugly on-ice incidents, including one in which forward Wilf Paiement clubbed a Russian player over the head with his stick—just a love tap in the eyes of supporters in Earlton, Ontario, his hometown. Team Canada was dubbed "Team Zoo."

Four years later, Esposito competed in the Canada Cup. This time he suited up for the United States and played a pivotal role in a 3–1 win over Sweden. "It's very, very tough on me," said Esposito, who had become an American citizen just before the tournament. "I'm still a Canadian," he said. "That's the way I feel. I'm not disowning my country by any means." But Canadians weren't convinced; there had been no trace of an *eh?* in his comments.

It was likely tough on him when the Canadians advanced to the final. Ultimately, the Soviet Union won.[29]

Even though he was a Hart Trophy finalist in the 1979–80 season—finishing second in wins (31) and save percentage (.930), and first in shutouts (6)—and recorded the third-most wins (29) the following season, his relationship with the Black Hawks front office grew strained, and he was convinced general manager Bob Pulford didn't want him on the roster.

In the 1983–84 season, Esposito played in just 18 regular-season games, while Murray Bannerman, 14 years his junior, played in 56. In March, Esposito asked management to let him out of his contract ahead of the NHL trade deadline, but they refused, fearing he would be picked up by another team. (The rival Minnesota North Stars were reportedly interested in him.)

Esposito was not amused. He refused to play in the team's last regular-season game, and a couple of weeks later, he publicly criticized then coach Orval Tessier. "The thing that really got me was the day he called a special meeting, trying to shake up the team," Esposito said. "So he goes on 10 minutes about me, about how I'm a detriment to his team. Right in front of 20 other players who respect me, he's swearing and cursing me." Esposito said he wouldn't play under those circumstances.[30]

He celebrated his 41st birthday a few days later, becoming the oldest player in the NHL. The Black Hawks front office was acutely aware of his age—advanced for an elite athlete, though not for a vampire, a leatherback sea turtle or an ordinary human. Management said he would not be invited to the next training camp. When no other playing opportunities came up, Esposito retired.

RETIREMENT

Even though his playing days were over, Esposito's future looked bright. He had a business degree and was president of the

NHL Players' Association, a position he had held since 1981, so most hockey insiders expected him to move into management. They were bang on.

In April 1988, he took a job as director of hockey operations for the Pittsburgh Penguins, and in one of his first moves, he offered himself a job as general manager. He accepted.

In his first season at the helm, the Penguins made the play-offs for the first time in seven years. (The Flyers eliminated them in the second round.) Esposito also oversaw the acquisition of two players who would end up playing a big role in the Penguins' success in the early 1990s: forward Mark Recchi and goalie Tom Barrasso.

Unfortunately, that brush with success was fleeting. With the Penguins hovering near the bottom of the Prince of Wales Conference in December 1989, the club's owners fired Esposito. But soon after that door shut, his brother opened another one.

Phil recruited him to be head of hockey operations for the Tampa Bay Lightning, an expansion franchise that Phil had helped establish. Tony eventually became assistant general manager of the Lightning, whose first season started in 1992. The brothers stayed with the team until 1998, when a new owner fired both of them.

Tony's success as a manager never eclipsed his accomplishments on the ice.

He was inducted into the Hockey Hall of Fame in 1988, four years after his brother. "I admire Phil very much, so it's very special for me to be in the Hall of Fame with him," he said. "There was never any doubt that Phil would make it," Tony said of his brother, who was one of the NHL's all-time leading scorers. "I wasn't so sure about myself."[31]

Also that year, the Blackhawks—the team changed its name to one word in 1986—honored him by retiring his jersey (No. 35) in a ceremony at Chicago Stadium. At the same time, the franchise retired the jersey of Glenn Hall (No. 1), the goalie whose style Esposito had emulated.

In 2008, the Blackhawks recruited Esposito to be an ambassador for the franchise and made the announcement during a special "Tony Esposito Night." Two of the team's goalies at the time, Patrick Lalime and Nikolai Khabibulin, wore Esposito's No. 35 on their jerseys in the pregame warm-up that night.

Decades after he retired, the tributes continued. In 2015, Canada Post issued a commemorative stamp in his honor, and two years later, a panel of hockey executives, journalists and NHL alumni named him one of the top 100 players in NHL history— another distinction he shared with his brother.

In 2021, the legendary goalie was diagnosed with pancreatic cancer and died soon after. His death sent shock waves across the hockey world. Former coaches and teammates, along with countless fans, mourned his passing. But aside from Marilyn, Jason and Mark, no one was more devastated than Phil.

"Gone so fast," his grief-stricken brother said from his home in Florida. "I was gonna go up to their summer place in Wisconsin to fish. I told Tony that. He said, 'Come anytime, but don't bother fishing. You've never caught a fish in your life. Fish don't like you.' And we laughed. Oh, did we laugh. All the time."[32]

|||||||||||||||||||||||||||||||||||||||||||||||||||||||||||||||||||||||||||||||||||||||||||||||||||||||||||||

TONY ESPOSITO • ALL-TIME RANKING

REGULAR SEASON			PLAYOFFS		
GAMES + RANK	WINS + RANK	SO + RANK	GAMES + RANK	WINS + RANK	SO + RANK
886 [10TH]	423 [10TH]	76 [10TH]	99 [21ST]	45 [26TH]	6 [28TH]

+ NHL ALL-STAR TEAM (1ST) 1969–70, 1971–72, 1979–80

+ NHL ALL-STAR TEAM (2ND) 1972–73, 1973–74

|||||| 6 ||||||

THE STRANGER
VLADISLAV TRETIAK

||||||||||||||||||||||||||||||||

A FEW WEEKS before the hotly anticipated Summit Series in 1972, two Canadian scouts arrived in Moscow to assess the Soviet players. The pair watched from the press box as the Soviet national team played the Central Sports Army Club in an exhibition game and were struck by how poorly Vladislav Tretiak performed. The goalie struggled in net, allowing eight goals. The scouts were sure Phil Esposito, Yvan Cournoyer and other Canadian sharpshooters would humiliate him.

But the scouts didn't know the 20-year-old had attended his bachelor party the night before. In fact, the scouts didn't know much about him at all.

In the 1970s, Tretiak's exploits in international competition and exhibition games against NHL teams made him a household name in Canada, but because he lived behind the Iron Curtain and didn't speak English, he remained an international man of mystery.

TRETIAK WAS born in April 1952 outside Moscow. His father, Aleksandr, was a pilot in the Soviet military, and his mother, Vera, was a physical-education teacher. She had played field hockey decades earlier and put the old stick in her son's hands at an early age.

Vladislav Tretiak, seen here in action in 1969, was so good in the Summit Series three years later that one of his critics, columnist Dick Beddoes, ended up eating his words—literally. **MICHAEL BURNS SR./HOCKEY HALL OF FAME**

Vladislav took swimming classes along with his older brother Valeri. He excelled in that activity and in the many other sports he took up, but hockey was his first love.

Anatoli Tarasov, the coach known as the father of modern Russian hockey, saw potential in Tretiak at a young age and invited him to try out for the youth wing of the Central Sports Army Club, colloquially known as the Red Army, when he was 12 years old. He made the cut. He started as a forward, but when the team's goalie got injured, Tretiak took over between the pipes and never left.

PROFESSIONAL HOCKEY

1969-72

Tarasov routinely pushed the young goaltender past the point of exhaustion, and Tretiak thrived under his tutelage. In 1969, he became the starting goalie for the Red Army team that played in the Soviet professional league. He also played for the national team in three world championships between 1970 and 1972, winning two gold medals and one silver. He returned from the 1972 Winter Olympics in Sapporo, Japan, with another gold medal. Thanks to him and other elite players such as Valeri Kharlamov and Alexander Yakushev, the USSR was becoming a hockey superpower.

HAVING DOMINATED international competition since the 1950s, the Soviets were chomping at the bit to take on the very best Canadian players—those who competed in the NHL. Negotiations between officials from both countries started in 1969, and when the NHL Players' Association gave its blessing, an eight-game tournament was set for September 1972.

It turned out to be one of the greatest moments in Canadian sports history, one that transcended sport. At the height of the Cold War, Canadian hockey fans viewed the series as a battle between democracy and communism—a clash between a collection of wholesome boys from the True North, strong and free, and Soviet androids wearing odd plastic contraptions called... helmets.

In the months before the series, Soviet hockey officials altered their players' training regimen to prepare them for the inevitable bumps and bruises they would suffer at the hands of aggressive Canadian opponents. The Soviets took boxing lessons and even participated in "cockfights," pecking at each other like caffeinated roosters.[1]

When the Canadian scouts returned from their trip to Moscow with news of Tretiak's mediocre performance in the exhibition game, Canadian coaches, players and even sports journalists squealed with delight, but Canadian goalie Ken Dryden had played against Tretiak in international competition and knew he was very quick, had a great glove hand and could play well standing up or down in a butterfly position.

Tretiak and his teammates knew little more about their opponents than the Canadians knew about them. "By 1972, I had enjoyed success in international competition, but I knew there were some very strong hockey players overseas whom we had never encountered," Tretiak says through a translator. "I wanted to find out who would be better, which team would play better hockey. I was anxious."

The Soviet players landed in Montreal on August 30, three days before the start of the series. The aliens disembarked from their spaceship—an Aeroflot plane—tucked their antennae behind their ears and went to a screening of *The Godfather*. (Much to their surprise, Canadian assistant coach and former NHL enforcer John Ferguson didn't make a cameo as a hit man.)

Players from both teams also attended a special banquet. "The Canadians didn't really interact with us. We were in one corner and they were in the other," Tretiak recalls. "They were having fun and looked relaxed. It was clear they thought the series would be a cakewalk."

Tretiak, who worked on his equipment with needles and scissors before games, remembers Canadian sports reporters being dismissive of him and his teammates. "They seemed involved in a contest to determine who could frighten our team the most," Tretiak recalled five years later, noting that sports columnist Dick Beddoes vowed to eat his own printed article if the Soviets managed to score even one goal.[2]

In the days leading up to the series, the Soviets fumbled through practices, looking like the Keystone Cops on ice. It was all part of a diabolical plot to deceive the Canadians—cue the ominous music—and lull them into a false sense of security. It worked. Watching one session, backup goaltender Eddie Johnston was convinced his team would send the Soviets back to Moscow with tears in their eyes.

IN THE Soviet dressing room before the opening game at the Forum, Tretiak greeted a visitor—Jacques Plante. The legendary NHL goalie gave him advice on how to handle Canadian stars such as Phil Esposito, Yvan Cournoyer and Frank Mahovlich. Plante drew diagrams on a blackboard. Tretiak was confused. "I didn't really understand him because I didn't speak English and there was no interpreter," Tretiak recalls. "He probably thought I would let in 15 goals, and he wanted to help me out of solidarity with another goalie."

As game time drew near, fans' excitement reached a fever pitch. "We were sitting in the dressing room, and suddenly it was as though the earth was shaking," says Tretiak. "There was a powerful rumble, and when our dressing room door opened, the din got even louder."

As millions of Canadians watched on television, the players were introduced to the capacity crowd at the Forum. Spectators gave the Soviet players the warmest welcome permitted during the Cold War—stony silence. Every Canadian player was greeted with rapturous applause.

Esposito opened the scoring just 30 seconds into the game, sending fans into a delirium; they almost blew the roof off the building and onto nearby Atwater Avenue. Almost six minutes later, Paul Henderson gave Canada a two-goal lead.

"The noise was overwhelming," Tretiak recounted a few years later. "It appeared that mass insanity had developed in the bleachers. Shouting, banging, whistling, sirens screeching, flashers flashing, and an organ playing some sort of funeral dirge. Until this day, I have wondered how we kept from being completely confused by this din." But, he added, after Henderson's goal, "everything fell into place."[3]

For Canadian players, everything fell apart. The Soviets' exceptional skating and intricate passing plays confounded the NHL stars—and so did Tretiak. Now fully recovered from his epic hangover, he made a series of excellent saves, some at point-blank range.

The Soviets slowly gained momentum and skated to a 7–3 victory, leaving Canadian fans dazed and confused, in the Forum and in bars and living rooms across the country. How on God's green earth, they wondered, had the brightest stars in the NHL constellation fallen to a group of ragamuffins in red helmets?

The Canadians regrouped and fared better in the next two games, beating the Soviets 4–1 in Toronto and then tying them 4–4 in Winnipeg.

But the Canadians struggled in the fourth game, in Vancouver, and boos rained down on them as they limped to a 5–3 loss. Esposito admonished fans during a televised interview on the ice after the game. "I am completely disappointed. I cannot believe it," he said as beads of sweat—teardrops?—streamed down his face. "Some of the guys are really, really down in the dumps."

"On my word of honor, I felt sorry for him," Tretiak wrote later. "He was dripping with perspiration, his eyes were sunken, and he seemed to be lost."[4]

Tretiak had enormous respect for Esposito. "He gave me the most trouble of all the Canadians," the Russian recalls today. "He was very big and strong. Alexander Ragulin was the only defenseman who could move him out of the crease so I could see the puck. Phil also had a strong shot. He was the best player on the Canadian team during that series."

THE SECOND half of the series started two weeks later in Moscow. The Canadians lost the first game at the Luzhniki Palace of Sports 5–4 because they had not slept well the night before— phones would ring in the middle of the night in their hotel rooms. Perhaps, though, the Soviets were just better. "A final word for the Soviet goalie, Vladislav Tretiak," one Canadian reporter wrote. "Marvellous."[5]

Tretiak was solid in the next two games, too, but the Canadians, desperate not to wear paper bags over their heads for the remainder of their careers, fought hard and won each by a single goal. With the series even at three wins apiece, the stakes were sky-high in the eighth and final game at the Luzhniki Palace on September 28.

It was tied 5–5 with 34 seconds remaining when Henderson, standing on Tretiak's doorstep, banged in a rebound. With the

Russian goalie lying on the ice, looking as helpless as an overturned tortoise, jubilant Canadian players leaped into each other's arms. Soviet fans sat stone-faced—more or less as they had throughout the series.

Millions of Canadians, who had stopped working, studying, eating and breathing during the game, were ecstatic. They sprang to their feet, shouted at the top of their lungs and flooded into city streets from coast to coast. Stewardesses on a flight from Los Angeles to Toronto broke out bottles of champagne, and a few dozen fans marched outside the Soviet embassy in Ottawa—which employed dozens of godless communists, apparently—chanting "Esposito for pope!"

"It was very difficult," Tretiak told an interviewer in 1983. "But I was satisfied. To play that well was a victory for us. They didn't consider us much of an opponent in Canada."[6]

The Soviets' surprising performance left a bad taste in the mouth of Dick Beddoes, literally. He had kept his promise and, after the first game, ate his printed column after coating it with borscht.

1973-79

In the next seven years, Tretiak competed in seven world championships, winning five gold medals, one silver and one bronze. He was also in the Soviet net for the 1976 Winter Olympics in Innsbruck, Austria, where he led the team to another gold medal.

Following the historic Summit Series, interest in the Soviet players grew, and fans clamored for more games between the top players in North America and those in the Soviet Union. That led to the 1974 Summit Series, which had the same format but a different outcome.

The Soviets beat the Canadian squad, which consisted entirely of players from the World Hockey Association. The Canadians' only victory was a 4–1 decision at Maple Leaf Gardens in Toronto. Tretiak played in all the games except the final. Having already clinched victory in the series, and concerned by rumors that Canadian players intended to brutalize Tretiak in the last game, Soviet coaches chose to start backup goaltender Alexander Sidelnikov instead.

Tretiak later identified Bobby Hull's notorious slap shot as the greatest challenge he faced in the series. He said he couldn't even see the puck when Hull shot it, because it came at him "like a bullet." He was less fearful of Canadian goalie Gerry Cheevers, whom he described as "an outstanding sportsman" because he tapped Tretiak on the pads with his stick before each game to wish him luck, but he was puzzled by Cheevers's game-day routine. "The one thing I can't understand is that he smokes," Tretiak said later. "Even before the game, one can see him in the locker room with a thick cigar between his teeth."[7]

Observers took note of the difference in the two goalies' playing styles. "Unlike Cheevers, Tretiak is chained to his net, much like the Communist rank and file is chained to their ideology," said a *Hockey World* writer doing double duty as a political commentator. "Tretiak is a machine, a robot programmed to keep pucks out of the Russian net. He is amazingly quick and uncommonly agile, a product of the rigorous Russian training program."[8]

THE FOLLOWING winter, fans were treated to the Super Series, in which two club teams from the Soviet professional league, the Red Army and the Soviet Wings, played exhibition games against NHL clubs.

The Wings lost to the Buffalo Sabres, but beat the Pittsburgh Penguins, the Chicago Black Hawks and the New York Islanders. Media and fans made note of those results, but were more interested in games involving the celebrated Red Army team.

On December 31, three days after beating the New York Rangers, Tretiak and his Red Army teammates faced off against the Montreal Canadiens in the Forum. The Habs were an offensive powerhouse and outshot the Red Army 38–13, but the game ended in a 3–3 tie, thanks to Tretiak, who stopped Jacques Lemaire from point-blank range twice in the final minute. Tretiak was named the first star of the game and received a standing ovation. Sports columnist Doug Gilbert conceded that Tretiak was, you know, pretty good. "And now we have Tretiak, this superbly balanced, cat-quick 23-year-old who can turn us on in the warmup with a limbering up drill that makes him look like he spent half his life in a Cossack dancing class," he wrote in the *Gazette*.[9]

The Red Army beat the Boston Bruins a week later, then took on the Philadelphia Flyers, the infamous Broad Street Bullies. When the Soviets arrived in the City of Brotherly Love, they were met with animosity. Flyers forward Reggie Leach later recalled that opposing players eyed each other suspiciously at a luncheon. "The Soviets kept to one side of the room and we kept to the other. We sized them up but didn't interact with them," he wrote in his 2015 autobiography. "There was no love lost between our teams."[10]

The game itself was so violent, with countless elbows thrown and sticks swinging in every direction, that the Soviets left the ice in protest during the first period, and didn't return until the NHL threatened to withhold payment for the series. Red Army coach Konstantin Loktev denounced his opponents as "a bunch of animals trying to physically destroy the players on opposing teams." The Flyers won 4-1. If not for Tretiak, who made 45 saves, the game would have been more lopsided. That led one Massachusetts-based sportswriter to state that Tretiak's performance in the series had been good enough to "make one wish he would defect and settle down somewhere in a Boston suburb."[11]

FANS WERE still talking about that game three years later, wondering whether Flyers defenseman Ed Van Impe had been honest when he said Soviet superstar Valeri Kharlamov had simply skated into his elbow, when the Soviet national team took on a squad of NHL stars in a three-game series in New York.

The NHL squad, which included 23 Canadians and three Swedes, beat the Soviets 4-2 in the first game of the NHL Challenge Cup, and were close to winning the second one when the tide turned and the Soviets won 5-4. Coach Viktor Tikhonov chose rookie goalie Vladimir Myshkin to start the third game instead of Tretiak, who had been in net for the previous two. Hockey fans are still scratching their heads over that decision. The "good little goalie," as Bobby Clarke called him, posted a shutout as the Soviets clobbered the NHL players 6–0.[12]

1980-84

Despite riding the pine in that decisive game, Tretiak was still the top dog. Between 1980 and 1984, he competed in three world championships (1981, 1982, 1983), winning gold in every one.

The Soviet national team, a dominant force in international hockey for years, arrived in Lake Placid, New York, for the 1980 Winter Olympics like original gangsters, packing heat and striking fear into the hearts of man and beast. They mowed down their first five opponents without blinking. They were so merciless, in fact, that they subjected the Netherlands to a Saint Valentine's Day Massacre—a 17–4 drubbing on February 14.

The American squad, which consisted mostly of college students, stepped onto the ice for the first game of the medal round looking heavenward, hoping divine intervention would save them from a grisly fate. But in the end, it was the Soviets who were bloodied. The Americans stunned the hockey world by beating the Soviets 4–3, sparking a nationwide celebration. The "Miracle on Ice" now has a hallowed place in the annals of American sports history. (Fans were treated to another miracle 24 years later, when Hollywood beefcake Kurt Russell transformed himself into Herb Brooks, the paunchy middle-aged man who had coached the Americans, for a movie.)

Many observers attributed the Soviet loss to a strategic blunder: Tikhonov had pulled Tretiak from the net after the first period, when the score was tied 2–2, and replaced him with Myshkin. Tretiak gave the US team credit for being well prepared and playing with "a lot of desperation," but when he was asked how many times that squad would have beaten the Soviets if they had played 100 games, Tretiak's educated guess was one.[13]

But the result might not have been the most unpalatable aspect of those Olympics for the Soviets. They didn't like the food in Lake Placid because it contained a lot of additives. "All we could eat were the eggs, because they were natural," said Tretiak, who admitted he didn't like most food in North America.[14]

THE SOVIETS were back in North America in September of the following year for the 1981 Canada Cup, a follow-up to the 1976 Canada Cup, which the host country had won by beating Czechoslovakia in the final. Teams from six countries took part in the 1981 tournament, which was held in Edmonton, Winnipeg, Ottawa and Montreal.

Tending net for the Soviets, Tretiak saw some unfamiliar faces on the Canadian squad. It included youngsters such as Ray Bourque and a pimply faced newcomer named Wayne Gretzky. The rising superstar led the tournament with 12 points, but Tretiak was named the most valuable player. The goalie was excellent throughout the competition, and in the final game, he stonewalled Canadian sharpshooters to help his team notch an 8–1 victory while spectators in the Forum desperately waved paper red-and-white maple-leaf flags.

The next day, the Gazette reported that Canada's hockey pride had been "stabbed in the heart." Sports columnist Red Fisher wrote that Canada's loss to a team that wasn't "the greatest Soviet group ever assembled" was something he couldn't explain unless he mentioned Tretiak. "What is it about this splendid athlete that has kept him No. 1 among the world's goaltenders for a decade?" he wrote. "NHL goaltenders can mutter about the pressure of an 80-game schedule and about the Stanley Cup playoffs and the collar-tighteners among them, but is there anyone anywhere who has been involved in more pressure situations than Tretiak? I don't think so."[15]

IN DECEMBER 1982, a team of Soviet stars arrived in North America to play a six-game series against NHL teams. The Soviets lost just two games, in Edmonton and Calgary. Hockey pundits felt it wasn't a coincidence that those were the only two games Tretiak, who had a fever, sat out.

He did play in a game against the Montreal Canadiens. That morning, both teams held an open practice and 15,000 fans headed to the Forum to watch. They applauded as the Habs did drills, but rose to their feet when Tretiak led the Soviet team onto the ice. Later, hundreds of them pushed through a police barricade surrounding the goaltender to ask for his autograph or just shake his hand. Tretiak ended up posting a shutout in a 5–0 victory over les Glorieux.

Aware of the wisdom in keeping friends close but enemies closer, Canadiens general manager Serge Savard made a bold move. That spring, he drafted the goalie who had inflicted so much pain on Canadian players and fans. Tretiak was selected in the seventh round of the 1983 NHL Entry Draft. Savard, a former Habs defenseman who had played in the 1972 Summit Series, knew firsthand how dominant Tretiak was in net. He described the Russian as "the best goaltender in the world."[16]

Soviet officials seemed fine with Tretiak heading to the NHL, but ultimately nixed the idea, saying Tretiak couldn't leave because he was an officer in the Soviet military and his father had also served. Tretiak was not pleased. After helping the Soviets win gold at the 1984 Winter Olympics in Sarajevo, Yugoslavia, he announced his retirement, citing his need to spend more time with his wife, Tatiana, and two children, Dmitri and Irina. The 32-year-old athlete had helped the Soviets win medals at 13 world championships and four Olympics since 1970.

RETIREMENT

Tretiak was gone from international hockey, but not forgotten in Canada. In 1989, he became the first European player to be inducted into the Hockey Hall of Fame.

Around that time, he made an appearance at a mall in Winnipeg, where one local girl stood in line for hours to get his autograph. "He was my hero," Sami Jo Small, who was about 10 years old at the time and went on to become one of the best goaltenders in the history of women's hockey, says today. "I was in awe of him. His book, *Art of Goaltending*, later became my bible. I fashioned my game after his and made my warmup routine more dynamic and acrobatic, based on his recommendations." A devoted fan, Small sported a shirt with his name on it.

Tretiak became the Chicago Blackhawks' goalie coach in 1990 and helped mold three future stars: Ed Belfour, Dominik Hašek and Jocelyn Thibault. Tretiak stayed with the team until 2006, when he was named head of the Russian Ice Hockey Federation.

That year, the governor general of Canada, Michaëlle Jean, awarded Tretiak Canada's Meritorious Service Medal in Ottawa. He was recognized for establishing the Friends of Canada organization to foster good relations between Canada and Russia. The ceremony received a lot of media coverage in Russia.

When the Montreal Canadiens retired Ken Dryden's jersey a year later, Tretiak attended the ceremony. In front of a national television audience and 21,000 spectators at the Bell Centre, the Canadiens' home since 1996, Tretiak walked to center ice wearing the jersey of the old Soviet national team. When the cheering subsided, he addressed the crowd. "I played against Team Canada in 1972 and in 1975 against the Montreal Canadiens. It was the best hockey I ever saw," he said in halting English, adding that Dryden was "a fantastic goalie and a great man." The two men embraced, then joined hands and pumped their fists in the air.

Six years later, Tretiak was on hand when Paul Henderson was inducted into the International Ice Hockey Hall of Fame, in Stockholm. "The organizers didn't tell me he was going to be there, so I was surprised when he showed up," Henderson recalls. "When he introduced me, he said 'Paul, I know why you scored that goal because I've watched the replay over and over.' Then he paused for what seemed like an hour and said, 'It was very bad goaltending.' The crowd just roared with laughter. Then he gave me a big bear hug."

Henderson won't forget that moment or the series that made both men household names in Canada. "You know, we hated him and his teammates back in 1972," he says, "but we've gotten to know them in the years since, and they're just terrific guys." Today, Henderson has nothing but respect and affection for the legendary goaltender who arrived in Canada as an alien and, in a few short years, became one of the most recognized and beloved hockey players in Canada.

||||||||||||||||||||||||||||||||||||||||||||||||||||||||||||||||||||||||||||||||||||||||||||||||||||||||

VLADISLAV TRETIAK

+ **WORLD CHAMPIONSHIP TITLES:** 10
+ **OLYMPIC TITLES:** 3
+ **EUROPEAN CUP TITLES:** 9

|||||||| **7** ||||||||

THE SHOOTING STAR
MIKE PALMATEER

|||||||||||||||||||||||||||||||

MIKE PALMATEER SUITED up for an alumni game between the Toronto Maple Leafs and the Detroit Red Wings in 2016. Three minutes into the outdoor game at BMO Field in Toronto, the 62-year-old made a diving save on a penalty shot by Red Wings alum Tomas Holmstrom. Palmateer looked like his former self—the youngster who had dazzled fans with his acrobatic saves four decades earlier—but only for a moment. After the save, he lay face down on the ice until a referee and former teammates skated to the rescue. That was the end of the game for him.

"That was classic Palmateer," teammate Lanny McDonald said. "It looked like he had no chance whatsoever, flipped over backwards, lay out as far as he could, obviously pulled something—maybe everything—but made the save. How cool is that?"[1]

Palmateer joined the Leafs in late October 1976 and soon emerged as one of the best goalies in the NHL. His star reached its zenith in the second round of the 1978 playoffs, when the Leafs beat the ascendant New York Islanders. His exploits in the seven-game series made him the toast of the town in Toronto, but he soon faded from view.

Playing on decrepit knees—he had more than a dozen surgeries on them during his career—and beset by countless other injuries, the diminutive goalie spent a lot of time on the sidelines and retired after just eight NHL seasons.

Palmateer made his mark on the ice but was less accomplished on the
domestic front. He once suffered an injury at the hands of a curtain rod.
DIMAGGIO-KALISH/HOCKEY HALL OF FAME

To this day, a generation of long-suffering Leafs fans ask themselves and each other, "What if Palmateer had stayed healthy?"

LONG BEFORE his knees became as brittle as matchsticks, Palmateer grew up in Toronto as part of a large family. His parents,
John and Lyn, raised three boys and three girls.

When he wasn't roughhousing with his siblings or fishing, Mike, who was born in January 1954, often had his nose in
a book, following the adventures of the Hardy Boys and, later,
James Bond. "He doesn't want to be a private eye," his mother
said years later. "He wants to be James Bond. So, he fantasizes.
That's the Michael I know... He likes the sophisticated spy type
with lots of girls and constant action, and that is the way he sees
himself."[2]

Palmateer was in constant motion, though not in pursuit
of Dr. No. He chased pucks and did it so well he became a top
scorer in two hockey leagues. During Palmateer's third season,

the coach of one of his teams asked for a volunteer to play net. Palmateer raised his hand and soon won his first game between the pipes. The father of the team's regular goaltender pulled his son from the team in a huff, and Palmateer became the starter.

When he was 11 years old, he joined the Toronto Marlboros, a storied athletic club that operated junior and senior teams in the OHA, and quickly made his mark with his unorthodox approach to goaltending.

While most goalies of that era stayed on their feet and cut down angles, Palmateer flopped on the ice, relying on lightning-fast reflexes to stop pucks. He would also come out of his net— way, way out—to challenge shooters, an approach he attributed to his experience as a forward and to the fact he didn't know any better; he had started playing net without the guidance of a goalie coach. "I just started sliding into everybody," he later said about the evolution of his style.[3]

The Marlies' early practices were bearable for him in part because they were held at Maple Leaf Gardens. Like most kids in Toronto, Palmateer bled blue and white. He idolized forward Frank Mahovlich and goalie Johnny Bower, whose poke check he emulated.

Palmateer was cocky. "I don't think he's been any other way," his mother said when her son was an NHL star. "When he was little there was nothing he thought he couldn't do. And there really wasn't. He could pitch a tent when he was five." She said he could also fish, hunt and drive a car without a single lesson.[4]

Palmateer played two seasons for the Junior B Markham Waxers, and in the second one, the 1971–72 season, he helped the team win the provincial championship. He joined the Marlies' OHA team the following season.

Many observers doubted he would excel because of his unorthodox style and diminutive size—he was about five foot eight and 155 pounds—but he proved them wrong. Not only did he lead the team to the OHA championship in 1973, but he also won the Dave Pinkney Trophy, which went to the goalies on the team with the lowest goals-against average.

By then, he had his eyes on the prize. "What will I do if I don't make it in the NHL? Rob a bank and live in Brazil, I guess," he told reporters during the Memorial Cup that year. "I want to play in the big league and that's what I'm going to do."[5]

"Palmy was very athletic. He was a good baseball player, a good golfer and a great hockey player," says Bruce Boudreau, who was one of Palmateer's teammates on the Marlies and, later, the Leafs. "But I think the biggest thing he had was his confidence. He believed in himself more than anybody. That belief is something I try to instill in players today. He had it in spades."

Boudreau, who joined the ranks of NHL coaches in the 2007–08 season, also remembers Palmateer as a fierce competitor. "He was as competitive as any athlete. He wanted to be the best at whatever he did, whether it was hockey, fishing or just playing cards."

The 1973–74 season wasn't quite as plummy for Palmateer. In a game just days after his 20th birthday, he twisted his knee and couldn't even stand afterward, but he just waved it off. "The doctor thinks I might have torn a couple of cartilages in my knee," he told reporters. "My knee just popped out but it can apparently pop back in anytime. Considering how many hours we'll have on the bus, it will probably do it then." But that proved to be wishful thinking. He had to sit out much of the season.[6]

Palmateer was out of sight for quite a while, but not out of mind. Four months after suffering that injury, the Leafs selected him in the fifth round of the 1974 NHL Amateur Draft, 85th overall. He was disappointed not to have been chosen earlier, but he was excited about being notified by one of his heroes. "It was a dream come true," he said. "I watched the Leafs on TV every Wednesday and Saturday. What was really cool was the phone call I got when they drafted me: Johnny Bower was the one that called."[7]

The Leafs sent him to the minors for seasoning. In the 1974–75 season, he divided his time between the Saginaw Gears of the International Hockey League and the Oklahoma City Blazers of the CPHL. He later regarded his time in Oklahoma fondly.

"We played in a great rink called The Myriad," he said about the multipurpose center. "It sat 10,000—not that we got that many, unless it was nickel beer night. But those were some of my best memories. The guys on that team—you only had each other."[8]

Palmateer spent another season in the Sooner State but soon reached his destination. He started the 1976–77 season playing for the Dallas Black Hawks of the CPHL, but it was just a pit stop. With Wayne Thomas struggling in the Leafs' net in the first three weeks of the season, general manager Jim Gregory decided to give Palmateer a shot. He called the goalie late one night, and Palmateer's response is now part of Leafs lore: "Fear not, Mr. Gregory. Your troubles are over."[9]

NHL

1976-77

Palmateer woke up at 5 AM the next day and headed to Detroit. He arrived there in the afternoon and, a few hours later, stepped onto the ice of the Detroit Olympia wearing the iconic Leafs jersey.

He made 25 saves and Toronto beat the Red Wings 3–1, ending a seven-game winless streak. The *Toronto Star* sang the praises of the "little" goalie, who confessed to being more tired than nervous in his NHL debut. "I thought I played a pretty solid game but don't forget that the guys in front of me played a great game," Palmateer said, possibly referring to star defenseman Borje Salming, who notched two assists. "Now there are a couple of things that have to happen—the chance to play in a few games and to show that I can do the job over a stretch. I think I can."[10]

Leafs coach Red Kelly thought so too. He kept Palmateer in net in the following games and the rookie didn't disappoint. On November 17, the Leafs took on the Montreal Canadiens, the defending Stanley Cup champions. With Guy Lafleur and Steve Shutt, two of the NHL's most prolific scorers, on the roster, Montreal had as much ammunition as a firing squad.

To make matters worse for opponents, Montreal also boasted an exceptional defense corps—here's looking at you, Guy Lapointe, Larry Robinson and Serge Savard—and a star netminder in Ken Dryden. In mid-November, Montreal sat at the top of the nine-team Prince of Wales Conference, six spots ahead of Toronto.

But the Leafs' new goalie stood tall—as tall as he could without platform shoes. (It was the 1970s, remember?) He stopped 39 shots and the Leafs shut out the Canadiens 1-0. It was the first time the Habs had been held scoreless in more than two years. "Shutting out the Montreal Canadiens is something like putting a lid on a smoldering volcano so that no smoke escapes," one journalist wrote. "The Habs have the most potent attack in hockey and disaster can come from anybody on the roster." But the sportswriter sang the praises of "the chubby, freckle-faced goaltender" who held Lafleur and *les autres* at bay.[11]

"He was a clutch goalie," says Mike Pelyk, a defenseman who played in front of Palmateer for two seasons. "Did he always have the best team in front of him? No. But he came to play every night. He would laugh and joke a lot, but once the puck dropped, he was on. He wanted to play and he wanted to win—and you wanted to play well in front of him because he was such a likeable guy."

He was also a chatty chap. The young goalie often taunted opponents, and in the heat of battle, he called games like a play-by-play announcer. "If a guy takes a hard shot and I catch it I'll yell, 'Great save!'" he explained. "Or when there's a pile-up I'll say, '... and the puck is loose and there's a scramble and now it's under me for a whistle!'" He was also inclined to sing, whistle and hum when the puck was at the other end of the ice.[12]

Palmateer continued to play well but was stopped in his tracks during a home game against the New York Rangers in December. In the third period, a teammate's stick found its way into the eye hole of the goalie's mask and scratched his cornea. The Leafs won the game 4-1. Palmateer celebrated the victory from a hospital bed. He sat out for almost two weeks.[13]

Even without him, the Leafs were a strong team that season. Toronto had a handful of the NHL's top scorers on the roster— forwards Darryl Sittler and McDonald, and defensemen Salming and Ian Turnbull. The team was considered a Stanley Cup contender.

The Leafs finished fifth in the conference with 81 points, the same number as the Pittsburgh Penguins. The two teams squared off in a best-of-three preliminary series. The Leafs beat the Penguins (2–1) and moved on to play the Philadelphia Flyers, who had finished first in the Clarence Campbell Conference with more points (112) than every team in the NHL except the Canadiens (132).

The Flyers, who had won back-to-back Cups in 1974 and 1975, were known as the Broad Street Bullies because they were stacked with players who were as happy to reconfigure their opponents' faces with fists, sticks and other weapons of opportunity as they were to put the puck in the net. The Flyers also had a lot of talent. Captain Bobby Clarke, Rick MacLeish and Reggie Leach were among the most feared snipers in the league. The Flyers also had Bernie Parent, one of the best goalies in the NHL, on the roster. He had finished second in wins (35) that season.

Palmateer's cornea was fine when the Leafs arrived in Philadelphia to start the quarterfinals, but his health problems weren't behind him. He played well for most of Game 1, performing the splits to make great saves, cutting down angles and clearing rebounds well. The Leafs were ahead by two goals in the second period when he left the ice and didn't return—a mic drop heard around the league. He claimed he was dizzy, but not everyone believed it. Some reports suggested he had left the game because he couldn't handle the pressure. "That's bull!" he insisted. "I'm the coolest guy under pressure that I know of. I had to leave that game because I had taken a whack on the head from a Flyer stick and I was seeing spots in front of my eyes."[14]

The Leafs won the opener 3–2, and Palmateer returned to the ice for the second game. Toronto won that contest 4–1, making the hearts of their fans go pitter-patter. Unfortunately for them, Philadelphia won the next game 4–3 in overtime.

Two days later, the teams met at the Gardens for Game 4. Palmateer made 39 saves, impressing everyone in the building with his agility. "Palmateer, a curly-haired rookie, not only looks like a soda jerk down at Baskin-Robbins, but he also looks as though he samples all 31 flavors every day," one journalist noted, apparently amazed that a man not fit for the cover of *Muscle & Fitness* magazine could be an elite athlete.

"On those rare occasions when the Flyers did penetrate Toronto's defense, they were further frustrated by Palmateer's brilliant goaltending. 'Nervous?' he was asked. 'Naw, no more than for a house league game.' The book says that the red-haired, green-eyed Palmateer is 23, but he looks 13. 'When I'm 40,' he says, 'I'll look 23, and all those other guys will be wrinkled and ugly.' The book also says Palmateer is 5'9", but he's barely 5'7"."[15]

Despite his heroics, the Flyers edged out the Leafs 6–5 in overtime.

In Game 5, Palmateer skated far out of his crease to confront Leach, who tripped over the goalie's stick and fell on him. Palmateer's leg was sore after the game, but the pain grew so intense that night that he returned to his old haunt, the hospital. Doctors diagnosed him with torn ankle ligaments and slapped a cast on him.

Unfortunately for Leafs fans, the Flyers won that game and the next, which Palmateer watched on a television in the Leafs dressing room.

1977-78

The ranks of Palmateer fans continued to grow as his statistics improved. He played in 63 games in his sophomore season, 13 more than in the previous campaign, and his goals-against average dropped from 3.22 to 2.75. He also finished third in the NHL in wins (34) and recorded the second-most shutouts (5).

After the Leafs beat the Los Angeles Kings 3–0 at the Great Western Forum in December, the Kings' star goalie, Rogie

Vachon, sent one of his own cigars to the Leafs dressing room to congratulate Palmateer on the shutout. "The cigar had his name on the wrapper," Palmateer said about the gift from the goaltender he had long admired. "It was great. I've put it away. I'll remember that for a long time."[16]

As the regular season drew to a close, Leafs fans started thinking about the playoffs and wondering if their favorite goalie would get there in one piece. By that point in his career, Palmateer had been knocked unconscious and suffered torn tendons and a broken nose. He had also narrowly escaped an eye injury so grave it would have forced him to wear a pirate's eye patch under his mask.

Palmateer conceded that playing with reckless abandon was risky. "I've had games where a guy has taken a shot and I've been down and I've stuck my face in the way. It was the only way I could make the stop. I see a guy wind up 10 feet in front of me and I figure the best way to cover the net is to go down in a spread eagle. I don't even think about it. But when it's over, I think, 'What am I? Nuts?'"[17]

Apparently, he also tackled home decorating with the same gusto. In March, he landed in hospital with a deep cut on his arm and received stitches. He told reporters he had been reaching for the drapery track—to close the curtains or to do some midnight dusting?—when the chair he was standing on collapsed. He fell against the window and cut his arm. There was speculation the injury had been the result of late-night revelry or a domestic disturbance, because he and his wife, Debi, were reportedly having marital problems. But Palmateer just rolled his eyes.

The Leafs finished the season fourth in the conference with 92 points, thanks in large part to Palmateer, McDonald and Sittler, who had finished third in league scoring (117 points).

Toronto played Los Angeles (77 points) in the opening round of the playoffs, winning back-to-back games and eliminating the Kings in short order. Palmateer notched a shutout in the second game, a 4–0 victory, but it's unclear whether he received another cigar from his counterpart.

The Leafs headed to Long Island to take on the New York Islanders, who had finished first in the Clarence Campbell Conference with III points. The team was an offensive juggernaut with three of the NHL's hotshots—forwards Mike Bossy and Bryan Trottier, who had placed second in overall scoring (123 points), and high-scoring defenseman Denis Potvin.

The Islanders' mustachioed goalie could be mistaken for a sprite, but he was a big deal. Glenn Resch was known as "Chico," a nickname bestowed upon him by a teammate who noted his physical resemblance to the titular character in the 1970s TV show *Chico and the Man*. Unlike Chico Rodriguez, however, Resch never struggled to find work. He had been a star in the minors and had posted the best save percentage in the NHL in the 1975–76 season, his first as a starter.

But Palmateer wasn't intimidated. "I'm learning. I'm constantly improving," he said. "I can honestly say now, I might be totally wrong, but I think I am one of the best. I don't think anyone is better than me."[18]

The Leafs' new coach, Roger Neilson, agreed, but he knew great goaltending and offense wouldn't be enough to beat New York, so he instructed his players to rough it up, Philly-style.

The series featured heavy doses of slashing, spearing, punching and, in some cases, mauling. The list of penalties was as long as Al Capone's rap sheet. The Leafs' strategy worked. The series was tied after four games.

Palmateer had been excellent in those outings and was in fine form heading into Game 5, but not all his teammates were in great shape. McDonald was wearing a helmet with a face mask—as common then as concussion protocol was—because his nose had been broken twice in a month. He was also nursing a fractured wrist bone.

Dave "Tiger" Williams had bite marks on his face, which surprised a grand total of no one because he was an enforcer. Broken bones and torn flesh were occupational hazards.

The Leafs' best blueliner was in the worst shape of all. Salming was in hospital because he had been struck in the face with a stick in Game 4, suffering a cut near his eye and a broken sinus bone. He was done for the series, leading some fans to worry that the team was done for the season.

Their concern deepened when New York beat Toronto 2–1 on Long Island. Islanders forward Bob Nystrom scored the winning goal in overtime, turning Leafs defenseman Brian Glennie inside out, then beating Palmateer on a shot from way out. After the game, a reporter asked Palmateer if he felt bad about letting the puck get past him. "Nah, why should I?" he said. "I played my normal great game. One time I stopped three straight shots with my mask."

Palmateer played with his usual intensity, too. Every Islander who trespassed on his property—the goal crease—paid a stiff fine. "He keeps the stick up and you expect him to drop it down," Nystrom said, "but if he doesn't, you're going to get it in the teeth."[19]

Despite the loss, Palmateer and his teammates were undaunted when they returned to Toronto. Sittler, McDonald and Turnbull, who had stepped up his game in Salming's absence, led the Leafs to a 5–2 win in another penalty-filled contest.

Two days later, the teams faced off in Nassau Coliseum for Game 7. Islanders fans welcomed the invaders from the north by booing the Canadian anthem during the pregame ceremony. All but four of the players on the Islanders' roster were Canadian, but, you know, logic is the first casualty of war.

With their seasons on the line, the teams fought tooth and nail. Potvin scored in the first period and Turnbull answered in the second. When the game went into overtime, fans on both sides of the border held their breath.

The Islanders almost won the series when forward Billy Harris stole the puck from Glennie in the Leafs' zone, broke in on net alone and took a shot. The puck was headed for the back of the net when Palmateer kicked out his right leg like a cancan dancer to block the shot.

Moments later, Turnbull fed the puck to McDonald, who, despite his broken wrist, managed to flip a shot over Resch's glove and into the net. The silence was deafening in the stands but not on the ice, where the Leafs celebrated. The team was headed to the semifinals for the first time since 1967. "We could have flown home on our own," McDonald said years later. "No fuel needed."

Bruce Boudreau, who played for the Leafs at the time, remembers that moment vividly. "I wasn't playing that night, so I was in the stands. When the game ended, I jumped right over a railing. I didn't realize it was a 10-foot drop. But I ran onto the ice and jumped on the pile of my teammates. It was pretty amazing."

After the game, Resch threw his glove against the wall in a fit of pique, swearing a blue streak. His counterpart was in much better spirits. Palmateer, usually not at a loss for words, sat crying tears of joy in the Leafs dressing room. Many observers credited him with forcing the game into overtime. His coach didn't dispute that. "Palmateer had a very big part in the win," Neilson said. "Any time a goalie holds the Islanders to 13 goals in seven games he's playing superbly." Palmateer had an impressive 1.85 goals-against average in the series.[20]

But Glennie was convinced the Leafs hadn't won because of their physical gifts and grit. No, it was his jockstrap. He had carefully—*very* carefully—lowered a white seashell into the sacred space between his legs before the game. "I wear it in my jock. I keep it for use in crucial games and this one certainly was," he said. "I was given it by a friend and it's been lucky."[21]

Either Glennie discarded the mollusk exoskeleton or its mystical powers diminished·the following week. His team's hard-nosed approach was not quite as effective against the Canadiens in the semifinals. With Salming on the sidelines, the Habs, the two-time defending champions, could focus on shutting down Sittler and McDonald—and it worked. The Canadiens swept the Leafs aside in four games.

Leafs owner Harold Ballard treated his players to champagne because their season had been a success in many ways. The Leafs had finished with the second-highest point total in franchise history and had reduced the number of goals scored against them from 285 in the previous season to 237 thanks, in large part, to their star goalie.

1978-79

In September, Palmateer slept in and missed the team's flight to Ottawa for its first exhibition game of the season. He finally made his way to the capital on a separate flight. His coach fared only a little better that day. Neilson drove around in circles at the airport in Toronto before locating the team's charter plane. The players faced more challenges on the flight home after their 5–1 loss to the Boston Bruins. The plane's oven didn't work, so the players had to eat cold, soggy lasagna.

That fall, the Leafs acquired goalie Paul Harrison, and he played so well in his early outings there was speculation he might soon become the starter.

Despite having two solid goalies on their roster, the Leafs seemed to suffer a slump every second month, and several players spent time on the sidelines with injuries. In November, Palmateer stopped taping his battered ankles because he wanted to be more mobile. Bad move. He aggravated an old ankle injury and missed several games.

In a 3–1 loss to the Buffalo Sabres three months later, Palmateer collided with Dave "the Hammer" Schultz, formerly of the Broad Street Bullies. The goalie left the ice. It was one of several blows to the head he suffered that week. They left him feeling dizzy and seeing double. Palmateer missed the next two games.

When the Leafs lost five straight games in March, the ill-tempered Ballard publicly declared that Neilson was done in Toronto. But he couldn't find a replacement in a hurry, so he bowed to pressure and reinstated the popular coach for the next game. Ever the showman, Ballard wanted to keep the public in suspense until the puck dropped. He ordered Neilson to take up his position behind the bench wearing a paper bag over his head. Neilson wouldn't cooperate, however, and showed up for the game against the Flyers without a bag, balaclava, harem girl's veil or any other item covering his face. The Leafs won 4–3.

Palmateer finished second in shutouts (4) and third in wins (26) and save percentage (.909). The Leafs ended in fifth place in the conference with 81 points.

They started the playoffs against the Atlanta Flames, who had finished fourth in the Clarence Campbell Conference with 90 points. High-scoring Flames forwards Bob MacMillan and Guy Chouinard were big offensive threats. Their goalie, Dan Bouchard, had more wins (32) than all his peers, including Palmateer, who had 26 victories.

But the Leafs beat the Flames in a preliminary round—in every sense of the word. The first game was so ugly that 47 penalties were called, including 36 in the second period alone. A massive brawl broke out at one point. Palmateer got in on the action, drawing a penalty for high-sticking.

Toronto moved on to play the Canadiens, the defending Stanley Cup champions, in the second round. They traveled to the Death Star, otherwise known as the Montreal Forum, where the Habs were lying in wait. Lafleur had placed third in league scoring (129 points), while Dryden had placed second in wins (30) and first among starters in goals-against average (2.30).

The Habs posted two resounding victories over the Leafs in the first two games of the series. Game 3 wasn't decided until the second overtime period, when Montreal forward Cam Connor put the puck past Palmateer to seal a 4–3 win. Palmateer made 44 saves in the Gardens that night, but he played injured after Habs forward Mark Napier fell on him and sliced his arm with a skate. Later that night, Palmateer headed back to the hospital, his second home, and learned he would have to undergo surgery to relieve pressure from internal bleeding.

Harrison found out the next day, when Sittler greeted him at the dressing room door and told him he would be starting in net for Game 4. He ended up making 30 saves that night and helped send the game into overtime, but neither he nor his teammates could counter the Habs' ferocious attack.

Early in the overtime period, referee Bob Myers sent Williams to the penalty box for high-sticking. Less than two minutes later, Robinson scored a goal to clinch a 5–4 win for the Habs. The Leafs' season was over, but Williams wasn't done. He charged out of the penalty box and, with his eyes glowing a fiery red, made a beeline for Myers. Teammate Dan Maloney restrained Tiger, saving Myers from a mauling.

After the Leafs were eliminated, Ballard fired Neilson again—this time for good.

Palmateer had been one of the team's best players for three seasons, but, much to his chagrin, he was one of the lowest-paid starting goalies in the NHL. When his contract ended that spring, he expected to negotiate a better one soon.

"Look, I'm the best goalie in the NHL. No, make it the world. That's not cockiness, it's reality," he told a reporter. "There may be some who do some things better than me, but overall I'm the best." Still, he ended up playing an entire season without a contract—a season that dissolved into a three-ring circus.[22]

1979-80

Ballard, whose bluster and disruptive management style were so extreme that legions of Leafs fans still regard him as an arch-villain, fired Jim Gregory in the summer and replaced him with George "Punch" Imlach, who had won the Cup as coach and general manager of the Leafs four times in the 1960s. He had served in the military in the Second World War, and he ran his teams like a drill sergeant.

Before the season began, Sittler and Palmateer were to participate in *Showdown*, a prerecorded skills competition featuring the NHL's best players. It aired during intermissions of Saturday night games. It was sanctioned by the NHL and the NHL Players' Association (NHLPA), but Imlach and Ballard ordered their star players to skip it. They responded by flipping their overlords the bird—though perhaps not literally—and attending the taping of the show.

The melodrama didn't bother Palmateer—at least not enough to ruin his appetite. He continued to eat spicy sausages in the dressing room between periods and inhale popcorn before games. Teammates would stare in wonder as he tipped a bag and poured the popcorn into his mouth or threw it in the air and caught it in his mouth. Sometimes, he would bounce it off the wall first. Occasionally, he mimicked normal human behavior by scooping up a handful of popcorn and putting it straight into his mouth. When a journalist documented his pregame ritual, a nickname was born. To this day, many Leafs fans refer to Palmateer as "the Popcorn Kid."[23]

Williams has vivid memories of the goalie munching on popcorn between periods and another one of his rituals. "He always put his sticks by the hydrocollator," Williams says, referring to a device that heats and stores hot packs for therapeutic use. "I think it was a superstition. He and some other guys put the sticks there to make them 'hot.' He felt if he had a hot stick, he would have a hot performance."

Superstitions aside, Harrison viewed his goaltending partner as a great asset in the dressing room. "He was a very fun guy to be around," he says. "He kept everything loose and he made it enjoyable to play hockey. It was fun for him."

But playing for Imlach wasn't a laugh a minute. He implemented a dress code requiring all players to wear a jacket and tie in his office. Alan Eagleson, executive director of the NHLPA and an agent representing Sittler, Palmateer and other NHL players, openly grumbled about the Leafs no longer being able to drink beer on planes and buses during road trips, and about a Ping-Pong table being removed from their clubhouse along with the private phone. "Imlach doesn't accept that the players have rights that all the other general managers have accepted," he said. "He has to realize that players' rights are crucial to the future of hockey and that the 1960s were 20 years ago."[24]

Tensions between Imlach and his strong-willed captain escalated until Imlach decided Sittler had to go. But the star had a no-trade clause in his contract, so Imlach traded away Sittler's linemate and best friend. When Sittler learned McDonald had been sent to the Colorado Rockies, he ripped the C off his jersey.

In Denver, McDonald said he was fortunate to have escaped. "Feel sorry for the guys staying behind on a disappointed, disorganized, disgruntled hockey team," he said. "The situation in Toronto boils down to Imlach against the world."[25]

That melodrama wasn't the only event that had Leafs fans crying in their soup as 1979 came to an end. Palmateer heard a snap in his leg while making a save in a game on Boxing Day and left the ice with a sprained ankle. He returned for a game against the Kings on January 24, but his ankle gave way 10 minutes into the contest. He didn't play again until early March.

While Palmateer was on the sidelines, Leafs management suggested he was faking the injury. He ended the regular season with just 38 games under his belt, a bloated 3.69 goals-against average and a bad taste in his mouth.

The Leafs placed fifth in the conference with just 75 points, and started the postseason by taking on the Minnesota North Stars (88 points) in a preliminary round. Led by fleet forward Bobby Smith, the Stars swept the Leafs aside in three straight games. Palmateer was in net for just one game—a 7–2 loss.

With contract negotiations at an impasse in the off-season and relations between management and Palmateer strained, the Leafs traded him to the Washington Capitals in a five-player deal. He signed a four-year deal with his new team.

The news hit many Leafs fans like a two-by-four in the face. "I was really upset and close to tears when I heard the news," said one 15-year-old girl. "I'm not going to support the Leafs anymore. I'm disgusted with what they did."[26]

The Capital Centre had the best popcorn in the NHL in Palmateer's opinion, but he wasn't happy about the trade. "Palmy was a Toronto boy and he loved playing there," says Boudreau. "He loved the excitement and the attention. Being sent to Washington was a tough pill for him to swallow. I think it kind of took the heart out of him."

But the Capitals were delighted. General manager Max McNab proclaimed that with Palmateer in the lineup, the team was "set in goal for the next 10 years." But you know what they say about the best-laid plans.

1980-82

The Capitals continued to struggle after Palmateer's arrival, and so did he. He spent much of the next two seasons on the sidelines.

He suffered several injuries in the 1980–81 season, including a strained hamstring, ankle ligament damage and bone chips in his wrist. He played in just 49 games.

His luck was worse the next season, when he crushed a bone in his right knee during a collision with a teammate at training camp. He underwent several surgeries and played in just 11 games.

He was hours away from one of those procedures when the Capitals called him back into service because backup goalie Wayne Stephenson had been injured. Palmateer had already taken medication to prepare for the surgery and was groggy when he arrived at the arena. He played in a deep purple haze and underwent surgery the next day.

But even with battered ankles and knees, Palmateer roamed as much as a free-range chicken. That irked coach Gary Green, who said the goalie jumped into the fray so often that his teammates spent more time retrieving his equipment than playing hockey. But the happy wanderer notched eight assists in his first season in Washington, an NHL record for goalies at the time.

When David Poile joined the Capitals as general manager in August 1982, he looked at the team's statistics—they had finished near the bottom of league standings twice during Palmateer's tenure—and promptly marked the goalie "return to sender." He sent Palmateer back to Toronto for cash.

1982-85

Since Palmateer's previous stint with the Leafs, Ballard, whose generosity of spirit was matched only by Attila the Hun, had cut Imlach loose and traded Sittler to the Flyers. Neither move had helped the team. The Leafs were eliminated in the preliminary round of the 1981 playoffs and missed the postseason entirely the following year.

Fans hoped Palmateer would help turn the team's fortunes around, but that didn't happen. The Leafs finished seventh in their conference (68 points) and advanced to the playoffs in Palmateer's first season back, but the North Stars (96 points) swept them aside in the division semifinals. Toronto missed the playoffs the following season.

Rick Vaive was one of the NHL's top goal scorers, but he didn't have a strong supporting cast, and Palmateer was hobbled by injuries again. He played in just 34 games in the 1983–84 season, and by the end of it, he wasn't even mobile enough to cover both sides of the net.

Still, the scrappy goalie showed up at training camp to start the 1984–85 season. He played half of an exhibition game and then had a run-in with Dan Maloney, his former teammate and the Leafs' new coach. Palmateer wanted to sit out practice the next day to rest his aching knees, but Maloney nixed that idea.

For the remainder of the season, Maloney relied on two young goalies, Allan Bester and Ken Wregget. Palmateer stayed off the ice and collected his salary. Relations between him and Leafs management grew so strained he stopped going to the rink. His days as a Leaf were coming to an end.

The Edmonton Oilers took the battered Palmateer for a test drive in the 1985–86 preseason, but it was clear his best days were behind him. Palmateer announced his retirement. By then, he had played in eight NHL seasons and undergone 14 knee operations. He had also suffered many broken bones and been knocked unconscious six times, suffering at least three concussions.

RETIREMENT

Soon after retiring, Palmateer settled in Aurora, a community 30 miles north of Toronto, to raise a family with Lee, his second wife. They had two daughters, Courtney and Tess. The retired goalie opened a restaurant in the community and got into the real estate business.

But Palmateer never ventured far from the ice. He worked for the NHL Central Scouting Services, an NHL department that ranks draft prospects, before the New York Islanders hired him as a goalie coach in 2001.

His stint with the Islanders was cut short because of—you guessed it—knee problems. He underwent yet another knee surgery, and because he couldn't return to the ice at the time, he left the job.

In 2002, the Leafs hired him as a scout. He stayed in that position until 2015 and, during that time, identified some talented young goalies before they made their NHL debuts, including Tuukka Rask and Connor Hellebuyck.

Despite his joint problems, Palmateer did return to the ice a few times. When Ken Dryden and Tony Esposito were unable to play in an old-timers game marking the 25th anniversary of the 1972 Summit Series, Palmateer stepped in. He knew any damage to his knees could be repaired the next day when he would undergo previously scheduled surgery. He arrived at Maple Leaf Gardens with the contents of his musty old hockey bag—his original equipment and a decades-old tube of an ointment used to treat pain. The 43-year-old goalie played in one period and didn't let the puck past him.

He was back on the ice for the alumni game between the Leafs and the Red Wings in 2016, but left the game after that spectacular save put him out of commission. "I was thinking, 'I killed myself,'" Palmateer said. "Then I realized I didn't. But I did wrench my back. It seized right up."[27]

"Palmy has never had good knees, and he's not the fittest individual in the world," Tiger Williams, the old enforcer, said about Palmateer, who has now undergone more than 20 knee surgeries, including two knee replacements. "But he still comes and competes, and that's what it's all about, you know?"[28]

MIKE PALMATEER · ALL-TIME RANKING

REGULAR SEASON			PLAYOFFS		
GAMES + RANK	WINS + RANK	SO + RANK	GAMES + RANK	WINS + RANK	SO + RANK
356 [143RD]	149 [137TH]	17 [140TH]	29 [109TH]	12 [113TH]	2 [92ND].

||||||| **8** |||||||

THE SURVIVOR
GRANT FUHR

|||||||||||||||||||||||||||

EARLY IN A playoff game between the St. Louis Blues and the Toronto Maple Leafs in 1996, a scramble in front of the Blues' net ended with Leafs forward Nick Kypreos barreling into Grant Fuhr, whose right leg got twisted in a tangle of bodies. The goalie managed to get back on his feet, and play continued. Moments later, he made a great pad save on star forward Mats Sundin. Fuhr then hobbled off the ice with two badly torn knee ligaments. He underwent surgery soon after and didn't return until the following season. Leafs players were amazed the goalie had been able to make a great save despite suffering a serious injury, but his teammates weren't. Having played alongside him all season, they knew that Fuhr was as tenacious as he was talented. His grit enabled him to overcome many setbacks during his career, on and off the ice. He was the ultimate survivor.

BORN IN September 1962, Fuhr grew up in Spruce Grove, Alberta, a village a few miles west of Edmonton. When Robert and Betty Fuhr adopted him as an infant, they were unsure they would be able to raise him to be comfortable with his heritage. Grant had Black roots, and they worried that he wouldn't be accepted in a lily-white community. As it turned out, there was no need for concern. "Soon my fears didn't matter," Betty later

Grant Fuhr, seen here in the 1985 Stanley Cup final, was considered a "money goalie," but he struggled to manage his finances early in his career. **PAUL BERESWILL/HOCKEY HALL OF FAME**

recalled. "The love was there. It came to me. And people accepted Grant." A few years later, the family adopted a girl, Debbie.[1]

Grant was cheerful and showed great athletic promise early on. "He had a natural ability from a tender age," Betty said. "He was very well coordinated. He went to Grade One, and the teachers were astounded at his coordination."[2]

Like his father, he was passionate about hockey. He got his first pair of skates when he was four years old, and he spent hours on a rink Robert had built in the backyard of a home in Saskatoon, where the family lived for 10 months.

Fuhr started playing in a league soon after and made a beeline for the net. "There was something about the [goalie] equipment I liked and something about the challenge," he said. "It's just something I took naturally to." He loved it so much, in fact, he grew determined to follow in the footsteps of Tony Esposito. To ensure his family members knew he was dead serious about playing in the NHL, he told them about his plans more than once.[3]

Fuhr was so good that he played for three teams at a time, some of which were in older age groups, and that gave him ample opportunity to hone his skills.

He excelled at many sports in his teens. The Pittsburgh Pirates of Major League Baseball drafted him as a catcher. He never pursued the offer because he was laser-focused on the NHL.

When he was 15 years old, two Tier 2 Junior A teams cut him. Fuhr just shrugged. "Getting cut wasn't that big a disappointment," he said. "I went back and played with kids my own age and got all the young stuff out." It's not clear what he meant by "young stuff," but some things are better left unsaid.[4]

Fuhr didn't have to wait long to play at a higher level. Two years later, in 1979, the Victoria Cougars of the WHL added him to their roster. He had two great seasons in Victoria. In the second one, he notched 48 wins in 59 games and led his team to the WHL championship.[5]

"I could do a little bit of everything," Fuhr says today. "I could cut down angles. I could be aggressive. I could rely on reflexes." He was also mentally resilient. "As a goalie, you have to be able to let go of a bad goal. A lot of guys will fret about them, but I wouldn't," he recalls. "After the puck goes into the net, there is nothing you can do about it, so you may as well just play on."

NHL scouts swooned more than teenage girls at an Elvis concert. Edmonton Oilers head scout Barry Fraser considered Fuhr the most promising junior goalie since Bernie Parent, and he urged management to draft the teen. Oilers general manager and coach Glen Sather was reluctant; Andy Moog had been excellent in the opening round of the 1981 playoffs, allowing just six goals in a three-game sweep of the Montreal Canadiens.

But Sather relented and selected Fuhr in the first round of the 1981 NHL Entry Draft. Fuhr was thrilled to have been drafted by a team so close to home.

NHL

1981-82

Fuhr made his NHL debut in October, allowing three goals on 36 shots as the visiting Winnipeg Jets beat the Oilers 4–2. Fuhr bounced back, however, going undefeated in his next 23 games and setting a record for a rookie goaltender. It still stands.

"We all knew he was great from the first day of camp," said goalie Ron Low, who was then in his third season with the team. He described Fuhr's approach as a combination of styles. "He would come out 15 feet to challenge the shot on one offensive rush. The next time he would be back in his crease. He could read the game so well."[6]

Fuhr wasn't the only record-setter on the team that year. In his fourth season in professional hockey, Wayne Gretzky set a single season record for goals (92) and became the first player in NHL history to reach 200 points. He ended up with a mind-blowing total of 212 points.

Gretzky and other emerging NHL stars, including forwards Mark Messier, Glenn Anderson and Jari Kurri and rushing defenseman Paul Coffey, led the Oilers up the standings. The team recorded 111 points, finishing first in the Clarence Campbell Conference and second in the NHL. Only the New York Islanders placed higher, with 118 points.

In a shocking upset, the Oilers lost to the underdog Los Angeles Kings (63 points) in the opening round of the playoffs, three games to two, and Fuhr allowed a whopping 26 goals. After the third game, which the Kings won 6–5 in overtime, a sportswriter noted that Fuhr blamed himself for the loss, and, "showing more emotion than he's ever been given credit for," vomited in the dressing room sink after the final buzzer sounded.[7]

But the digestive mess didn't detract from his success in the regular season. He finished second in wins (28) and third in save percentage (.898) and was a finalist in voting for the Calder Trophy as well as the Vezina Trophy, whose winners have been determined by a vote among all NHL general managers since 1982.

1982-84

The Oilers became one of the NHL's best teams over the next two seasons, finishing first in the conference in 1983 (106 points) and first in the NHL a year later (119 points). Most observers attributed their success to explosive offense.

In the 1982–83 season, Gretzky led the NHL in scoring (196 points), while Messier, Anderson and Kurri also placed in the top 10. Gretzky was unstoppable the following season, when he led the NHL in scoring (202 points). Coffey finished one spot behind him (126 points) and Kurri was in the top 10 on the scoring ladder.

Fuhr didn't have a banner year. In fact, he played so poorly that season, frustrated Oilers fans booed him after a 4–3 loss to the Detroit Red Wings in January. After serious contemplation in the dressing room, Fuhr described them as "jerks."[8]

At the end of the month, the Oilers sent Fuhr to the Moncton Alpines, their affiliate in the AHL, hoping he would get his groove back. He played 10 games, then returned to Edmonton.

That spring, he watched from the sidelines as Moog, who had played almost 20 more games than him during the regular season, helped the Oilers eliminate the Jets (3–0), the Calgary Flames (4–1) and the Chicago Black Hawks (4–0) to advance to their first ever final. Mike Bossy, Bryan Trottier and their band of merry men had won the Cup in three consecutive seasons, and they weren't prepared to loosen their grip on it just yet. They swept aside the Oilers in four games.

FUHR RETURNED to form in the 1983–84 season. Despite suffering a knee injury early on, he played in 45 regular-season games, seven more than Moog. Not only was he solid in net, notching more wins (30) than all his counterparts, but he also proved to be an offensive threat—though maybe not enough to win the Art Ross Trophy as the highest scorer in the league. He recorded 14 assists, setting a record for most points by a goaltender in a season. It has yet to be broken.

Fuhr was in the Oilers net for the better part of three playoff series—victories over the Jets (3–0), the Flames (4–3) and the Minnesota North Stars (4–0).

Sather started him in the final against the New York Islanders, who were vying for their fifth straight Cup, and Fuhr thanked him by posting the Oilers' first ever playoff shutout. He stonewalled Islanders sharpshooters, and in one memorable save, he popped a hard, rising shot into the air and then jumped up to catch it. "I don't know if there was a better performance from an NHL goalie that season," Moog says today, recalling the 1–0 victory. "He was determined to win the game, whatever it took. If he had to win the game 5–4, he could do that. But he had to win that one 1–0, and he did that."

The good times ended for Fuhr five days after that victory. He injured his shoulder in a collision with New York forward Pat LaFontaine in Game 3. Moog took his place and helped the Oilers pry the Islanders' sticky little fingers from Lord Stanley's mug. Edmonton won the series in five games—the franchise's first NHL championship. Elated fans jammed the streets around the Northlands Coliseum to celebrate, one of whom loudly declared, "The Oilers dynasty has begun!"[9]

IN SEPTEMBER, Fuhr and a handful of his teammates competed in the Canada Cup, an international six-team tournament held in seven cities in Canada and the US. Canada came out on top by winning the best-of-three final over Sweden. Fuhr suffered a knee injury and ended up playing in just two of the team's eight games.

1984-85

Through most of the regular season, the Oilers stormed across the league like Vikings raiding the British Isles, laying waste to all that lay before them. Gretzky brandished the biggest broadsword, finishing at the top of the scoring ladder with 208 points, one spot ahead of Kurri (135 points). Coffey placed fifth (121 points).

The Oilers finished first in their conference with 109 points and second in the league behind the Philadelphia Flyers (113 points).

They struggled in the final stretch, but they didn't disappoint in the playoffs. They eliminated four teams in rapid succession—the Kings (3–0), the Jets (4–0), the Black Hawks (4–2) and the Flyers (4–1)—to win their second consecutive Cup.

Fuhr played in every game and notched all 15 wins, more than any other goalie. He also stopped two penalty shots in the final, including one in the last game.

His playoff exploits amazed opponents. "He even stood on his head to stop shots," the Kings' Terry Ruskowski said after a 4–2 Oilers win in Game 2 of their series. "He blocked some that no goalie should have. It's the best goaltending we've faced this year."[10]

Fuhr also made an impression on opposing teams' fans, including one Winnipeg girl who would later play goal for medal-winning teams in three Olympics and four world championships. "When Fuhr took his mask off, I could see that he was Black, and that made me think about hockey in a new way," says Sami Jo Small. She decided that it was okay to be different, whether that meant being a dark-skinned player or a female one. "I would secretly cheer for him when the Oilers played the Jets."

1985-87

The Oilers were dominant over the next two seasons, finishing at the top of the standings in 1985–86 (119 points) and 1986–87 (106 points). Their firepower was awe-inspiring.

Gretzky's feats continued to traumatize fans in arenas around the league, who covered their eyes whenever he touched the puck. He finished atop the scoring ladder in both seasons, notching 215 points and 183 points, respectively.

Proving he was no slouch either, Kurri placed fourth (131 points) and then second (108 points) in points. Coffey placed third (138 points) in the first of those two seasons, and, in the second one, Messier finished fourth with 107 points.

Fuhr placed third in the league in wins (29) in the 1985–86 season.

BUT IT wasn't the players' accomplishments that made headlines in May 1986. That month, *Sports Illustrated* published a story stating that drug use was rampant on the team, and that five players had cocaine problems. Had the pressure of playing in Edmonton really driven players to drugs? Not according to NHL president John Ziegler and NHL Players' Association president Alan Eagleson. Both pooh-poohed the notion.

The article also stated some players had financial problems, Fuhr particularly. It claimed he had spent money as recklessly as a college freshman in a strip club and that a local collection agency had settled a $468.69 debt he owed a video store for unreturned tapes. But Fuhr didn't mean to deny fellow citizens the chance to rent *Back to the Future*, honest. "When my clothes were dirty, I just threw them in the closet and went out and bought something else," he explained a couple of years later. "Some of [the tapes] ended up in the closet under the dirty clothes."[11]

The article that shall not be named—it was called "The Joyless End of a Joyride"—also noted that Sather managed Fuhr's finances. "The problems Grant's got come from a kid that is dumb," the manager said.[12]

Fuhr later insisted that "it wasn't so much being a dumb kid as being a kid who did some dumb things." He also insisted he "was never that bad. I was living life to have some fun. I wasn't worrying about the responsibilities that go along with life. I was just young."[13]

The 1986 postseason was a rough ride for the team and for Fuhr personally. He helped the Oilers notch a 7-3 victory over the Vancouver Canucks (59 points) in the first game of the opening round, then headed to the hospital to be with his father, who had been diagnosed with cancer late in the season. Robert died less than 24 hours later. His grieving son missed the second game of the series, which the Oilers won 5–1, but he returned for the third and deciding game. The Oilers posted another 5–1 victory. "I wanted [a shutout] for my Dad," Fuhr said after the game. "I'll get one for him though... somewhere somehow. It's only a matter of time."[14]

The Oilers then took on their provincial rivals, the Flames (89 points). The "Battle of Alberta" was a physical series to say the least. In Game 4, Oilers enforcer Dave Semenko exchanged blows with Tim Hunter, another heavyweight champion. Before the game ended, Flames forward Nick Fotiu got into a heated exchange with the referee and tried to attack Sather behind the bench. Fortunately for "Slats," a row of his players separated him from the raging bull.

The series went the distance. Game 7 was tied 2–2 early in the third period when rookie Oilers defenseman Steve Smith accidentally banked a pass off Fuhr's left skate and into the Oilers' net.

The crowd in the Northlands Coliseum fell silent. Jaws dropped, shoulders sagged and plastic cups fell to the floor. The Oilers fought hard to come back, but it was no use. The Flames skated to a 3–2 win and advanced to the conference finals. "Flukes do happen," Fuhr later said of the mishap. "That's just part of the game. It was just destiny. It wasn't our time."[15]

THE OILERS tallied more than 100 points for the sixth straight year in the 1986–87 season, and weren't about to be sidelined by another fluke. They lost just two games in the first three rounds of the playoffs, rolling over the Kings (70 points), the Jets (88 points) and the Red Wings (78 points), while barely breaking a sweat.

Fuhr was excellent in the fourth game against Detroit, when he made sensational saves late in the second period and throughout the third. He was so good that not even Detroit coach Jacques Demers could stay silent. "The hero of this series is Grant Fuhr," he said. "He was outstanding. I don't know how he stopped some of the shots. We've said all along that he's the best goalie in hockey. When he gets in the one-goal games he always comes up with the big saves. He's the best goalie I've seen in a long time."[16]

Gretzky agreed. "You don't win in this league unless you absolutely have the best goalie," he said. "The teams are pretty even when you get to the last three or four. It's the most important position in the playoffs."[17]

Unfortunately for the Oilers, they ran into a hot goaltender in the Cup final, against the Philadelphia Flyers, who had finished first in the Prince of Wales Conference with 100 points. Ron Hextall swung his stick like a hatchet, striking opponents who dared to approach his net. He was also an emerging star.

Hextall helped his outgunned team push the series to seven games, but Fuhr was not about to roll over and play dead. He was great in Game 7, helping the Oilers secure a 3–1 victory and win the Cup for the third time. The crowd erupted when Gretzky held the trophy over his head. He then passed it to Smith, a sweet treat for the blueliner who had managed not to score on his own net this time around.

Hextall won the Conn Smythe Trophy over Fuhr, but only, said Oiler assistant head coach John Muckler, because "Grant had a better team in front of him."[18] Oilers fans, their faces painted orange and blue as they celebrated on the streets of Edmonton, agreed. "Why are we here?" asked Dave Shields, a fan who had driven 125 miles to join the festivities. "Because of Fuhr."[19]

1987-88

That summer, Fuhr and two other goalies were added to the roster of the Canadian team competing in the Canada Cup. But Hextall, who had just won the Vezina Trophy, and the Islanders' Kelly Hrudey never saw action. Fuhr played in all nine games and cemented his reputation as a goalie who was at his best when the chips were down.

He faced a blistering Soviet attack in the three-game final and played a key role in the deciding game on September 15 at Copps Coliseum in Hamilton, Ontario. He made two incredible saves early in the second period to keep the Canadians in the game when they were on their heels. He was solid throughout and was watching from his goal crease when Gretzky and Mario Lemieux combined to score the game winner with less than two minutes remaining in the third period. Fans whooped it up in the stands, and the team crowded around Fuhr to celebrate.

While fans across Canada cheered the 6–5 win, the players doused each other with champagne in the dressing room. Fuhr was spotted spraying the sparkling wine over everyone within a two-foot radius. "You don't mind if I ruin someone's suit, do you?" he asked, inching toward coach Mike Keenan. There's no record of what happened next, but it's safe to assume the episode ended with Keenan paying a visit to a dry cleaner.[20]

Fuhr, who played the final round with an injured stick hand and a rash all over his body—*ewww!*—was named to the tournament's all-star team along with Gretzky, Lemieux and defenseman Ray Bourque. The Canadian team, which included several future Hall of Fame players, is still considered one of the best ever assembled.

HOCKEY FANS across the country were in high spirits following the Canada Cup, but the bonhomie didn't last long for those in Edmonton. Several Oilers refused to report to training camp. Coffey was so unhappy with his contract that he skipped camp entirely and was soon sent to the Pittsburgh Penguins as part of a seven-player deal. A few months later, the Oilers sent Moog to the Bruins in a four-player deal that brought Bill Ranford to Edmonton as Fuhr's new goaltending partner. Moog had been unhappy playing second fiddle to Fuhr in the playoffs.[21]

Looking back, Moog thinks he could have benefited from taking Fuhr's approach to the game. "I ran my mouth one day about lack of defensive coverage," he recalls. "The coach said, 'Why can't you be like Grant? He wouldn't say sh*t if he had a mouth full of it.'"

As it turned out, the Oilers' 1987–88 season was not one for the ages. They finished second in the conference with 99 points, six fewer than the Flames. It was the team's lowest point total since the 1980–81 season, when they recorded 74 points. One factor in that dip was the absence of Gretzky, who suffered a knee injury and missed 16 games.

Despite his team's troubles, Fuhr posted the best numbers of his career in the regular season, leading NHL goalies in games played (75), wins (40) and shutouts (4). He continued to shine in the playoffs, when he played in more games (19) and notched more wins (16) than any other goalie.

He wasn't as impressed by his statistics as everyone else was. "All I cared about was winning," he says today, adding that he didn't mind allowing five goals in a game as long as the other team allowed one more. "The object of the game is to win. It's not about personal accomplishments."

"I've never seen reflexes like Grant's," Gretzky said at the time. "I think he's the best goaltender in the history of the NHL."[22] More than three decades later, Fuhr considers the comment to be hyperbole. "I don't know if I would have gone quite that far," he says. "You could have put a few guys ahead of me. But if you play well enough for your teammates to appreciate you, that's all that really matters."

The Oilers returned to form in the playoffs, running roughshod over the competition. They beat the Jets (77 points), the Flames and the Red Wings (93 points), before sweeping aside the Bruins, who had finished second in the Prince of Wales Conference with 94 points, in the final. The Oilers lost just two playoff games en route to their fourth Cup victory, making fools of pundits who had doubted that the team could bounce back from a rocky regular season. "I think what this does," Gretzky said, throwing shade at critics, "is teach people that you never bet against a winner."[23]

Although Fuhr had played in every postseason game, he wasn't exhausted. Oh, wait. Maybe he was. "Yes, I'm tired. I can finally admit it," he said. "But I'm going to have a helluva time being tired."[24]

The victory parade was held two days later, and the celebrations continued for Fuhr at the NHL Awards banquet in June. The goalie, who was a finalist for the Hart Trophy, won the Vezina Trophy. His acceptance speech was short on words but long on sentiment. "You don't win awards without the 20 guys you play with," he said. "And I had a great time playing with them. They're the greatest bunch of guys. Thank you."

More than three decades later, Fuhr believes that camaraderie was as much a factor in the Oilers' success as skill. "As teammates, you have to like each other," he says. "You have to play for each other. And the best way to do that is to treat the team like a family."

Fuhr and some teammates once traveled to Hawaii for a vacation. It was a great time, sure, but did he go surfing? Hell, no. "I don't swim that well, so surfing was out of the question." Besides, he says, "in the ocean you're not at the top of the food chain. The beach was the best spot for me."

1988-91

To say the next three seasons were eventful for the Oilers is like saying some stuff happened during Donald Trump's term as US president.

The saga started in August 1988, when the Oilers dispatched Gretzky to the Los Angeles Kings in an eight-player trade that sent shock waves through the sports world. Oilers fans were apoplectic. Some of them even burned an effigy of Peter Pocklington, the Oilers' owner. Messier and some of the other players considered going on strike.

A member of Parliament urged the federal government to block the trade or buy Gretzky's contract and sell him back to a Canadian team. "The Edmonton Oilers without Gretzky is like apple pie without ice cream," Nelson Riis said, "like winter without snow, like the *Wheel of Fortune* without Vanna White."[25] Gretzky didn't even have to host a television game show to earn high praise.

But in the end, politicians turned their attention back to the upcoming federal election and hockey fans were spared the spectacle of their heroes picketing the Northlands Coliseum holding placards bearing the words NO WAYNE? NO WAY!

The Oilers' productivity dipped after Gretzky moved to California, but they were still an offensive threat. Kurri and forward Jimmy Carson, who had joined the team in the trade that would live in infamy, were among the NHL's top 10 scorers in the 1988–89 season, and Messier was second in scoring (129 points) behind Gretzky (142 points) the following season.

The Oilers didn't finish at the top of the conference standings in any of the first three seasons after the big trade, but they placed second in the 1989–90 season with 90 points and beat the Jets (85 points), the Kings (75 points) and the Blackhawks (88 points) en route to the final against the Bruins. Boston had finished first in the NHL with 101 points, but the Oilers were up to the task—and they won the Cup for the fifth time. In the dressing room at the Boston Garden, Messier stood on a platform and tilted the trophy, drenching a group of sports reporters.

Fuhr, who had announced his retirement the previous summer, apparently because of a financial dispute with management, only to change his mind, didn't play in the postseason. He had suffered a case of appendicitis the previous fall, and when he returned to action, he hurt his shoulder so badly he had to undergo reconstructive surgery. He looked on as Ranford took a star turn in the Oilers net and won the Conn Smythe Trophy.

Three months after the Cup victory, Fuhr found himself in the middle of a scandal that made international headlines. The *Edmonton Journal* ran a story stating that he had a drug problem. It included quotes from his first wife, Corrine, whom he had married in 1985 and recently divorced. She said she had often found cocaine hidden in his clothes and claimed to have received threatening phone calls from drug dealers.

Fuhr admitted he had used an illegal substance from 1983 to 1989, but said he had stopped after spending time in a rehab facility the previous summer. The NHL suspended him for a year. Sather was critical of the move, stating that Fuhr had tested negative for cocaine use three times in the previous 12 months. Messier and others spoke up too, saying the NHL should have been helping, not punishing, players with substance abuse problems.

Fuhr wasn't even allowed on the ice during his suspension, but he managed to stay close to his teammates. "I would often stop by their homes to have coffee in the morning. When we finished, I went to the gym and they went to the rink," he says. "If you have good friends, believe in yourself and don't get down on yourself, you can get through pretty much everything."

In February 1991, the NHL lifted the suspension. To sharpen his skills before his return, Fuhr played a few games for Edmonton's AHL affiliate, the Cape Breton Oilers. During road games, fans taunted him from the stands. In New Haven, Connecticut, one inspired spectator approached the goalie near the bench, holding a plastic bag filled with a white powdery substance. He also held up a sign that said, "Pay me later." The substance may have been sugar, but the message wasn't sweet.

That didn't rattle Fuhr. He helped Edmonton finish fifth in the conference (80 points) and advance to the third round of the playoffs, the conference finals. Unfortunately, their season ended when they lost to the Minnesota North Stars (68 points) in five games.

1991-94

Before the start of the 1991–92 season, Oilers management continued dismantling the team to cut costs. Four months after they traded away Jari Kurri, they did the same to Fuhr. He headed to Toronto in a seven-player deal that also included Glenn Anderson.

Fuhr "played his rear end off for this team for a lot of years," Oilers forward Craig MacTavish lamented. "The trade had been talked about so much, it didn't catch anybody by surprise, but it shouldn't detract from all the great years Grant had with us. He was cool, calm, great under pressure."[26]

True to form, Fuhr just shrugged. "Billy Ranford wants to play a lot and he's done all the things he had to do," he said. "Economics say you can't play two goalies, though."[27]

He stayed in Toronto for a season and a half, but when rookie Félix Potvin became a sensation, Fuhr was sent to Buffalo in a five-player deal in February 1993. He took the trade in stride, saying his stint in Toronto had been "fun while it lasted."[28]

The Sabres had great offense—Pat LaFontaine and Alexander Mogilny were among the NHL's top scorers—but they needed a seasoned goaltender.

The Sabres placed eighth out of 12 teams in the Prince of Wales Conference (86 points) and then prepared for the postseason. Coached by John Muckler, who had left Edmonton in 1991, the Sabres met the Bruins in the first round of the playoffs, the division semifinals. Boston had recorded 109 points in the regular season, finishing second in the conference and in the NHL, so they were heavily favored. But snipers Adam Oates and Joe Juneau didn't intimidate Fuhr.

He was exceptional in the first three games, helping the Sabres win them all. He was at his best late in Game 3, when he dove to stop a shot and then did a reverse somersault to get back on his feet. "Grant's a special person when it comes to hockey," said Muckler. "The more pressure he has, the more enjoyment he gets out of it. He feels he can win a game all by himself, and he's probably right."[29]

Early in Game 4, Fuhr caught his skate in the mesh of his net and strained his right knee. He stayed between the pipes for the rest of the period, but during the first intermission, Dominik Hašek, then in his first season with the Sabres, prepared to replace him. Fuhr must have performed a Vulcan mind meld on the Czech in the dressing room; the transition between the two goalies was seamless. Hašek stood his ground and made spectacular saves in overtime to help the Sabres win the game, 6–5, and the series. It was a major upset.

The Sabres then took on the Montreal Canadiens (102 points) in the division final. Fuhr was back in net for the series, but with Mogilny and LaFontaine sidelined by injuries, Buffalo was no match for the Canadiens. Their goalie, Patrick Roy, was a standout. The Habs swept aside the Sabres in four games and ended up winning the Cup.

That spring, Fuhr applied for membership at the Transit Valley Country Club, in a Buffalo suburb. It turned him down even though some of his teammates were already members there. Critics said Fuhr had been rejected because of his skin color. Club officials denied it, claiming his application had contained "incorrect and incomplete" information. Still, the club got threatening phone calls, and vandals burned a swastika into the grass on the 14th green of the club's golf course. The club reversed its decision and apologized. Fuhr had joined another club by then, but he wasn't bitter. "You're never too big to accept an apology," he said.[30]

The snub didn't affect his performance. In the 1993–94 season, he and Hašek won the William M. Jennings Trophy as goalies on the team that allowed the fewest goals (218) in the regular season. (This used to be the criterion for the Vezina Trophy.) Hašek soon emerged as a superstar, and just as he had in Toronto, Fuhr found himself taking a back seat to a one-time protégé. In February 1995, he was sent to the Kings in a six-player deal.

1994-96

Fuhr was happy to be reunited with Gretzky in Los Angeles, but his time there turned out to be a disappointment. He played in 14 games and won just one of them. When the Kings missed the playoffs, it was clear his days in La-La Land were numbered.

But Gretzky's faith in Fuhr was unwavering. That summer, Mike Keenan, then general manager and coach of the St. Louis Blues, was enjoying a glass of wine on a patio in New York when Gretzky spotted him from a passing taxi and jumped out to join him. When their conversation turned to goaltending, Gretzky recommended Fuhr, who was then a free agent.

Soon after, Fuhr joined the Blues. He was 33 years old, with a surgically repaired left knee, screws in both shoulders and a lot of wear and tear on other joints. He often moved as awkwardly as c-3po on the Death Star. Few people expected him to be as good as he had been in his heyday.

Skepticism deepened when he arrived at training camp in September 1995 looking more like a giant panda than an elite athlete. Keenan was alarmed by the weight gain. "I said, 'Oh sh*t. I just gave you an opportunity to get back in and now this?'"[31]

Keenan suspended Fuhr for a week. That persuaded him to start working with a conditioning coach. Fuhr soon returned to human form, checking in at 188 pounds. Still, he continued to indulge in the odd burger and put cream in his morning coffee. "Not two-percent milk. Not whole milk," he said. "Cream."[32]

St. Louis wasn't an offensive powerhouse; the team finished near the bottom of the NHL in goals scored in the 1995–96 season. But they were fourth in the Western Conference with 80 points, 19 more than the season before—and most of the credit went to Fuhr.

"If he didn't have a good game, he'd say, 'Oh well, no worries, I'll be better next game.' A bad outing never seemed to bother him, which is the perfect demeanor for a goalie," Blues teammate Al MacInnis said later. "The one thing about Grant was, when you needed a save, he'd give you a save. Late in periods. Late in games. Late in overtime."[33]

Giving Father Time a swift kick in the rear, Fuhr was outstanding in most of the games he played in—and he played in a lot of them. In fact, he played in 79 games that season, and all but three were consecutive. In doing so, he set two NHL records that still stand.

Many people thought Keenan, whom a sportswriter once described as "Supreme Dictator for Life," was meting out cruel and unusual punishment, but Fuhr was happy with the workload.[34] "I liked playing every day," he said years later. You prepare to play every day. So, the fact that Mike let me play every day was great."[35]

In February, the Kings traded Gretzky to St. Louis in a six-player deal. With the Great One on the roster and Fuhr at the top of his game, Blues fans were optimistic about the team's prospects.

The Blues faced off against the Leafs (80 points) in the first round of the playoffs and won the first game, 3–1, in Maple Leaf Gardens. Fuhr started in net for the second game two nights later, but he didn't finish it.

Nick Kypreos slammed into him like a wrecking ball in the first period, destroying the goalie's knee and ending his season. As Fuhr prepared for surgery, Jon Casey took his place. The Blues fought hard—Gretzky had nine points in the series—but they couldn't overcome the loss of their star goalie. The Leafs eliminated the Blues in six games.

Kypreos landed on the naughty list of just about everyone in St. Louis, including Fuhr. The goalie insisted the Leafs forward had jumped on him. He said he had no respect for Kypreos and, to prove it, called him a "no-mind." No doubt, Kypreos found a lump of coal in his stocking that Christmas.[36]

1996-2000

Over the next three seasons, Fuhr became one of the winningest goaltenders in Blues history, but he never fully recovered from that injury, and he even suffered more.

In September 1999, after the Blues acquired a new starter in Roman Turek, Fuhr agreed to waive his no-trade clause and the Blues traded him to the Calgary Flames in exchange for a draft pick.

Calgary fans were willing to forgive Fuhr for inflicting so much pain on them during the Battle of Alberta a decade earlier; they were excited about the possibility of him helping their team make the playoffs for the first time since 1996. But Fuhr suffered another knee injury and played in just 23 games that season, posting only five wins. His biggest contribution to the team was being a mentor for young goalie Fred Brathwaite.

By September 2000, Fuhr had undergone three knee surgeries in two years. He finally called it quits. "The time is right for me to retire," he said. "There is nothing like playing, but the body is telling me it's time."[37]

Tributes poured in from around the hockey world. "Grant Fuhr, diving, lunging, contorting, was as expressive a goaltender as ever lived," sports columnist George Johnson wrote. "To him, a goal crease was what a canvas was to Monet, a pulpit was to Billy Graham, a blank sheet of paper in a typewriter to Hemingway. It was where he felt most alive."[38]

RETIREMENT

Fuhr stayed with the Flames organization as goaltending coach for the next two seasons and, soon after, filled the same role with the Phoenix Coyotes. He stayed in that position until 2009.

In 2003, the Oilers retired his jersey number, 31. Once again, former players and coaches sang his praises. "The Oilers back then played wide-open, offensive hockey and they abandoned Grant for periods every night," Keenan said. "They could do it because they knew he would backstop them."[39]

A month later, in November, he was inducted into the Hockey Hall of Fame. Many observers noted that he was the first Black player to win the honor. Fuhr said he was proud of that, but just as he always had, he downplayed the significance of his skin color. "The reason you get into the Hall of Fame is for what you have accomplished on the ice and I probably take the most pride in that," he said.[40]

Fuhr now lives in Palm Springs, California, where he spends time with his current wife, Lisa, and pursues his passion for golf despite having several joints replaced since his retirement from the NHL. He has fared well in celebrity golf events and has played in some PGA-sanctioned events. A few years ago, the scratch golfer became director of golf at a local country club.

That didn't surprise Coffey, who remembers Fuhr playing golf during the playoffs. (Years ago, a reporter asked Fuhr how he could play as many as 36 holes between game days. He replied, "Because it usually gets too dark to play 54.")[41] "I don't know how he ever found golf to be relaxing because I've always found golf is just a lot of hard work," Coffey said. "But he was just so good at it."[42]

Fuhr—who is the father of four kids, Janine, Rochelle, R.J. and Kendyl—gets a warm, fuzzy feeling when he looks back at his NHL career, despite all the challenges he faced on and off the ice. "I enjoyed being in the show every day," he says. "I never looked at it as a job. I got to play a game for a living. I was able to treat it as a game and enjoy it."

||||||||||||||||||||||||||||||||||||||||||||||||||||||||||||||||||||||||||||||||||||||||||||||||||||||||||||||

GRANT FUHR • ALL-TIME RANKING

REGULAR SEASON			PLAYOFFS		
GAMES + RANK	WINS + RANK	SO + RANK	GAMES + RANK	WINS + RANK	SO + RANK
868 [12TH]	403 [12TH]	25 [98TH]	150 [5TH]	92 [3RD]	6 [28TH]

+ NHL ALL-STAR TEAM (1ST) 1987–88

+ NHL ALL-STAR TEAM (2ND) 1981–82

||||||| 9 |||||||

THE CROWD-PLEASER
ROBERTO LUONGO

||||||||||||||||||||||||||||||

HOURS AFTER A flip shot from the blue line bounced slowly past Florida Panthers goalie Roberto Luongo in a game in 2015, he took to Twitter. He posted a photo of himself in the dressing room after the game, a 6–2 victory over the Anaheim Ducks. He appears in a crouch position wearing goalie pads, holding a puck in his glove hand. The caption reads, "Problem solved."

Brilliant in some games and mediocre in others, Luongo both delighted and tortured fans—sometimes in back-to-back games. Yet he was a fan favorite for much of his career because of his dedication, perseverance and self-deprecating humor.

He retired in 2019 after making his mark in the NHL and in international competition, but he continues to tickle the fancy of fans with his colorful tweets.

LUONGO WAS born in Montreal in April 1979 and grew up in in Saint-Leonard, a community with a large Italian population, under the watchful eye of his parents, Antonio and Lina.

Antonio had grown up in a community in southern Italy and, like many Italians, was passionate about soccer. He introduced his sons, Roberto, Leo and Fabio, to the game. They excelled at it, but, growing up just 12 miles from the Montreal Forum, they were obsessed with hockey.

Luongo was a standout at the 2004 world championship in the Czech Republic. He was described as being "head and shoulders" above any other goalie in the tournament—not surprising given that he was six foot three.
JIRI KOLIS/HOCKEY HALL OF FAME

Roberto loved watching Montreal Canadiens goalie Patrick Roy strut his stuff, but he looked farther afield for inspiration. He idolized Grant Fuhr and spent hours pretending to be the Edmonton Oilers goalie, making spectacular glove saves on toys and other small household items—except for those with sharp edges.

When he played ball hockey on the street in front of the family home, Luongo tended goal and imagined he was the heir apparent to Fuhr.

"I just loved to watch him. He just made it so much fun and I tried to mimic him every time," Luongo recalled years later, adding that he emulated the legendary Fuhr because of his fast glove hand, and not because of his collection of Stanley Cup rings.[1]

Luongo started skating when he was eight years old and was far from steady at first. "I remember I was crying," he said. "It was a tough day."[2]

When he started playing hockey, his parents discouraged him from being a goaltender because they wanted him to work on his skating, so he played forward. But he was more interested in stopping pucks than chasing them, and he continued to pester his parents to let him play goal. When the goalie on his peewee team failed to show up for a game, a ray of sunshine poked through the clouds and an angel caressed Luongo's cheek with a feathered wing. His parents allowed him to strap on the pads. The 11-year-old notched a shutout in his first game between the pipes. "In the end you can't stop destiny," his mother said years later. "It was just meant to happen and it did."[3]

Shy and withdrawn in school, Luongo would trip over his words whenever he had to speak in front of the class. But he was more than happy to be in the spotlight on the ice. A big kid with excellent reflexes, he was a standout—and he took his craft seriously.

"The other boys, 12, 13 years old, [would be] fooling around, whatever, and Roberto would be in the corner, getting ready," said Tony Canuto, who was his coach at the time. "He was so serious in the room and on the ice, such a competitor. He hated to be beat."[4]

By the time he was 15 years old, Luongo was playing for Montréal-Bourassa, a team in the Quebec Midget AAA hockey league that had already produced elite NHL goaltenders such as Martin Brodeur and Félix Potvin.

Luongo caught the attention of scouts in the Quebec Major Junior Hockey League. The Val-d'Or Foreurs selected him second overall in the 1995 QMJHL draft.

He starred in the league for four seasons—three with the Foreurs and one with the Acadie-Bathurst Titan, a team based in Bathurst, New Brunswick. He excelled, tying a league record with seven shutouts in the 1997–98 regular season and setting a record for most playoff victories (38). He helped both teams win the league title, one year apart.

The league named Luongo its top professional prospect in 1997, and sure enough, the New York Islanders selected him fourth overall in that year's NHL Entry Draft. At the time, it was the highest a goalie had ever been selected in the current draft format.

Sports reporters were suddenly very interested in the 18-year-old, who was developing into a tall butterfly goaltender with a great glove hand. "I never put pressure on myself to the point where the game is no longer fun. It's always a challenge, but it's fun, not a job," he told them about his future job.[5]

Six months later, Luongo suited up for Team Canada in the 1998 world junior championship in Finland. He played backup to Mathieu Garon of the Victoriaville Tigres, going winless in three games. Canada finished eighth.

Despite that disappointment, Luongo was named the starter for the Canadian team that competed in the 1999 world junior championship in Winnipeg. He appeared in seven of eight games and posted four wins, two of which were shutouts. Canada lost to Russia 3–2 in the final, but Luongo was named the tournament's best goaltender.

NHL

1999-2000

Just a few days after the gold-medal game, the Islanders signed Luongo to a three-year contract. He marked the occasion by buying himself a Jeep.

Luongo started the season with the Lowell Lock Monsters, the Islanders affiliate in the AHL, but he didn't have to wait long to make his NHL debut. On November 28, the Islanders came calling. They needed a goalie for a game against the Boston Bruins. "I found out a few hours before," Luongo recalled later. "My parents [in Montreal] didn't even have time to get down there. They had to watch on TV." No doubt, they were pleased with what they saw. Their son stopped 43 shots in a 2–1 victory at the FleetCenter.[6]

Luongo was so good in his first few games, the Islanders sent their starter, Potvin, to the Vancouver Canucks in exchange for backup goalie Kevin Weekes—and Luongo started looking for accommodations nearby.

When he allowed seven goals in a 7–3 loss to the Bruins on January 4, Islanders general manager Mike Milbury took Luongo to task for apartment hunting on a game day. "You can't do that in the NHL. You have to prepare yourself," Milbury told reporters. Luongo defended himself, claiming he had looked at just one apartment that day and had not departed from his usual game-day routine.[7]

Luongo struggled in subsequent weeks, and Weekes replaced him as the team's starter. In March, the Islanders sent Luongo back to Lowell, Massachusetts, saying he needed more playing time than he would get with the Islanders.

When the Islanders took goaltender Rick DiPietro as the first overall pick in the 2000 Entry Draft, it was clear Luongo didn't have a future on Long Island.

After the Islanders finished the season third from the bottom with 58 points in the 15-team Eastern Conference, management sent Luongo to the Florida Panthers in a four-player deal. Despite his inconsistency that season, Panthers general manager Bryan Murray trumpeted him as a franchise player.

2000–06

The Panthers had lost in the first round of the playoffs in the season preceding the trade, and their fortunes only worsened after Luongo arrived in Sunrise, Florida.

The team missed the playoffs in every one of the next five seasons—the 2004–05 season was canceled because of a labor dispute—and Pavel Bure was the only forward on the team to make an impact during that span. The Russian Rocket was one of the NHL's top scorers (92 points) in the 2000–01 season.

Luongo split the workload with Trevor Kidd that season, but he later emerged as the Panthers' starting goaltender. In the 2003–04 season, he recorded the third-best save percentage in the league (.931) and was a finalist for the Vezina Trophy. Two years later, he led the NHL in games played (75).

His backup that season, Jamie McLennan, attributes Luongo's success to hard work. He recalls seeing Luongo on the ice the morning after a bad game. "I got to the rink really early, and he was already on the ice by himself. He was going through the paces, doing his routine. This was an hour and a half before practice. That means he arrived at the rink while the rest of us were still at home eating breakfast," McLennan says today. "Now, that is dedication."

The two goalies shared a lot of laughs during their season together. McLennan remembers one incident vividly. "Lou once came to the bench during a break in play. He said he had stopped a shot so hard, his hand was likely broken. I didn't want to go in. I was probably sitting there eating popcorn," McLennan says. "So I said, 'Nah, you're fine. Get back out there!' He still tells that story."

Luongo didn't spend all his time in a Panthers uniform between 2000 and 2006. He also donned the national team jersey for six international tournaments—four world championships, one Olympics and one World Cup. He played second fiddle in most of those competitions, behind Fred Brathwaite, Sean Burke or Martin Brodeur, but he had a star turn in the 2004 world championship in the Czech Republic.

He played in seven of Canada's nine games, recording six wins to help clinch the gold medal. Before the final, a wire service assessed Canada's chance of beating Sweden. "In the end, the difference may reside where it often does: in goal," it reported. "Roberto Luongo is head and shoulders above any other goaltender in this tournament." He made 28 saves, and Canada won the game 5–3.[8]

With contract negotiations at an impasse, the Panthers traded Luongo to the Vancouver Canucks in a six-player deal in June 2006. Canucks general manager Dave Nonis was enthusiastic. "We believe that, in Roberto, we're getting a player who has represented his country at the highest level, has been nominated for the Vezina Trophy and has proven that he is among the elite goaltenders in the world." The Canucks signed Luongo to a four-year contract.

In the eight years preceding his arrival, goaltenders had filed in and out of the organization like holiday shoppers at a

Canadian Tire on Christmas Eve. Almost 20 netminders had played for the club. Brian Burke, the Canucks general manager during those years, once called his team a "goalie graveyard."

2006-10

Luongo's trip through the next four seasons in Vancouver was a roller coaster; he experienced many highs and lows.

Early on, he emerged as one of the game's biggest stars. He notched more wins (47) in the 2006–07 season than in any other season of his career, and it was the second-highest total in the NHL that year.

One of those victories was especially rewarding.

On January 15, he was hit in the throat by a puck during a practice in Montreal. He spent the night in the intensive care unit of a hospital, sleeping in an upright position to ensure his windpipe didn't swell. He was discharged the next day, looking worse for wear and speaking in a raspy voice. But he suited up for a game against the Canadiens that night.

Luongo could barely communicate with his teammates on the ice, but he stopped all 30 shots fired at him and the Canucks notched a 4–0 win. "He sounded like the Godfather but played like a god," sports columnist Iain MacIntyre wrote. "Vancouver Canuck Roberto Luongo is not only a goaltending marvel, he's a human marvel, too."[9]

With Luongo between the pipes, the Canucks finished third in the conference with 105 points and made the playoffs—not bad for a team that pundits and fans had expected to crash and burn.

The Dallas Stars were their first-round opponent. With Eric Lindros and Mike Modano on the attack and goaltender Marty Turco in net, the Stars had fared well that season, finishing sixth in the conference (107 points).

The opening game of the first round was a pitched battle. Luongo, making his playoff debut, was shaky at times but got better as the game went on—and it went on for a very long time. It was tied 4–4 at the end of regulation time, and didn't end until

Canucks forward Henrik Sedin scored late in the fourth over-time period. By then, Luongo had stopped 72 shots, one shy of a record set by Kelly Hrudey in 1987.

Spectators were sleepy, but his teammates were animated. "Before games, you come in the room and you look at the other team's lineup," said Canucks veteran Trevor Linden. "You go 'OK, they've got this guy and that guy and that guy.' And then you go: 'But we've got this guy.' When the best player from either team is in your net, that's pretty significant."[10]

Sports reporters also sang Luongo's praises. One credited him with transforming the Canucks from "an erratic, offensive team that thought defence was a railing in Chicago, into one of the National Hockey League's soundest, most disciplined contenders."[11]

The Canucks eliminated the Stars in seven games and moved on to play the Anaheim Ducks, who had placed second in the conference with 110 points. With two seasoned stars, forward Teemu Selanne and defenseman Chris Pronger, on the roster, the Ducks proved too hot for the Canucks to handle and eliminated them in five games in the conference semifinals. Luongo made 56 saves in the deciding game, which went into double overtime.

When he missed the first few minutes of the first overtime period, fans assumed it was because of a wardrobe malfunction. Wrong. The malfunction was much more disruptive. Luongo had responded to the call of nature during intermission, and was still in the bathroom when the puck dropped.

"I was there doing my business and I hear the play starting in the arena," he said later. "So I panicked there. I don't remember if I wiped. I just put my gear back on, tried to get out there as soon as I could." He attributed the gastric disaster to caffeine. "Bad stomach. Coffees don't help, but I need those," he said. "Some-times you've got to pay the price."[12]

Years later, he returned to the scene of the crime in Ana-heim—yellow police tape had been removed—and tweeted a photo of a toilet with the caption "And this is where the magic happened."

As the Ducks steamed toward a Cup victory that season, Canucks fans took stock of their team's surprising playoff run and drifted off to sleep whispering the words "Lou! Lou!" They were delighted when Luongo was a finalist for the Hart Trophy and the Vezina Trophy.

THAT SENSE of optimism faded the following season when the Canucks missed the playoffs, but Luongo played well and was third overall with six shutouts.

In September 2008, Canucks management named him captain. It was an unconventional decision—only six other NHL goaltenders had ever filled that role. And it was challenging for Luongo. According to league rules, he couldn't perform any of the on-ice duties required of captains. Two teammates were responsible for communicating with on-ice officials and taking part in ceremonial face-offs and other formalities. Forbidden to wear the C on his jersey, Luongo instead had it incorporated into the artwork on one of his masks.

The *Globe and Mail* applauded the move and called on the league to be more accommodating. "The NHL should adjust its rulebook to allow Mr. Luongo to wear the C on his sweater," an editorial asserted. "Mr. Luongo is not only one of the finest goaltenders in the league, he is the best player on the Canucks, and has the best work ethic. In other words, he does what is often required of leaders: He leads by example, a key attribute of Mark Messier, the standard for a great hockey captain."[13]

In November, Luongo appeared to make a routine save on a shot in a game against the Pittsburgh Penguins, but he collapsed to the ice after the play and needed help getting to the dressing room. He was diagnosed with a groin injury, and didn't return until mid-January. Despite that setback, Luongo managed to post nine shutouts—second best in the NHL.

The Canucks finished fourth in the conference with 100 points, so fans were optimistic heading into the first round of the playoffs against the St. Louis Blues (92 points).

Their faith was rewarded when the Canucks swept aside the Blues. Much of the credit went to the rangy goaltender with excellent reflexes. Luongo allowed just five goals on 131 shots over four games. "If there was any doubt before about just how important Luongo is to the Canucks' hopes of a long and glorious playoff run, there must.certainly not be any now," wrote sports columnist Gary Mason. "Against the Blues he was sublime—as good as a goalie gets in the playoffs."[14]

The conference semifinals weren't as kind to Luongo or his team. The Chicago Blackhawks defeated the Canucks in a six-game series. Luongo allowed seven goals on 30 shots in the deciding game. After the 7–5 loss, Luongo said he had let his teammates down, and he left a media scrum with tears in his eyes. Not every fan was sympathetic. Some even called for him to be traded.

In August, Luongo attended Team Canada's training camp for the 2010 Winter Olympics in Vancouver. While there, he told reporters he wanted to sign another contract with the Canucks before the start of the regular season. The team granted him his wish, signing him to a lucrative 12-year deal.

LUONGO SUFFERED a rib injury during a game against the Detroit Red Wings early in the 2009–10 season, but returned to the ice after missing a handful of games, and was primed and ready for the start of the Olympics, whose hockey games would be played on the Canucks' home ice.

He recorded a shutout in Canada's first game, an 8–0 win over Norway, then prepared to spend long stretches on the bench as a backup. But when Martin Brodeur played poorly in a 5–3 loss to the US in the preliminary round, Team Canada coach Mike Babcock made Luongo the starter.

When Babcock delivered the news, Luongo was more nervous than excited. "He was literally sick to his stomach," says sports broadcaster James Duthie, who got to know the goalie well by interviewing him and working with him on segments for TSN. "When he shared the news with family members, they remarked that he looked white as a ghost. He knew he would be under intense pressure."

Luongo ended up playing five games, three more than Brodeur and five more than Marc-André Fleury, who may or may not have been playing solitaire on the sidelines. Luongo was stellar in the semifinal against Slovakia, making a crucial save on Pavol Demitra, his Canucks teammate, in the dying seconds of regulation time to seal a 3–2 win.

He was also in net for the historic gold-medal game against the US. He made 34 saves, including one on Joe Pavelski, moments before Sidney Crosby scored in overtime to seal a 3–2 victory as almost 17 million viewers, half the Canadian population, tuned in. (According to a national audience measurement organization, the game was the most-watched television broadcast in Canadian history.)

"[Luongo] was amazing," exclaimed Team Canada forward and Blackhawks captain Jonathan Toews. "That's another thing, I told him I was kind of sick and tired of hearing the 'Looo' chants when Chicago would come here to Vancouver, but it never sounded better than tonight, that's for sure."[15]

"It was probably the pinnacle of my career," Luongo said years later. "In the highest-pressure moment imaginable, to be able to come out and win like that, I think, is insane."[16]

Luongo was on a high after the Olympics, but it didn't last long. He struggled in the second half of the NHL season and finished with mediocre statistics.

The Canucks finished fourth in the conference with 103 points and opened the playoffs by taking on the Los Angeles Kings (101 points) in the opening round. Led by Mikael Samuelsson and Daniel Sedin and his brother Henrik, who had finished at the top of the NHL scoring ladder (112 points) that season, the Canucks eliminated the Kings in six games.

A reporter who covered the final game pointed to a great pad save Luongo had made when his team was trailing 1–0, and concluded that the goalie, "playing in one of the biggest games of his career," had "lived up to all the hope and hype" he had generated since his arrival in Vancouver.[17]

The Canucks then took on the Blackhawks (112 points) in the conference semifinals for the second straight season and came up short *again*. Toews had lost the lovin' feeling he had enjoyed during the Olympics; he notched four goals and eight assists over six games to help his team eliminate the Canucks. The Blackhawks went on to win the Cup.

2010-11

During the summer of 2010, speculation was rife that Luongo wouldn't continue as team captain. Critics noted that, late in the series against the Blackhawks, he had refused to do pregame interviews. That is standard operating procedure for goaltenders, who are notoriously elusive before big games—but not for captains, who are required to speak to reporters even when their thousand-yard stare makes it clear they would rather be trapped in a fiery car wreck.

In September, Luongo stepped down as captain and was replaced by Henrik Sedin. Looking relaxed in a T-shirt, plaid shorts and sandals at a news conference, Luongo told reporters he wanted to focus on goaltending without having to handle the captain's responsibilities.

As Luongo ended his stint as designated team leader, he started his stretch as a pupil of Roland Melanson, a former NHL goalie whom the Canucks had hired to work with him. Under his tutelage, Luongo started playing deeper in the crease instead of moving out to challenge shooters. The change gave him more time to react to tips and other plays close to the net. It also kept him safe from players like massive blueliner Dustin Byfuglien, who had barreled through the goalmouth in the playoffs like a monster truck at a mud-bogging event.

Luongo was no longer the team's captain, but he was still *da man*. Between December and February, he went 21 games without a loss in regulation time. He and promising rookie Cory Schneider proved to be an excellent goaltending tandem. As the regular season wound down, Luongo asked Melanson to start Schneider in two more games, so the newcomer could reach the total (25) required to be eligible for the William M.

Jennings Trophy. At the end of the season, the pair shared the award.

Luongo's statistics spoke volumes about his performance. He finished first in the NHL in wins (38), second in goals-against average (2.11) and third in save percentage (.928).

Thanks to strong goaltending and the contributions of Daniel and Henrik Sedin, who finished first (104 points) and fourth (94 points), respectively, on the NHL scoring ladder, the Canucks finished atop the NHL standings with 117 points. They started the playoffs by taking on the Blackhawks (97 points). (Luongo wasn't disappointed that Byfuglien had been traded to the Atlanta Thrashers the previous June.)

Duncan Keith, a two-way player who had won the Norris Trophy as the NHL's top defenseman the previous season, led the Blackhawks' charge, but the Sedin twins and Alex Burrows matched them almost goal for goal.

Luongo was in net for the first three games, all Vancouver victories, and posted a shutout in the opener, but he stumbled after that. He allowed 10 goals over the next two games, both Chicago wins. He started Game 6 on the bench, but when Schneider got injured early in the third period, Luongo was called into service. He made 12 saves and allowed one goal, but Chicago won the game 4–3 in overtime. Both Vancouver goalies were available for Game 7, but coach Alain Vigneault took a chance on Luongo and was rewarded for his faith. Luongo made 31 saves, including one in which he slid across his net to block a shot by Patrick Sharp in overtime. The Canucks won the game 2–1, and the series.

"Last three games, four games I felt like I was tested," Luongo said afterwards. "They always say tough times is when you see the true character in somebody, so obviously, it was a big day in my career today." Sports columnist Cam Cole agreed, saying the goalie had "nearly pitched a perfect game in the most pressure-packed game of his NHL career."[18]

Two days later, the Canucks opened the conference semifinals against the Nashville Predators (99 points). Luongo went head-to-head against Pekka Rinne, one of the league's best netminders, and came out on top. He allowed just 11 goals, two fewer than Rinne, helping the Canucks eliminate the Predators in six games.

Excitement in Vancouver reached a crescendo. A local butcher shop added a "Big Lou-ongo" sandwich to the menu, and fans ate it with gusto, wiping remnants of meatballs from their chins as the melted cheese dripped onto their Canucks jerseys. Elsewhere, a van embossed with the team logo drove through the streets, honking at enthusiastic passersby. Not to be outdone, a family in Kelowna, 250 miles east of Vancouver, painted their house to resemble a Canucks jersey.

Almost 19,000 fans crammed into Vancouver's Rogers Arena for the start of the conference final against the San Jose Sharks (105 points). They and Canucks fans across the country were in for a thrilling ride. The Canucks lost just one game as they eliminated the Sharks in five games.

Luongo was in net for the entire series, allowing just 13 goals on 189 shots. He made 54 saves in the final game, which was decided in double overtime. Fans danced in the streets as Canucks players celebrated in the dressing room and looked ahead to their first Cup final in 17 years.

The Canucks then took on the Boston Bruins in the final. Boston, which had finished third in the Eastern Conference with 103 points, was a tough, defensive team with an excellent goaltender. Tim Thomas had won the Vezina Trophy and the William M. Jennings Trophy in recent years.

Vancouver fans were hoping Luongo would be solid in net again, and they weren't disappointed. He stopped 36 shots as the Canucks posted a 1–0 victory in the first game. He made 28 saves in the next one, and the Canucks won 3–2.

The party ended in Boston two days later, when Luongo let in every Bruins goal in an 8–1 loss in Game 3. Vancouver fans took down the streamers, popped the balloons and threw the last piece of cake in the garburator. They hoped for better times ahead.

But Luongo didn't fare much better in the next game. He surrendered four goals on 20 shots and was pulled in favor of Schneider. "The weak link the crowd really jumped on, and took every opportunity to mock-serenade, was Roberto Luongo," Cole wrote, before noting that "even the faithful are having grave doubts. And they should—because the Vancouver Canucks aren't going to win the Stanley Cup with what Luongo gave them on this trip to Boston."[19]

His ego was battered and his body was bruised, but Luongo managed to bounce back in Game 5 and post another shutout in a 1–0 victory to give his team the series lead.

After the game, he critiqued his counterpart's positioning on Vancouver's winning goal, suggesting it wouldn't have happened if Tim Thomas had stayed in the crease rather than moving out to challenge the shooter. His comments struck many as offside, so he tried to explain himself a day later. "I've been pumping his tires ever since the series started and I haven't heard one nice thing he had to say about me, so that's the way it is," Luongo said.[20]

Thomas responded during a press conference before Game 6. "I guess I didn't realize it was my job to pump his tires," he said with a grin. "I guess I have to apologize for that. I still think I'm the goaltender on the union side and I stick with all the other goalies. In being one and knowing what it takes to perform at this level and with this amount of pressure, I understand to a certain extent what every other goaltender is going through."[21]

Heading into Game 6, the Canucks were positioned to clinch the series and hoist the Cup for the first time in franchise history, but they ended up falling short—and no one fell shorter than their starting goalie. Luongo allowed three goals in three minutes in the first period, and was replaced by Schneider. The Bruins notched a 5–2 victory to even the series.

Luongo was back between the pipes for Game 7, but despite the fervent prayers of the Vancouver faithful, he put in another poor performance. He allowed three goals on 20 shots. Bruins forward Brad Marchand scored two goals and an assist, tying him with teammate Mark Recchi as the highest scorer in the series, with seven points, and the Bruins won the game, 4–0, and the Cup. Spectators at Rogers Arena slumped in their seats and the Canucks watched in stunned silence as the Bruins gathered around Thomas, whose tires were fully inflated, to celebrate.

In his column the next day, Cole noted that Boston had out-scored Vancouver 21–4 in the last five games. "Given that pau-city of offence, Roberto Luongo would have had to be all-world for the Canucks to win the series," he wrote, "and among critics who thought the team stood a better chance with rookie Cory Schneider between the pipes, he wasn't even all-Vancouver."[22]

Luongo was a finalist for the Vezina Trophy on the strength of his regular-season statistics, but that didn't take the sting out of losing the final.

2011–14

That loss was a big blow to the Canucks, but not a fatal one. The following season, they finished at the top of the NHL standings again, this time with 111 points. Henrik Sedin played a big role in that success; he was one of the league's highest scorers once again. But there was no magical playoff run this season. The Los Angeles Kings (95 points) eliminated the Canucks in the confer-ence quarterfinals, four games to one, and went on to win the franchise's first Cup.

A year later, the San Jose Sharks swept the Canucks aside in the first playoff round of the shortened 2012–13 season, after the NHL and the players' union quibbled over player salaries until early January. And Vancouver missed the playoffs altogether the following season.

Luongo's performance during that span was spotty, and he battled Schneider for top spot in net during the first two seasons after the team's trip to the final. Schneider emerged as the team's starter in the 2012–13 season. Luongo may have been gnashing his teeth and sticking pins in a Schneider voodoo doll in private, but he handled his rival's success graciously in public. He called the Canucks "Cory's team."

He went a step further and took part in a cheeky TSN segment that made light of the battle for the starter's job. It featured the two men tussling in the dressing room and Schneider taking a whack at Luongo with a goalie stick. "Luongo didn't just want to have fun with it," said Duthie at the time. "He wanted to let everyone know, 'Forget whatever you believe. We're actually good buddies.'"[23]

If there was one activity Luongo enjoyed as much as poking fun at himself, it was playing cards. In November 2011, he participated in his own charity poker tournament and finished second out of 300 people. "Just like his goaltending, he's a cool cat," said fellow participant Christian Oonk, who was seated next to Luongo for much of the night. "He's pretty relaxed. He proved he could play poker." The event raised almost $100,000 for Canucks for Kids Fund, an organization that supports charities dedicated to improving children's health and wellness.[24]

Around that time, a Twitter account by the name of @strombone1 started producing a steady stream of hysterical tweets about Luongo. The profile picture on the account was a silhouette of a goalie, and the account was followed by several Canucks players, so fans suspected it was the goaltender who was providing the comic gold. They turned out to be right.

When the 2012–13 season finally started in January, he treated followers to a memorable tweet: "Can't wait!!! Canucks fans, are you ready to see Cory Schneider as No. 1 in net?"[25]

After giving up a game-winning goal in a shootout against the St. Louis Blues in February, he took to Twitter. He posted a photo of Blues forward Andy McDonald in front of the net in his team's 4–3 win, with the caption "Almost had him…"

Then, after allowing eight goals in an 8–3 loss to the Red Wings a week later, Luongo wrote a tweet that referred to a novelty toy—a miniature red goal light that sounded every time a goal was scored in a game. The message read, "I just wanted to apologize to all the people who had to replace their Budweiser Red Light bulb after yesterday's debacle."

"I just wanted to keep it a little bit different, a little bit light, and to show more of my personality that sometimes is hard to bring out in front of the cameras," Luongo later said, explaining his motivation for his tweets. "Because when you're in front of the cameras, you want to keep it politically correct and don't stray too far away from the hockey terms everybody uses."[26]

"He was a shy guy early on, and that was misconstrued as aloofness," Duthie says today. "He didn't really know how to communicate with a bunch of microphones in front of him. Maybe that's why Twitter was perfect for him."

When the season ended, Luongo believed his days in Vancouver were numbered, even though he had nine years left on his contract. He put his penthouse up for sale, but that proved to be a waste of time. The Canucks traded Schneider to the New Jersey Devils in June 2013, securing Luongo's status as the starter the following season.

The 2013–14 season turned out to be unremarkable for the Canucks and their star goaltender, but Luongo had the chance to go to Sochi, Russia, for the Winter Olympics in February. Sportswriters were uncertain whether he or Montreal Canadiens star Carey Price should be Team Canada's starter. The coaches went with Price, choosing Luongo to start in just one game—a preliminary round contest against Austria, which Canada won 6–0.

Luongo returned from Russia with a gold medal, but he didn't get much love from John Tortorella, who had replaced Vigneault as Vancouver's head coach after the 2012–13 season. The coach, known for being as compassionate as Cinderella's stepmother, chose rookie Eddie Läck to start in goal in the Heritage Classic against the Ottawa Senators. It was a slap in the face to Luongo, who had looked forward to playing in the outdoor game at BC Place in Vancouver.

A day before the NHL trade deadline on March 5, the Canucks sent Luongo back to Florida in a four-player deal. It was a happy homecoming for Luongo. During his first stint there, he had met his wife, Gina, and started a family, which had grown to include a daughter named Gabriella and a son named Gianni.

The Panthers and their fans welcomed him back with open arms, hoping the 34-year-old goaltender would help the team become a strong contender.

2014-19

Luongo was so determined to make that happen that he took on a heavy workload and even played hurt. In March 2015, he injured his shoulder in a home game against the Toronto Maple Leafs. By the end of the first period, he was barely able to lift his arm, so he left the game and headed to the hospital for an assessment. In his absence, chaos ensued. Backup goaltender Al Montoya suffered a groin injury, forcing goaltending coach Rob Tallas to suit up. Luongo was following events through—what else?—Twitter and realized his team was in dire straits. He high-tailed it out of the hospital, leaving physicians and nurses disoriented, and rushed back to the arena to find his ashen-faced goalie coach preparing for battle. "I was like, 'Holy sh*t! What's going on?'" Luongo later explained. He didn't wait for an answer. He played the second half of the third period and, despite his ailing shoulder, didn't allow any goals. The Leafs won 3–2, but Luongo was heralded as a hero. "It just shows a lot about him," Panthers forward Jonathan Huberdeau said afterwards. "When we needed him, he came back hurt and did the job."[27]

BY THE end of that season, the Panthers had missed the play-offs for the third straight year. But they bounced back in 2015–16, when they finished third in the Eastern Conference with 103 points and took on the Islanders in the first round of the play-offs. Luongo made some spectacular saves in Game 2 to help the Panthers even the series with a 3–1 win. He stopped a shot from point-blank range in the second period, and during an Islanders power play in the third period, he stopped two shots by John Tavares, who had notched three points in the first game of the series. Despite the goalie's best efforts, the Islanders came out on top of the six-game series.

Incredibly, Luongo had made those memorable saves while injured. He had started feeling discomfort in his lower body months earlier, but had dismissed it as a mild groin injury. But it was his hip that was the problem, and the injury wasn't mild. After being examined by doctors, he underwent hip surgery. He did extensive rehab during the summer and was back between the pipes in the fall.

His hip continued to need TLC over the next three seasons, so he modified his routine to include a dynamic warm-up and strengthening exercises. He maintained that routine, but as he inched closer to his 40th birthday, he suffered more injuries and saw less playing time.

The Panthers missed the playoffs in the 2016–17 season and the next one. Luongo finished third in the NHL in save percentage (.929) in the 2017–18 campaign, but when he stepped onto the ice before a game against the Washington Capitals in late February, his mind was not on hockey.

The Panthers held a special service to pay tribute to the 17 people who had died in a mass shooting at a high school in Parkland, Florida. Standing on the ice and holding a microphone, Luongo addressed the crowd. He told fans his children went to school in Parkland, and that his wife had been born and raised in the area. "It's heartbreaking," he said, holding back tears. "You guys are in our thoughts. We've been thinking about you every day constantly for the last week. Just know that we're there for you if you guys need anything. You'll be in our prayers." He also said the teachers who had jumped into action to protect students should be "put on a pedestal."

Although his mind was elsewhere that night, he managed to make 33 saves, and the Panthers beat the Capitals 3–2. "I think in one game, you can kind of get that from a guy that means so much to people," said teammate Keith Yandle, "not just the way he plays on the ice, but what he does off the ice."[28]

Six weeks later, Luongo hit a milestone. He made 26 saves in a game against the Bruins, joining Brodeur and Roy as the only goaltenders in NHL history to play in at least 1,000 games.

Unfortunately for hockey fans in south Florida, the Panthers failed to make the playoffs again in the 2018–19 season, which ended with a 4–3 loss to the New Jersey Devils. Luongo made

23 saves that night, and he would never make another one in an NHL game.

RETIREMENT

In June, the 40-year-old announced his departure in the most fitting way. He tweeted a photo of goalie pads hanging over a power line between two buildings, with a caption that read, "I've decided to take my talents to a South Beach retirement home." It was a cheeky reference to NBA star LeBron James, who had used similar language to announce he was leaving Cleveland to play for the Miami Heat in 2010, and it was vintage Luongo.

Following his retirement, he took a job as special advisor to Panthers general manager Bill Zito. Luongo told media that working for the franchise was "awesome." The river of love flowed both ways. In 2020, the Panthers retired his jersey (No. 1), making him the first player in franchise history to receive that honor.

Two years later, he was inducted into the Hockey Hall of Fame. In his acceptance speech, he recalled his agent telling his parents that their eldest son wouldn't be living at home for much longer. He said they had been shocked. "I don't know if you guys understand what Italian families are like. You don't move away when you're 15 years old. You do that when you get married and some of my friends are still living at home."[29]

A month later, the Canucks announced that Luongo, who holds several of their franchise records, would be inducted into the club's Ring of Honour, a display that celebrates players who have made a big impact on the team.

While preparing for that tribute, Luongo got set for a brief return to action. He took part in the breakaway challenge event in the 2023 NHL all-star skills competition. He faced three shooters on the ice in Sunrise, Florida, and stopped just one of them—Leafs sniper Mitch Marner.

Wearing sunglasses and holding a pool noodle instead of a stick, Luongo allowed a goal by Panthers forward Matthew

Tkachuk, who was dressed for the beach in shorts, a floral print shirt, swimming goggles and a white bucket hat like the one sported by Gilligan on his famous island.

But the highlight-reel goal came from superstar Alex Ovechkin's four-year-old son, Sergei, who tucked the puck between the goaltender's legs after skating up the ice with his father and fellow superstar Sidney Crosby.

Luongo shared his thoughts about the event on his favorite social media platform. "One stop on 3 shootout attempts last night," he wrote in a tweet. "It's like I never left!"

||||||||||||||||||||||||||||||||||||||||||||||||||||||||||||||||||||||||||||||||||||||||||||||||||

ROBERTO LUONGO • ALL-TIME RANKING

REGULAR SEASON			PLAYOFFS		
GAMES + RANK	WINS + RANK	SO + RANK	GAMES + RANK	WINS + RANK	SO + RANK
1,044 (2ND)	489 (4TH)	77 (9TH)	70 [40TH]	34 [39TH]	5 [44TH]

+ NHL ALL-STAR TEAM (2ND) 2003-04, 2006-07

||||| 10 |||||

MISTER CONGENIALITY
MARC-ANDRÉ FLEURY

|||||||||||||||||||||||||||||||||||

ON THE MORNING of one game day, Marc-André Fleury took part in the Pittsburgh Penguins' optional skate. When it ended, the team's goalie coach, Mike Bales, spotted him chatting with a trainer, who was behind the bench. Bales turned away but looked back a moment later when he heard laughter. Much to the delight of onlookers, Fleury had leaped over the boards in a single bound to tackle the trainer. "Many starting goalies are tense on game days, and there you have Marc doing a Superman routine," Bales says with a laugh, looking back on the goalie's time in Pittsburgh. "It's goofy things like that that endear him to everyone."[1]

Indeed, Fleury has a reputation for being as cheerful as he is talented. He helped the Pittsburgh Penguins win three Stanley Cups and then cemented his star status by leading the Vegas Golden Knights to one of the best inaugural seasons in sports history. "A couple of years ago I was being told I was too old to play," the Man of Steel said after that season ended, in June 2018. "But I still love it. I still have a lot of fun."

THE GOOD times started in November 1984, when Fleury was born in Sorel-Tracy, Quebec, a small port city on the bank of

Fleury posted a 1.57 goals-against average in the world junior championship in January 2003—not bad for a kid battling the stomach flu. **DAVE SANDFORD/HOCKEY HALL OF FAME**

the St. Lawrence River, about 50 miles north of Montreal. His parents, André and France, raised Marc-André and his younger sister, Marylène, in a modest home his father, a carpenter, had helped build.

Marc-André was passionate about hockey at a young age. When the weather was warm, he played road hockey with his friends and cousins in a nearby cul-de-sac. In the winter, he skated on a rink one of his uncles had built. "I loved the outdoor rink," Fleury said years later. "Being outside, and skating all night. When it gets dark and it's snowing, that was the best time to play hockey."[2]

He started playing organized hockey when he was seven years old and soon found his calling between the pipes. He twice attended a goalie school run by François Allaire, who helped shape Patrick Roy and Jean-Sébastien Giguère into elite NHL goalies.

On many winter mornings, Fleury woke up before dawn to put on his equipment. The boy then waddled outside, where his father hoisted him into the family truck. They drove to the local arena and waited for the doors to open at 6 AM. Once inside, goalie coach Stéphane Ménard put the boy through his paces, teaching him the dark arts of goaltending. Fleury was a quick study. "If you told him to do something, he wouldn't argue," Ménard later recalled. "He just did it."[3]

Playing in the NHL seemed like a pipe dream at the time, but Fleury worked on his game, drawing inspiration from NHL stars such as Martin Brodeur and Roy, the Montreal Canadiens' brash netminder. "The Canadiens were my favourite team," Fleury later recalled. "I adored them."[4]

Fleury soon made his mark in the junior ranks. When he was 15 years old, the Cape Breton Screaming Eagles selected him 16th overall in the 2000 QMJHL draft. He was excited at the prospect of playing in the prestigious league, but was also apprehensive. He didn't know where Cape Breton was, but he was certain it wasn't in French Canada—and Fleury spoke almost no English. But he packed his bags, found Cape Breton on a map and headed 900 miles east, to the northeastern tip of Nova Scotia.

He moved into the home of Bob and Angela Hawkins. The couple, who had two young children, didn't speak French but managed to communicate with Fleury by using facial expressions and gestures—two mimes performing without face paint on a hilly island in the North Atlantic. They managed to convey an important message: if Fleury didn't understand what people were saying to him, he should just smile and nod his head. That wasn't a problem for the teen. Smiling came as naturally to him as breathing.

"He still has that same smile and that same sweet personality [as] when he lived with us," Angela Hawkins said in 2018. "As you can see in the games, he still likes to have a lot of fun just like when he was 15 years old. He's still the game guy."[5]

Despite the language barrier and a sense of homesickness, Fleury adjusted well to life in Sydney, the largest urban area on Cape Breton. On his first day there, he played road hockey with the neighborhood kids. He soon learned how to wear formal attire, which was required on his team's game days. Angela showed him how to tie a necktie and ensure it matched his shirt and pants.

During his tenure with the Screaming Eagles, Fleury often returned to Sorel-Tracy in the summers to be reunited with family and his childhood sweetheart, Veronique. Spending a few months at home speaking *en français* did wonders for him. He returned to Cape Breton every fall season, ready to do battle on the ice.

Fleury emerged as one of the top players in the QMJHL. The teen was rail thin, but he was tall and took up a lot of space in net, making it difficult for shooters to find an opening. He also read plays well and had lightning reflexes. He was excellent at cutting down angles and dropping into a butterfly position when needed, leaving shooters banging their sticks on the ice in frustration.

He became the starting goaltender in his second season with the Screaming Eagles, and led the team to its first ever semifinal appearance. (The Acadie-Bathurst Titan won that series in five games.) Early in the 2002–03 season, he made an incredible 60 saves in a 3–3 tie with the Rimouski Océanic.

THAT YEAR, Fleury spent the holiday season close to his new home. He played in the world junior championship in Halifax, on a team with future NHL players such as Brooks Laich and Joffrey Lupul.

Fleury was battling the stomach flu when the tournament started. He was on the sidelines when David LeNeveu allowed a pair of soft goals in the second period of a round-robin game against Finland. Instead of making another mad dash to the bathroom, Fleury skated onto the ice and replaced his beleaguered teammate. He stopped every shot he faced, helping Team Canada notch a 5–3 victory.

Fleury stayed in net for the rest of the tournament and recorded a 1.57 goals-against average—a good outing for a kid with abdominal cramps. His team had to settle for silver—the Russians won the title for the second straight year—but Fleury was named the tournament's top goalie and most valuable player.

He gained momentum, and at the end of his third full season wearing goalie pads painted Screaming Eagles yellow, he was named the QMJHL's top defensive player and its top professional prospect.

In May 2003, the rising star met one of his heroes. He and some other top prospects stood in the hallway near the New Jersey Devils locker room just hours before Game 2 of the Stanley Cup final. When Martin Brodeur appeared, Fleury was dumbstruck. He fumbled through his suit jacket pocket, looking for his Brodeur hockey card, but by the time he found it, Brodeur had come, greeted the young players and gone. An NHL employee took the card from the teen and headed into the Devils' equipment room. He handed it back moments later with Brodeur's autograph.

Fleury regained his composure in time for the NHL Entry Draft in Nashville a month later. The Pittsburgh Penguins had the first overall pick and selected him. When the team's general manager, Craig Patrick, called his name, Fleury stood up, embraced loved ones and headed to the dais. His megawatt smile dimmed only slightly as he focused on pulling the Penguins' black-and-gold jersey over his head. He then posed for photographs with Penguins executives. Fleury was just the third goalie to be selected first overall in the NHL draft. (The others were Michel Plasse in 1968 and Rick DiPietro in 2000.)

That summer, Fleury packed up his belongings at Chez Hawkins and headed for greener pastures. He was gone when the Screaming Eagles started their next season, but not forgotten. His sunny disposition and on-ice heroics had endeared him to Sydney residents.

"Whenever he finishes his hockey career, he would get 100 per cent of the vote for mayor here," Stuart MacLeod, who sits on the team's board of directors, said in 2018. "He's that popular."[6]

Angela Hawkins keeps in touch with Fleury, sending him text messages after each game to congratulate or console him, depending on the outcome. He always responds.

NHL

2003-04

Fleury turned heads at the Penguins' training camp that fall, and the club signed him to a three-year contract. He took his place in net for the first game of the season, playing behind a porous defense corps. The Penguins fell 3-0 to the Los Angeles Kings, but Fleury made 46 saves, including one on a penalty shot. The hometown crowd gave the 18-year-old a standing ovation and chanted his name.

Two decades later, Fleury still views that game as one of the highlights of his career. "It was just incredible to skate with all those guys and to stop that penalty shot with a poke check. I heard the crowd calling my name," he says. "Amazing!"

Kings forward Luc Robitaille chimed in after the game. "Could you believe some of those saves?" he said while on a stationary bike. "That was sick."[7]

FLEURY WAS flying high when he arrived in Finland for the world junior championship that December, but he made a play in the final against the US that Canadian hockey fans only wish they could forget. With five minutes remaining in a 3-3 game, Fleury tried to clear a puck, but it bounced off a teammate and into his own net. No one was more surprised than his opponents. "We saw [Fleury] come out and play the puck and then all of a sudden [Patrick O'Sullivan] was celebrating," said American star Zach Parise, who was on the bench at the time. "We looked at each other and said, 'What just happened?'" The Canadians had to settle for another silver medal.[8]

Fleury had made some big saves in the game but endured a public thrashing. His gaffe was broadcast on Canadian television in an endless loop. A national newspaper devoted its front page to a photo of him sprawled face down in the crease like roadkill. The headline read, STAR GOALIE'S GAFFE HANDS GOLD MEDAL TO AMERICANS.

FLEURY SUFFERED another setback at the end of January, when the Penguins sent him back to Cape Breton. Many hockey insiders believed the club made the move because it would have had to pay the rookie a bonus if he had stayed on and met several performance goals. Fleury finished the regular season with the Screaming Eagles, and after they were eliminated in the playoffs, he headed to Wilkes-Barre, Pennsylvania, where he played two games for the Penguins' AHL affiliate.

While he honed his game elsewhere, the Penguins plummeted to the bottom of the NHL standings (58 points), setting an NHL losing-streak record (18 games) in the process. Superstar Mario Lemieux missed all but 10 games with a back injury and, at the end of the season, could only stare in horror at the smoldering ruins of his team's season.

The next NHL season was cancelled because of a labor dispute, so Fleury played in the AHL.

2005-06

Fleury split this season between the AHL and the NHL. Pittsburgh had three good goalies on its roster, but Fleury played in more games (50) than Sébastien Caron (26) and Jocelyn Thibault (16). In a home game in December, he helped his team notch a 6-2 victory over the Devils. He dazzled spectators with his acrobatics and great reflexes, leading them to chant his name. The crowd roared when he was named the first star of the contest, and he was elated for hours. "When you hear the crowd like that, you get those goose bumps," he said in halting English. "I think that's why I love so much to play."[9]

He was smiling again two months later, when his father skated in the annual Penguins Adult Hockey Fantasy Camp, on a team that included former Penguins Phil Bourque and Alain Lemieux. "It was pretty fun. He was pretty pumped up just about coming," said Marc-André, who chirped at his father during the action. What did he say? That will remain one of life's enduring mysteries. "I was yelling at him in French so nobody else could understand what I was saying," the goalie explained.[10]

The Penguins ended the season with the same point total (58) they had recorded in the previous campaign, but they didn't win the "worst in league" designation this time around. That honor went to the St. Louis Blues, who had finished one point back.

2006-07

The Penguins' fortunes improved the following season, thanks to the contributions of budding stars Sidney Crosby and Evgeni Malkin, who combined for 205 points. Crosby finished first in NHL scoring (120 points), and Malkin won the Calder Trophy. Forward Jordan Staal and defenseman Sergei Gonchar formed a strong supporting cast.

Fleury, who had signed a two-year contract extension before the season, also played a big role in the team's rise from the ashes. He posted 40 wins, including five shutouts. He attributed much of his success to Gilles Meloche, a former NHL goalie who had become the Penguins' full-time goalie coach. He worked with fellow French speakers Fleury and Thibault all season. "I think it's good to have a guy from [Quebec] to let us be more comfortable to explain things," Fleury said. "I get along with Gilles and Jocelyn very well. It's fun. It's a good atmosphere."[11]

The Penguins finished third in the Eastern Conference (105 points) and met the Ottawa Senators (105) in the first round of the playoffs. Fleury notched his first NHL playoff win in Game 2, making 34 saves in a 4-3 decision. It turned out to be his team's last victory of the season.

2007-08

Fleury sprained his ankle during a game in December and was out for three months. During that time, Ty Conklin took over in net and played well enough to raise doubts about Fleury's status on the roster.

Despite the chatter and his tender ankle, Fleury had a spring in his step when he rejoined his team. "We all get along very good," he said about his relationship with Conklin and Dany Sabourin, the other goalie who shared the workload with him that season. "I'm sure we'll find ways to adjust to it and show everybody we'll be fine."[12]

Weeks later, Fleury said that he hadn't been thinking about how he might stack up against other goalies when he returned to the team. "I was away for so long, so I was getting frustrated not being able to be with the team, to play or practice," he said, "so the first thing in my head was to go play hockey, you know, go have some fun and don't worry about anything else." That meant avoiding media coverage of the team, he added. Would he ignore a story that cast him in a positive light? a journalist asked. Yes, the goalie replied with a laugh, "I'll have my Dad read it."[13]

Fleury's first game back following his injury was a showdown with the Atlanta Thrashers on March 2. He skated onto the ice sporting pads the color—though not the texture—of cheesecloth. Months earlier, an optometrist had informed him that yellow is the most distinguishable color. She recommended he wear white pads, which would blend in with the ice, the rear boards and the netting, making it harder for opposing shooters to spot him in traffic. He followed her advice and ditched his golden goalie pads. The Penguins beat the Thrashers 3–2.

Malkin, second in NHL scoring (106 points), led the Penguins' charge up the standings. The team ended the regular season second in the conference (102 points), just two points back of Montreal. They steamrolled their way to victory in the first three rounds of the playoffs, making quick work of the Senators (94 points), the New York Rangers (97 points) and the Philadelphia Flyers (95 points).

After posting a shutout in a 6–0 romp over the Flyers in Game 5 of the conference final, Fleury remarked on how far the Penguins had come since his rookie season, when they finished at the bottom of the standings. "I think everything is a lot more fun now... I guess everyone is always happy and it's pretty cool that altogether we lived those tough days. And I think everybody improved together. As a team, we're winning, so it's big fun."[14]

The fun continued when the Penguins advanced to the Stanley Cup final to meet the Detroit Red Wings, who had finished first in the Western Conference and the league with 115 points. But the laughter came at Fleury's expense.

Before Game 1, he charged out of the locker room and led his teammates to the ice, but his right pad got caught on the entrance gate as he ran past and he tumbled forward. The goalie stood up immediately and continued on his way, not even stopping to brush the ice chips off his pants, but there was no use in pretending nothing had happened. Spectators in Joe Louis Arena were heaving with laughter.

"Me and my buddy were kneeling down and all of a sudden Fleury comes running out," said Alec Thieda, a member of the ice crew. "His pad catches the corner of the boards and he just eats it. I've never seen something that funny in my life. I've gotten 25 phone calls already. I've never been that close to something like that, it's awesome."[15]

But that wasn't Fleury's worst mishap of the series. Two days after making 55 saves in a 4–3 triple overtime victory, he made a mistake in Game 6 that still makes Penguins fans wince. Detroit was leading 2–1 when, seven minutes into the third period, Red Wings forward Henrik Zetterberg put a shot between Fleury's pads. The goalie appeared to have the puck covered, but looks can be deceiving. It was behind him, and when Fleury leaned back, he pushed it into the net. That goal ended up being the game winner. When the game ended, the Penguins could only console each other as Detroit players celebrated their Stanley Cup victory.[16]

Fleury played in more games (20), notched more wins (14) and posted more shutouts (3) than any other goalie in the playoffs that year, but when legions of Penguins fans look back at that postseason, they see only Fleury lying flat on his back in the goal crease, looking dazed.

2008-09

The uproar about that goal subsided the following season as Fleury put in one solid performance after another. Pittsburgh won 10 of their 13 games in March, and Fleury played in all but one of them.

"I can only say what I see and it looks like he's having a blast out there right now," defenseman Mark Eaton said about his goalie. Added longtime teammate defenseman Brooks Orpik: "He is just as immature as he was when he was 18 but I don't mean that in a bad way. He's just a guy who is carefree. He doesn't really have a lot of worries. He's always got a smile on his face. He's always here to have a good time and at the same time he's always working hard."

Malkin led the NHL in scoring that season (113 points), while Crosby finished third (103 points). Pittsburgh placed fourth in the conference with 99 points. The Penguins had a core of talented youngsters and some veterans who added grit to the roster. All the players were confident heading into the playoffs.

Fleury played a pivotal role in the opening round against the Flyers (99 points). Late in Game 2, he extended his leg as far as it would go without detaching and sliding into the corner boards, and made a spectacular toe save on Jeff Carter, one of the league's top goal scorers, who was on the left side of the crease in front of an open net.

The Penguins won that game 3-2 in overtime. They also posted a 3-1 win in Game 4 thanks in large part to Fleury, who made 45 saves. It took the Penguins six games to eliminate the Flyers—but it took more than that to defeat their next opponent.

Led by Alexander Ovechkin, who had finished between Malkin and Crosby in league scoring (110 points) that season, the Washington Capitals (108 points) pushed the Penguins hard in their series; three games were decided in overtime. Early in Game 7, Ovechkin blew past Penguins defenseman Rob Scuderi and bore down on Fleury alone. With a flash of his glove hand, the goalie stopped "Ovi" cold. The Penguins went on to record a decisive 6-2 victory.

The Penguins swept the Carolina Hurricanes (97 points) in the conference final, then took on the Red Wings (112 points), who had finished second in the Western Conference. Fleury managed to make the journey from the locker room to the ice without incident to start the final, but he stumbled in Game 5— badly. The Penguins were hoping to take the lead in the series, which was tied at two games apiece, but it wasn't to be. Fleury imploded in the second period. He allowed four Detroit goals in 14 minutes of play before coach Dan Bylsma put him out of his misery and yanked him from the game. The Penguins lost 5–0.

Somehow, Fleury managed to walk away from that car wreck bruised but intact. He was back in net for Game 6 in Pittsburgh. The Penguins were leading 2–1 with less than two minutes remaining in regulation time, when Red Wings forward Dan Cleary took a clearing pass and broke in alone on Fleury. He faked a forehand, then took a backhand shot. Fleury made a stretch save, and Pittsburgh hung on for the win.

The series went back to Detroit for Game 7. Once again, Fleury rose to the occasion. Penguins forward Maxime Talbot— who often shadowboxed with Fleury before they stepped onto the ice—scored twice in the second period. Detroit responded with a goal in the third, then came close to tying it up. Zetterberg fired a shot from the right face-off circle. Fleury made the save but sent a rebound to the left face-off circle, where legendary defenseman Nicklas Lidström was lying in wait. He took a shot with less than two seconds remaining. Fleury made a diving save and the crowd at Joe Louis Arena fell silent—including Muhammad Ali, who watched the game in a Detroit jersey. The Penguins won the game, the series and their third Stanley Cup.

"I knew there wasn't much time left," a beaming Fleury said after the game. "The rebound was wide. I just decided to get my body out there and the puck hit me in the ribs—so it was good."[17]

Fleury had again played in more games (24) and recorded more wins than any other goalie in the playoffs.

A few days later, almost 400,000 people gathered in downtown Pittsburgh for the Stanley Cup parade. Fans lined the streets to catch a glimpse of their hockey heroes. Fleury and Crosby flanked the Cup while perched on a dark SUV, wearing white Penguins jerseys, matching ball caps and dark sunglasses. Only the iconic trophy gleamed brighter in the sunlight than Fleury's pearly white teeth.

But this celebration might not be Mathieu Garon's most vivid memory of that series. He was the team's backup goalie that season and roomed with Fleury on the road. The men tried to take an afternoon nap in their Detroit hotel room one game day but couldn't because some Red Wings fans were whooping it up in a room nearby. Fleury did what any professional would do: he filled a garbage can with water, leaned it against the revelers' door, knocked on it and then bolted.[18]

2009–12

Pittsburgh fell short of expectations in subsequent years. With two of the NHL's top scorers on the roster, the team finished no lower than third in its conference in three consecutive seasons. But Crosby and Malkin couldn't lift the Penguins past the second round of the playoffs. (Injuries sidelined Crosby for many months during that time, which didn't help matters.)

Yet those seasons weren't without good moments for Fleury. He was on the roster of the Canadian team that competed in the 2010 Winter Olympics. Roberto Luongo was the team's starter and Brodeur was his backup. Fleury didn't see any ice time in Vancouver, but he was still enthusiastic. In fact, he was excited just to be breathing the same air as Brodeur. The men spent a lot of time together, and Brodeur gave his protégé some tips.

Fleury didn't compete in the Games, but his competitive fire was evident. In Canada Olympic House, he and speed skater François-Louis Tremblay met at a Ping-Pong table in the athletes' lounge, raised their paddles in salute and then got down to business. Fleury won the first game, but Tremblay won the rematch. The speed skater took on Crosby next and beat him too. But "Sid the Kid" regrouped to beat several challengers, including Fleury.

The goalie later proved he could bounce back from setbacks in table tennis and hockey. He had a rough start to the 2010–11 season—he allowed two goals on five shots against the Phoenix Coyotes in November and was pulled from the ice early in the game—but he proved to be resilient. Three weeks after the train wreck in Arizona, he made 43 saves in a 2–1 win over the Senators.

Fleury was pivotal during his team's 12-game winning streak in November and December. "When he is having fun and smiling, he is usually going to play well," observed Meloche. But the goalie coach added that Fleury's fun-loving personality belied an intensity. Meloche said Fleury had to be dragged off the ice at the end of practices because he wanted to stay and hone his skills. "What fans don't see with him," said general manager Ray Shero, "is how much he cares and how competitive he is."[19]

2012-13

This season didn't start until January because of another labor dispute. Fleury, who had placed second in wins (42) the previous season, shone early on, posting some of the best numbers of his career. He won 23 games and lost just eight in the shortened regular season, helping his team finish first in the conference (72 points).

The Penguins entered the postseason as one of the NHL's hottest teams, having won eight of their previous 10 games. Fans expected the team to go the distance. It didn't, and their starting goalie was partly to blame.

He posted a 5–0 shutout against the New York Islanders (55 points) in the opening game, but he was shaky in the next three. Backup Tomáš Vokoun took over in Game 5 and stayed in net for the rest of the series, which the Penguins won in six games.

Fleury watched from the sidelines as the Penguins defeated the Senators (56 points) in a five-game series, and he stayed there for most of the conference final, against the Boston Bruins (62 points). He was in net for part of Game 2, which the Bruins won 6–1. Vokoun was back between the pipes in the next game, and Bylsma's decision to bench Fleury raised questions about the goalie's standing on the team.

"That tells you something about how they felt about Marc-Andre," said analyst Joe Micheletti, who worked for NBC and NHL Network. "He's such a great, likeable kid, and so popular with everybody, but there is an issue that they have to figure out and I think it's right at the top of the list."[20]

When the Bruins swept aside the Penguins in four games, Fleury's future with the team seemed uncertain. With some players cleaning out their lockers and others getting fitted for new golf clubs, Bylsma assured inquiring minds that Fleury was still the team's starter and described him as a "franchise goalie."

2013-14

Fleury proved to be as resolute as the old man in *Monty Python and the Holy Grail*, who refused to be placed on a cart full of corpses and famously insisted, "I'm not dead!" The goalie was very much alive. With help from new goalie coach Mike Bales, Fleury improved the technical aspects of his game. He notched 39 wins and was back in the good graces of his fans by the end of the regular season. What had accounted for the turnaround—Bales's feedback, a good luck charm or a realignment of the stars? Fleury didn't know. "I just go out and play and have fun," he said, "and my team's been doing great in front of me. I don't think too much."[21]

Fleury posted the second-most wins (39) in the NHL during the regular season, but his performance in the postseason was uneven. The Penguins, who had placed second in the conference with 109 points, were leading the opening round against the Columbus Blue Jackets (93 points) when the teams squared off at Nationwide Arena for Game 4. The Penguins were ahead 3–2 with less than a minute left in regulation time when Fleury wandered behind his net to play the puck and missed it. That allowed hard-charging forward Brandon Dubinsky to score the tying goal. Nick Foligno won the game for Columbus in overtime with a long-distance wrist shot that, in the opinion of one journalist, could have been stopped "by nine out of 10 road hockey goalies."[22] But Fleury and his teammates recovered and went on to win the series in six games.

They then prepared to meet the New York Rangers (96 points) in the second round. Built around one of the best goalies in the game, Henrik Lundqvist, the Rangers weren't an offensive powerhouse; none of the players on the roster had more than 60 points in the regular season. Despite that weakness, the Rangers had Penguins fans smacking their foreheads in frustration at the end of Game 1.

The Penguins battled back from a two-goal deficit, only to lose in overtime when Derick Brassard beat Fleury cleanly with a wrist shot. But once again, Fleury insisted he wasn't dead yet—and it turned out to be true. He posted shutouts in the next two games and held the Rangers to two goals in Game 4, which his team won 4–2. Despite his contribution, however, New York won the next three games and the series.

2014-15

The Penguins had a strong start to the next season, winning all but three of their first 13 games. With a 1.89 goals-against average and a .931 save percentage, Fleury was the star of the show. The club rewarded him with a four-year contract extension. But it was more than his performance that made him a hot commodity. His presence in the dressing room was a boost to team morale. The secret sauce? His personality.

Fleury always showed up at the rink with a smile on his face and even managed to make practices fun. Players enjoyed bantering with him on the ice, and, according to Bales, the goalie did "a lot of goofy things" that amused his teammates. He would do jumping jacks during breakaway drills. When he gave up a couple of goals, he would drop to the ice and do push-ups as penance. "As soon as you meet him, you know why he is popular," new Penguins GM Jim Rutherford said.[23]

A few weeks after signing the contract extension, Fleury recorded his 300th NHL win. The team suffered a spate of injuries and illnesses that season, including a mumps outbreak. Several players were spotted with swollen cheeks, including Crosby, who scurried around the rink looking like Alvin the Chipmunk. But Fleury continued to shine. He recorded a league-leading 10 shutouts and kept his team's playoff hopes alive. The Penguins finished eighth in the conference with 98 points.

The Penguins squeaked out just one win against the Rangers (113) in the first round of the playoffs, but no one blamed Fleury. He made 34 saves in Game 5, just three fewer than Lundqvist. "The King" tipped his crown to his rival after the Rangers won 2–1 in overtime. "Fleury played really well," he conceded. "He kept them in this one."[24]

2015–16

Fleury had a great start the following season. By mid-November, he had a sparkling 1.93 goals-against average, and his save percentage was .933. The Penguins won 10 of their first 15 games and spirits were high in the dressing room. Fleury was feeling the love, even from his backup goaltender. Jeff Zatkoff recounted an incident in which Fleury switched the wrappers on the spray deodorant and hair spray in the locker room, forcing Zatkoff to contend with "rock hard armpits."[25]

By then, Fleury had mastered the art of practical jokes. He had proven adept at filling cars with foam packing peanuts and rearranging hotel room furniture. He had also sprung out of equipment bags like a jack-in-the-box, simultaneously startling and delighting teammates.

His agent, Allan Walsh, is very familiar with Fleury's affinity for practical jokes.

"We decided to grab a bite to eat after one game, so we walked to his car. It was full of giant bags of foam peanuts," recalls Walsh. "I asked him what was going on. He just looked at me, smiled and said, 'I'm planning something.'"

Fleury insisted that "life is nicer when you're having fun and laughing," and his teammates appreciated his joie de vivre. "It's probably not easy for a goalie to be like that," Crosby said.

"There's a lot of responsibility. But it's just natural for him to be like that, and I think it's important. When guys see your goalie that relaxed, it definitely has a calming effect."[26]

Fleury's positive outlook was put to the test later that season. He suffered a concussion in mid-December and didn't return until early January. He was a man on a mission when he returned. He posted excellent numbers and the future looked bright—until it didn't. He suffered another concussion in a game against the Nashville Predators in late March and missed the rest of the regular season.

Despite Fleury's limited ice time that season, fans saw a lot of him. He appeared in a popular television commercial for a hospital in Pittsburgh. In the ad, he changes his daughter's diaper with a goalie glove, then uses a stick to push the soiled item into the garbage. He also tries to feed the baby with his water bottle. "One thing I love about my husband, Marc-André, is how he separates hockey from family," his wife, Veronique, says. "Here at home, he's just like any other dad. Well, most of the time." When the commercial first aired, Fleury fielded questions about his daughters, three-year-old Estelle, and Scarlett, the infant who had costarred with him in the ad. "It's something you really don't know about until you get into it," he said about fatherhood. "It's work… but when you see them smile and happy, it's priceless."[27]

No doubt, Fleury was happy with his team. The Penguins finished second in the conference (104 points) and were in fine form heading into the playoffs. Zatkoff, whose armpits had recovered from the hair spray incident, was in net for the first two games of the opening series against the Rangers (101 points). Fellow backup Matt Murray took over for the rest of the series, which Pittsburgh won in five games.

Murray played well in the next series against the Washington Capitals (120 points)—so well that he stayed in net even after Fleury was cleared to return. Fleury seemed unfazed. "I haven't played in a month now," he said after Game 3. "What's important is us winning. Matty's giving us a chance to win every night he's been in there. I'll stay ready. I'll encourage him. It's not a personal game. It's a team game."[28]

The Penguins wrapped up the series in six games, then squared off against the Tampa Bay Lightning (97 points) in the conference final. Fleury returned to the ice in that series, playing part of Game 4 and all of Game 5. Tampa won both. Murray then headed back to the crease and helped the Penguins win the series in seven games.

They moved on to play the San Jose Sharks, who had placed sixth in the Western Conference (98 points), in the final. Sharks forward Joe Thornton had placed fifth in NHL scoring during the regular season (82 points), two spots behind Crosby (85 points), but he recorded just three assists in this six-game series. The Penguins came out on top. When the game ended at the SAP Center in San Jose, the Penguins crowded onto the ice to celebrate in front of 18,000 heartbroken Bay Area hockey fans.

Murray had performed so well that there was speculation he might replace Fleury as the team's starter. But Fleury wasn't panic-stricken. He told journalists he might "worry about that in a few weeks."[29] Two months later, he returned to his hometown with the Cup. He filled it with his daughters' breakfast to start the day, but later swapped out the Cheerios for ice cream.

2016-17

In September, Murray broke his hand in a World Cup of Hockey game. Fleury was the Penguins' sole starter until Murray returned in November. For the rest of the regular season, the two goalies shared the workload. Murray started in 47 games, 13 more than Fleury.

Despite battling for ice time, the men formed a close bond and were spotted sharing a laugh during practice. "It's because of how good of a guy he is," Murray said when asked about their rapport. "He definitely took me under his wing when I got here. I'll be forever grateful for everything he's done for me."[30]

Murray wasn't the only goalie to form a bromance with Fleury while battling for top spot. In late 2016, a newspaper ran a story that included quotes from several of his former backup goalies.

Mathieu Garon, who spent one season with the Penguins, gushed about Fleury. "Most No. 1 goalies do their own thing," he explained. "They don't really pay attention to the other guys. With him, he was always asking questions, always talking to me. We would talk about basically anything. It was just fun to be around him."

Brent Johnson, who was on the Penguins roster for three seasons, said he socialized with Fleury even after they were teammates. He said he wished Fleury the best—and he actually meant it. "It's that common bond of knowing what a goaltender goes through. He understood that more so than anyone I ever played with," Johnson said. "I want that guy to be happy."[31]

Perhaps the highest praise of all came from Jocelyn Thibault, who clearly had a sweet tooth. "Marc-Andre Fleury's like chocolate," Thibault said. "Everybody likes chocolate. You can't *not* like him."[32]

Fleury has rough days like everyone else, but he is never unpleasant. "I'm not always very energetic, and after rough games, I keep to myself a little," he says today, "but I try to brush it off and show up at the rink the next morning with a smile on my face. I know I'm just lucky to be playing hockey."

The Penguins won four of their last six games of the regular season and finished second in the conference (111 points). The immediate future looked bright, but it wasn't for Murray. He tweaked a groin muscle during the warm-up before the first postseason game.

Fleury started against the Columbus Blue Jackets (108 points) and had the goal crease to himself for the rest of the series, which the Penguins won in five games. The veteran was so good that he outshone Blue Jackets star Sergei Bobrovsky. The Russian goalie had led the NHL in save percentage and goals-against average in the regular season and was about to win his second Vezina Trophy, but in this series, Fleury had a better save percentage (.933) than his young counterpart (.882).

Columbus kept Fleury on his toes in the series and he loved every minute of it. Penguins defenseman Brian Dumoulin heard him "hooting and hollering" during one fusillade of shots. "He loves the atmosphere and he loves kind of getting peppered," Dumoulin said. "It makes you feel better when he's stopping those pucks."[33]

Fleury remained the starter in the second round against the Capitals (118 points). He stonewalled Ovechkin and his teammates in Game 7. The Penguins won that game 2–0 and headed home to take on the Senators (98 points) in the conference final. It was one of many instances during Fleury's time with the Penguins in which they proved to be a roadblock the Capitals couldn't get past.

The Senators notched a 2–1 overtime win in the first game of the series, but the Penguins bounced back. They scored one goal in the second game, and that proved to be enough. Fleury notched another shutout, but the good vibrations didn't last for long. In the third game, he allowed four goals in less than 13 minutes and was pulled from the ice. Murray took over and stayed in net for the rest of the series. The Penguins eliminated the Senators with an exciting double-overtime win in Game 7. Spirits were soaring in Pittsburgh as the Penguins prepared to play in their second straight final.

Murray was solid in the first two games of the series against the Predators (94 points), who had placed fourth in the Western Conference, and the Penguins won both of them. But he faltered in the next two games, which the Predators won. His poor performance led to speculation that Fleury would return for Game 5. But Mike Sullivan, who had become head coach the previous season, stuck with Murray. The goalie showed his appreciation by helping his team crush the Predators 6–0. Murray posted another shutout in Game 6, when the Penguins beat Nashville 2–0 to win their second straight Stanley Cup.

As Nashville fans filed out of Bridgestone Arena, more than a few seeking the warm embrace of Jack Daniel's Tennessee whiskey, the Penguins celebrated. Someone handed the Cup to Fleury and he, in turn, handed it to Murray. "The fact that he handed me the Cup there says a lot about who Flower is," Murray said, choking up. "That meant so much to me for him to do that. I don't know what made him do that, but I'm very thankful for having him around, to call him a friend and a mentor. He's a special human being."[34]

Fleury proved just how special he was when he agreed to waive the no-movement clause in his contract. The Penguins were allowed to protect only one goalie in the upcoming NHL expansion draft and Fleury felt it should be his protégé, who was a decade younger. The Stanley Cup parade would be his last with the Penguins.

On June 14, more than 650,000 fans lined Grant Street, the main government and business corridor in Pittsburgh, to watch the Penguins' motorcade pass. The players drank beer, took selfies and raised the Cup as the roar from the crowd became deafening. Thousands of fans chanted Fleury's name.

When it was Fleury's turn to spend a day with the Cup, he traveled to Montreal. He took the trophy to Ronald McDonald House, where the families of kids being treated at nearby hospitals were staying. He then placed it in the passenger seat of his open-air Jeep, fastened the seat belt around it and headed north. When he rolled into his hometown with his glistening travel companion, passing drivers honked their horns, and people lined the streets to cheer or snap photos from open windows. "It was quite the trip," says Allan Walsh, recalling that visit to Sorel-Tracy.

That summer, the Vegas Golden Knights selected Fleury in the expansion draft. He got a standing ovation at the draft ceremony in T-Mobile Arena in Las Vegas, and later had dinner at a restaurant with his wife, some of his new teammates and one old one—Crosby.

The two had been tight as teammates, spending hours together busting terrorist operations, rescuing hostages and executing other feats of derring-do—all part of a popular video game. "I've made so many great friends over the years," Fleury says, reflecting on his time with his teammates.

Penguins fans had to bid farewell to a three-time champion, the winningest goaltender in club history and one of the most popular athletes in town. But spirits were high in the Mojave Desert. Vegas had acquired a veteran who was popular with teammates and fans—the perfect face for a new franchise.

2017-18

Many Pittsburgh fans viewed Fleury's departure as a sad but inevitable event—as inescapable as putting an aging racehorse out to pasture to spend its golden years grazing on grass and long-stem hay. But they were in for a surprise. In an indication of what lay ahead, Fleury stopped 45 shots and led his team to a 2–1 victory over the Dallas Stars in the Golden Knights' debut.

He sat out for two months with a concussion but ended up playing more games (46) than the four other goalies vying for his job, and posted the best goals-against average (2.24) of his career to that point. It was the third-best average in the league.

His new team played his old one twice that season, and both games were memorable. During the warm-up before a home game in December, Fleury and Murray met at center ice and shared a hug. The crowd at T-Mobile Arena included a lot of Penguins fans, who gave him a standing ovation when starting line-ups were announced. Fleury made 24 saves in that game, as the Golden Knights notched a 2–1 victory.

Two months later, the Golden Knights played in Pittsburgh. Spectators roared when a tribute to Fleury played on the video board during the game. He tapped his heart with his glove and clapped with his goalie stick before returning to the net. But the fans continued to cheer, moving him to tears.

With Fleury holding the fort and forward William Karlsson scoring bushels of goals (43) that season, the Golden Knights surpassed the expectations of even their most optimistic supporters. They smashed two NHL records by recording the most wins (51) and points (109) by an expansion team in its inaugural season. They also placed third in the Western Conference, becoming the first team since 1980 to advance to the playoffs in its first season.

At the end of the regular season, the Bellagio Hotel and Casino erected a life-sized statue of Fleury in action. It featured 90 pounds of chocolate on a base of crispy rice treats. Fleury, who saw photos of the sculpture, said he planned to take his kids to see it, and to sneak a bite when they weren't looking.

The Golden Knights started their postseason by dispatching the Kings (98 points) in less than a week and becoming the first team in NHL history to sweep a first-round series in its inaugural season.

Vegas then beat San Jose (100 points) in six games to advance to the conference final against the Winnipeg Jets (114 points), which had sniper Patrik Laine and one of the league's top scorers in Blake Wheeler. Goalie Connor Hellebuyck had tied for most wins (44). But it turned out to be much ado about nothing. The Golden Knights eliminated the Jets in five games.

The only figure standing taller than Fleury at that point was the replica Statue of Liberty that stood on the Las Vegas Strip wearing a 28-foot-long Golden Knights jersey—just one size too small for Bruins defenseman Zdeno Chára.

Vegas prepared for the final against Washington, which had tied for third in the Eastern Conference with 105 points and managed to eliminate the Penguins. Ovechkin arrived in Las Vegas for the first game as a man on a mission—to win the franchise's first Cup. Braden Holtby, who had won the Vezina Trophy two years before, was also determined. Vegas thrilled the crowd, which included at least one Elvis impersonator, by winning the contest 6–4. But the team's first win of the series turned out to be its last. The Capitals won the next four games, igniting wild celebrations in the US capital. Ovechkin and his teammates partied all night in Las Vegas. They were seen dancing (poorly) at a club, and just before dawn, defenseman John Carlson was spotted with hockey's holy grail in the lobby of the MGM Grand.

The loss was disappointing for Vegas players, but not crushing. The team's first season had been magical, and their goalie had been golden. Fleury said he loved playing in Las Vegas, and it was clear the franchise wanted him to stick around. In July, Vegas re-signed him to a three-year contract.

2018-20

Vegas played well over the next two years but failed to recapture the magic of the team's first season.

In the 2018–19 season, Fleury posted eight shutouts, the second-best total in the NHL, and the Golden Knights tied the Dallas Stars for sixth in the conference (93 points) but lost to San Jose (101 points) in the first round of the playoffs. The Golden Knights had a 3–0 lead in the third period of Game 7 but imploded after the referee called a five-minute major penalty against forward Cody Eakin for a dangerous hit. Vegas proceeded to allow four goals in as many minutes and the Sharks won the game, 5–4, in overtime. The Golden Knights cried foul, accusing officials of making an "embarrassing call."[35]

Early in the following season, Fleury made a save for the ages. Toronto Maple Leafs forward Ilya Mikheyev took a shot that ricocheted off the crossbar and onto the stick of forward Nic Petan. His backhand shot was headed to the back of the net when Fleury dove and plucked the puck out of the air.

"When Fleury's illustrious career comes to an end," reported the Las Vegas Sun, "it won't be possible to string together highlights without that save." Fleury answered questions about it after the home game, which his team won 4–2. "Just enjoy it I think, little giggle, little smile, just happy it didn't go in," he said. "Those are the saves I love to play for."[36]

Just days after that spectacular save, the man who had appreciated it most passed away. Fleury's father, André, lost his battle with lung cancer, and his son headed home to be with his family. Marc-André continued to grieve after returning to Las Vegas, knowing he would never again speak to his father after games, something he had been doing throughout his career. He struggled for the rest of the season.

In many ways, the 2019–20 season was challenging for everyone in the hockey world. The COVID-19 pandemic cut the season short. Players hung up their skates and donned personal protective equipment in mid-March. None returned until early August, when the top 12 teams in each conference (according to points percentage) competed in modified playoffs. Games were held in two hub cities, Toronto and Edmonton. Spectators were *verboten*.

The Golden Knights, who had placed third in the conference (86 points), eliminated the Chicago Blackhawks (72 points) and the Vancouver Canucks (78 points) before taking on the Stars (82 points) in the conference final. The Stars won the series in five games.

Fleury, who had recorded the second-highest number of shut-outs (5) in the league during the regular season, started in just four of the team's 20 postseason games. Robin Lehner, who had joined the Golden Knights in February, assumed the top job during the playoffs. He posted three shutouts against the Canucks.

Seeing Fleury on the sidelines enraged his agent. Walsh posted a tweet that showed a photoshopped sword plunged into the goalie's back. The weapon was embossed with the name of Vegas head coach Peter DeBoer. The tweet caused a stir. Fleury told journalists it was just Walsh's way of defending him. True to form, Fleury said he liked Lehner. "We have a good friendship and I think he's a very good goalie also," he said on a Zoom call. "No hard feelings."

2020-21

With COVID-19 wreaking havoc worldwide and the Canada-US border remaining closed, the NHL realigned into four divisions, with no conferences, when the next season started in January 2021. Each team played only division rivals. The 56-game season was short but sweet for Fleury.

Lehner was sidelined for a month with a concussion, so Fleury saw a lot of action. He won all but 10 of the 36 games he started, the third-best total in the league, and posted some of the best numbers of his career. He finished third in the NHL in goals-against average (1.98), save percentage (.928) and shutouts (6). He attributed his success in part to goalie coach Mike Rosati, who persuaded him to remain deeper in the crease to better han-dle rebounds and cross-ice passes.

At the end of the regular season, the Golden Knights and the Colorado Avalanche led the NHL standings with 82 points each. Vegas opened the playoffs at home against the Minnesota Wild (75 points). Before the puck dropped, the lights dimmed, flowers were projected onto the ice and the public address announcer introduced the most popular hockey player in the desert. "He's No. 29. He's Marc. André. Fleury!" The crowd gave the goalie a rapturous welcome—one that was several decibels higher than the one Mark Stone, the team's captain and leading scorer, received.

Vegas lost the game 1–0 but ultimately won the series, in which momentum seemed to be shifting constantly, clinching it with a convincing 6–2 victory in Game 7. Fleury played in all seven games and was in good spirits when the team's plane landed in Denver to take on the Avalanche. Lehner, who had returned to the lineup in March, started in the first game but lived to regret it. The Avalanche buried the Golden Knights, 7–1. Fleury took over, winning four of the next five games as the Golden Knights eliminated the Avalanche.

The Golden Knights then ventured out of their division to take on the Montreal Canadiens (59), who had finished fourth in the North Division. This semifinal featured a showdown between two of the NHL's best goalies—Fleury and Carey Price. The Habs goalie emerged as king of the castle in the six-game series. Fleury, the dirty rascal, hit a low point in Game 3. Vegas was leading 2–1 in the third period when he skated behind his net and mishandled the puck. It landed on the stick of Montreal for-ward Josh Anderson, who put it in the empty net and then, just for fun, scored the winner in overtime. Fleury sat out two of the next three games and the Habs eliminated the Golden Knights.

Despite the mishap in Montreal, Fleury had been exceptional that season. He and Lehner shared the William M. Jennings Trophy. Fleury's numbers were too good for NHL general man-agers to ignore, and they rewarded him with the Vezina Trophy. Martin Brodeur presented it to Fleury online—which passed as in-person during the pandemic—and Fleury thanked everyone but the snack bar attendants at T-Mobile Arena for his success.

Winning the award made him the most celebrated goalie in the NHL, but the Golden Knights needed space under the NHL salary cap and they had Lehner, who was younger and less expensive than Fleury, in the lineup—so they plucked "Flower" from their roster and sent him to the Blackhawks in exchange for a minor-league player. Fleury found out about the trade via Twitter.

2021-23

The 36-year-old goalie considered retirement. His family, which now included two-year-old James, was thriving. But he soon confirmed he would be leaving Las Vegas. "I thought I was going to maybe retire [in Las Vegas] and finish it out, maybe live there after hockey. So it was a little bit of a change of direction," he said when he donned the Blackhawks uniform in September. "But the [Blackhawks have] been great helping me make myself comfortable in the city. The school has been great for the kids. They love it. They're playing soccer. The wife loves it. So yeah, no complaints."[37]

Fleury reached a milestone three months later, in a game in Montreal. With family and friends cheering him on at the Bell Centre, he helped lift the Blackhawks to a 2–0 win over the Canadiens. It was the 500th victory of his career—a milestone reached by just two other goalies: Martin Brodeur and Patrick Roy.

Fleury's winning ways on and off the ice endeared him to his new teammates. "He is just a fun, uplifting person to be around," said Blackhawks star Jonathan Toews. "He has that look in his eye and that big smile. He's a special player and an incredible teammate." Had the Blackhawks captain ever seen Fleury in a bad mood? "Rarely, but maybe a couple of times. He can get fired up occasionally."

Fleury never dropped the gloves while playing for the Blackhawks, who missed the playoffs that season, but he did while playing for the Minnesota Wild, who acquired him in March 2022, two months before bowing out in the first round of the playoffs.

In a game in St. Louis in March 2023, Fleury took exception to Blues goalie Jordan Binnington throwing a punch at Wild forward Ryan Hartman. Fleury tossed off his mask and made a beeline for Binnington. The amiable Fleury did his best to look menacing for a minute or two before an official separated the two netminders. No punches had been thrown. "I just gotta get my stuff," Fleury told the linesman, nodding toward his mask. "I don't like to have my hair like this."

After the Wild's 8–5 victory, Fleury expressed his disappointment about being denied the chance to make his mark as an enforcer. "It would have been fun," he said, smiling. "The crowd was up on their feet. I never had a fight in my career, so it would have been pretty cool. Too bad."[38]

The Wild finished sixth in the 16-team Western Conference (103 points) and opened the playoffs against the Dallas Stars (108 points). Fleury saw action in just two of the six games in the series, allowing seven goals on 37 shots. Minnesota was eliminated and there was soon speculation Fleury would go to another team. But he insisted he would stay put even if it meant being a backup goaltender the following season.

At that point, it seemed unlikely Fleury would ever get the chance to put up his dukes in an on-ice skirmish, but he had already made his mark in the NHL. "How would I like to be remembered?" he says, when asked about his legacy. "As someone who gave their best every night, made some acrobatic saves and was fun to watch. To me, hockey is fun."

MARC-ANDRÉ FLEURY • ALL-TIME RANKING

REGULAR SEASON			PLAYOFFS		
GAMES + RANK	WINS + RANK	SO + RANK	GAMES + RANK	WINS + RANK	SO + RANK
985 [4TH]	544 [3RD]	73 [12TH]	169 [3RD]	92 [3RD]	16 [3RD]

+ NHL ALL-STAR TEAM (2ND) 2020–21

THE CLASS ACT
HENRIK LUNDQVIST

||||||||||||||||||||||||||||

HENRIK LUNDQVIST WAS so good in his seventh NHL season that his New York Rangers teammates awarded him the Broadway Hat at least five times. It was a black fedora with a ribbon and a bow that, after each win, was bestowed upon the Ranger who had played the most pivotal role in the victory. The hat's origins were unknown, but its sartorial shortcomings were clear to Lundqvist. "It looks terrible," he said in January 2012. "I'm going to say it looked O.K. the first couple of games, but now…" *Yeesh.*[1]

Throughout his NHL career, Lundqvist made an impression on the ice, where he proved to be one of the best European goalies in league history, and off. His fashion sense was as exceptional as his reflexes, and he devoted a lot of time to charitable causes. By the time he retired in 2021, he had established himself as the consummate class act.

LONG BEFORE he donned his first designer suit, Lundqvist grew up in a tiny village in Sweden, not far from the Arctic Circle. Åre was so small, its only toy store consisted of a few shelves in a flower shop. Henrik lived with his parents, Peter and Eva, older sister Gabriella and twin brother Joel.

The boys, born in March 1982, were so inseparable that family members and friends often referred to them as one entity,

Lundqvist played a key role in Sweden's gold-medal victory at the 2017 world championship. He celebrated the gold medal with his brother, Joel, who was team captain. **ANDRE RINGUETTE/INTERNATIONAL ICE HOCKEY FEDERATION**

Joel and Henrik. When they were toddlers, Joel was admitted to hospital with a bad cough and, during his brief stay, Henrik was so distraught he refused to eat.

All the Lundqvist siblings loved music and formed a band. Like the Partridge Family before them, they practiced at home, where Henrik played guitar, Joel plucked his bass and Gabriella kept the beat on drums. Unlike the Partridge kids, they didn't perform in lounges in crushed velvet jumpsuits. Their first love was sports.

The boys skied competitively. Joel recalls one race that took place during a heavy snowfall. He managed to get down the hill in good time, but Henrik, unable to see well, stopped short of the finish line. When he realized his mistake, he finished the race, but his final time was horrible. "Henrik didn't think it was very funny but the rest of us sure did," Joel says. "It was not a good day for him."

The brothers also played tennis, which Gabriella excelled at, but focused most of their energy on soccer and hockey. In both sports, Joel was a forward and Henrik was the goalie. The boys were so competitive that after one loss they ran screaming into the woods in protest. They sat and stewed for an eternity—about 15 minutes. "The other kids were probably wondering what was wrong with us, but we were just so upset," says Joel.

JoelandHenrik spent most of the winters skating on a frozen pond. Their time was limited because the sun set in midafternoon, but they slowly improved, and when they were eight years old, they started playing organized hockey in the nearby community of Järpen. At one practice, their coach asked if anyone wanted to try playing between the pipes. Henrik was shy, so his brother raised his hand for him.

Joel knew that his brother was obsessed with goaltenders. Henrik saw the goalie mask and glove as the epitome of cool and the bulky pads as an accessory to die for. He watched videos of his favorite goalies, Patrick Roy and Dominik Hašek, in an endless loop.

A few years later, the Lundqvist family moved to Båstad, a small city in southern Sweden, to support Gabriella's tennis career. (She later competed for Sacramento State University.)

When the boys were 16 years old, they turned heads at a tournament in Gothenburg. Västra Frölunda, a hockey club with a team in the Swedish Elite League, asked them to play for its junior team, so they moved to Gothenburg and donned the red and green colors of the Frölunda Indians.

The twins excelled there too and competed for Sweden at the 2000 World U18 Championship. Six months later, they traveled to Calgary for the NHL Entry Draft. The Dallas Stars selected Joel in the third round (68th overall). Henrik sat on pins and needles in the Saddledome while the names of almost two dozen goaltenders were called. Finally, the New York Rangers took him in the seventh round (205th overall).

"I will never forget it," Lundqvist said later. "There was a scout from Sweden who wanted to draft me from Round 2 on, and everybody was, like, 'No, no, no.' Finally, Don [Maloney, the Rangers' assistant general manager] stepped in and said, 'Let's do it.' At that point, I was just happy to get drafted."[2]

The scout was Christer Rockstrom. He had rated Lundqvist as the top European goalie, but fellow Rangers scout Martin Madden thought Lundqvist lacked consistency. Late in the draft, Maloney, who was seated between the men, turned to Rockstrom and noticed Lundqvist's name on the scout's list. He then turned to Madden and said, "We're looking for a goalie. Why wouldn't we take a flier on him?" Madden relented, and without knowing it, the Rangers chose a franchise player. "I knew some of the top-end players, but I had no knowledge of Henrik Lundqvist," Maloney admitted. "I wouldn't have known him if I tripped over him. As you get deeper into the draft, you're basically looking for anyone with a heartbeat who can stand up and skate."[3]

Lundqvist returned to Sweden determined to prove he should have been selected higher in the draft—*much* higher. He started working with goalie coach Michael Lehner, who applied the principles of Kyokushin, a form of karate, to improve Lundqvist's mental strength and ability to cut down angles and challenge shooters. Under his tutelage, Lundqvist developed into an excellent butterfly goalie who had lightning reflexes and a great glove hand.

As a teenager, Lundqvist didn't yet have the mental toughness and confidence that would later help him become an elite NHL goalie. Thomas Magnusson, head of goaltending development with the Swedish Ice Hockey Association, recalls speaking to Lundqvist in the lobby of a hotel where the junior national team was staying for a tournament. The lanky adolescent was feeling unsure of himself because, despite having played some games for Frölunda's team in the Swedish Elite League, he hadn't been able to secure a permanent spot on the roster.

"He was a great goalie, but he wasn't playing to his potential because he doubted himself. He was not having fun at all. We knew we had to bring him to his feet, help him believe in himself," says Magnusson, who has been referred to as the godfather of Swedish goaltending. "The other coaches and I assured him that we had faith in him. That seemed to help. He ended up playing well in that tournament."

In a few years, Lundqvist became a starter for Frölunda's Elite League team and helped it win two league titles. He also won the Honken Trophy as Sweden's best goalie in three straight seasons.

In 2004–05, an NHL labor dispute led several of the league's goalies to lace up for teams in European countries, including Sweden. Lundqvist outshone Miikka Kiprusoff (Calgary Flames) and José Théodore (Montreal Canadiens) to win the Golden Helmet as the MVP in the Swedish Elite League and the Golden Puck as the country's top player. "I'm thinking, 'Can I make it in the NHL?'" Lundqvist said later. "And then all those guys from the NHL come over and played against me. I had my best year, and I'm like, 'I can do this.'"[4]

Lundqvist also made his mark internationally during his time with Frölunda, playing for Sweden in two world junior championships U20 (2001, 2002) and two world championships (2004, 2005).

In his third season with Frölunda HC, Lundqvist visited a local hospital and spent time with a 10-year-old patient who had terminal cancer. The boy died a few days later, prompting his mother to send a letter to Lundqvist thanking him for bringing some joy into her son's life before he died. The experience had a profound effect on Lundqvist, who would later devote much time and energy to charitable initiatives.

NHL

2005-06

Lundqvist arrived in New York in the fall of 2005, when the Rangers added him to the roster as a backup to Kevin Weekes. When Weekes got injured in the second game of the season,

Lundqvist had a chance to strut his stuff. He made his NHL debut on October 8, in a game against the New Jersey Devils in East Rutherford. He stopped 24 shots in a 3–2 overtime loss.

The teams met again five days later at Madison Square Garden. Veteran Martin Brodeur, one of the best goalies in NHL history, stood tall in the Devils' net, but Lundqvist wasn't intimidated. He was excellent in his home debut, stopping 20 shots in a 4–1 Rangers win. The capacity crowd was impressed and gave the rookie a standing ovation when he was announced as the first star of the game.

Lundqvist was great in a home game against the Atlanta Thrashers a couple of days later. In the third period, the puck bounced off a teammate's skate into the Rangers net. Spectators rose to their feet, but instead of booing the goalie and pelting him with beer cups or brisket sandwiches, they chanted, "Hen-*reek*! Hen-*reek*!" The Rangers won the game 5–1 and Lundqvist was named the first star. The coronation of "King Henrik" was complete.

LUNDQVIST BECAME a national hero in his homeland when he helped Sweden win the gold medal at the 2006 Winter Olympics in Turin, Italy. The Swedes won five of the six games he played in, including a 3–2 win over Finland in the final. Lundqvist made 25 saves in that game, one of which was a spread-eagle stick save against Olli Jokinen in the dying seconds of the game. The save was so stunning that Jokinen raised his arms in celebration before realizing he hadn't scored.

The Swedish team, which included NHL stars such as Peter Forsberg, Mats Sundin and Nicklas Lidström, flew to Stockholm, where they received a hero's welcome. Lundqvist soon returned to New York and wore his medal while doing television interviews and posing for photos at a charity event at Madison Square Garden.

LUNDQVIST WAS the master of his domain all season, notching 30 wins—a team record for wins by a rookie goalie—and finishing in the top third of the league in goals-against average and save percentage. He was named to the league's all-rookie team and was a finalist in voting for the Vezina Trophy.

The Rangers hadn't competed in the playoffs in almost a decade and most fans expected more mediocrity this season. But thanks to Lundqvist and veteran forward Jaromir Jagr, who finished second in NHL scoring (123 points), the Rangers posted the most wins (44) since the 1993–94 season. They finished sixth in the Eastern Conference with 100 points and met their rivals from across the Hudson River in the first round of the playoffs.

Brodeur, who led all goalies in wins (43) for the seventh time in his career, helped the Devils (101 points) sweep the Rangers aside in four games. Lundqvist played in three games in that conference quarterfinal but was far from great. He had trouble tracking the puck. He was suffering from migraines and blurred vision, which, he later discovered, was due to grinding his teeth.

Despite the playoff disappointment, Rangers fans were smitten with Lundqvist by the end of the season. The goalie himself was in a New York state of mind. In the summer, he moved from White Plains, a suburb where Rangers rookies were required to live, to Manhattan with his Swedish girlfriend, Therese. The couple spent time exploring Gotham's side streets, restaurants, movies and shows. Fans often spotted the goalie around town, with his trimmed beard and designer duds.

Lundqvist also made plans to spend time in Sweden, visiting family and friends and jamming with Box Play, a band he had formed with three Frölunda teammates, including his brother. Lundqvist, whose first purchases in New York were a guitar and a harmonica, admitted his band was "not really that good."[5]

He may not have been as good a guitarist as he was a goaltender, but music was a big part of his life throughout his career. "I used to listen to high-energy music while preparing for games," Lundqvist says, citing Blink-182, the Foo Fighters and AC/DC as three of his favorite bands. "I would listen to music, check my equipment and do my stretching," he says, describing the routine he adhered to religiously. He was also specific about what he ingested before games and between periods—water, energy drinks and bananas.

2006-07

In mid-December, the Rangers took on the Dallas Stars at the American Airlines Center. It was an ordinary game by most standards; Rangers forwards Matt Cullen and Karel Rachunek scored two goals each to seal a 5–2 victory and Lundqvist made a whopping 43 saves. But the game was special for Lundqvist and his family. The Stars had called up Joel from their AHL affiliate because star forward Mike Modano was injured.

Joel spent less than six minutes on the ice and didn't take a shot on net but his brother paid close attention to him anyway. "I never see players out there but I noticed every time he was on the ice," Henrik said. "I was nervous every time he was out there. Getting the chance to play against him in the NHL is a special feeling." (Joel spent three seasons with the Stars before returning to the Swedish Elite League.)[6]

"It was a very weird feeling to see him in the net at the other end of the ice after all the years we played on the same team," Joel says, looking back. He adds that their parents watched the game from their home in Sweden. Which son's team did they cheer for? "I don't know the answer to that," he says with a laugh. "I only know they wanted both of us to play well."

Despite losing several players to injury in March, the Rangers won 10 of 15 games that month. Lundqvist played a pivotal role in their success. He impressed everyone who watched him play—with the exception of one of the women charged with cleaning the ice during games at Nassau Coliseum on Long Island.

During a TV time-out in a game between the Rangers and the New York Islanders on April 3, Kelli Higgins skated onto the ice in her black two-piece uniform. Moments later, she tried to clear snow from the Rangers goal crease. Lundqvist refused to step aside and, to add insult to injury, he took a swipe at her squeegee with his stick. Higgins was indignant. She told media Lundqvist was the only visiting goalie who refused to cooperate with the Ice Girls. "He absolutely refuses to move so we're always having to go around him," she said. "That's not fair because he hides the snow in there." The Islanders ended up winning the game 3-2, proving beyond a reasonable doubt that karma is a bitch. "We don't want an apology," Islanders vice president of operations Tim Beach said afterwards, "but flowers would be nice."[7]

The Rangers finished sixth in the conference with 94 points and met the Atlanta Thrashers (97 points) in the first round of the playoffs. New York swept the Thrashers aside in four games. Lundqvist allowed six goals overall and posted a shutout in Game 3—the first Rangers goalie to notch a playoff shutout since Mike Richter in 1997.

A week later, the Rangers squared off against the league-leading Buffalo Sabres (113 points) in the conference semifinals. Forward Daniel Brière, one of the NHL's top scorers, led the Sabres to victory in the six-game series.

Had one of the Ice Girls put a curse on Lundqvist? If so, it didn't have any staying power. The goalie, who was a finalist for the Vezina Trophy again, signed a one-year contract extension with the Rangers in the summer, cementing his status as the team's starting goalie.

2007-08

The Rangers also signed Chris Drury and Scott Gomez that summer, and the acquisition of the star forwards seemed to be a great move by the end of November, when the Rangers sat in second place in the conference behind the Ottawa Senators. But the team lost its footing in December and tumbled down the standings. Lundqvist floundered along with his teammates.

In December, his father had surgery for a brain aneurysm, and his eldest son—Henrik is 40 minutes older than Joel—felt helpless on the other side of the Atlantic Ocean. "You don't really think when it happens that it affects you," the goalie said later. "But afterwards, when [my father] started to recover, I thought back about those weeks after [the aneurysm] and it was a really tough time. I think it affected me a little bit."[8]

Still, the franchise had faith in Lundqvist and proved it by signing him to a six-year contract extension that would see him earn almost $7 million per season. That made him the highest-paid goaltender in the NHL on average over the length of his contract. The dollar signs must have put a spring in his step. His play improved and he ended the season with more shutouts (10) than any other goalie in the league. He was also a finalist for the Vezina for the third straight season.

The Rangers finished fourth in the conference with 97 points and squared off against the Devils (99 points) to start the postseason. The Rangers won the series in five games.

Lundqvist allowed 12 goals in five games, four fewer than Brodeur. The veteran may have been surprised by those statistics; earlier in the season he said he didn't really like Lundqvist's style—a reference to his goaltending, not his formal wear—and described it as "weird."[9]

The Rangers had high hopes heading into the conference semifinals against the Pittsburgh Penguins (102 points). But the Penguins had too much firepower. Evgeni Malkin, who finished second in NHL scoring that season (106 points), notched seven points, and superstar Sidney Crosby, who had sat out much of the season with an ankle injury, added another six points as the Penguins beat the Rangers four games to one.

2008-09

In the summer, the Rangers lost their captain and highest scorer. Jagr left to play with Avangard Omsk, a team in the Kontinental Hockey League (KHL), a newly formed professional league based in Russia. A couple of months later, the Rangers followed him to Europe—not because they missed him, but because New York was one of four NHL teams that started the season there.

The Rangers first headed to Bern, Switzerland, and played an exhibition game against a team from the top Swiss league. The Rangers skated to an easy 8-1 victory.

The next day, the Rangers took on Metallurg Magnitogorsk, a KHL team that had recently won the European Champions Cup. Reebok, which supplied gear to the NHL at the time, wanted the Rangers to wear the company's tracksuits on and off the team bus in Europe. Steve Valiquette, the team's backup goalie at the time, later recalled that Lundqvist wasn't pleased. He said Lundqvist wouldn't feel prepared to play unless he was wearing a great suit on game day. Sure enough, Lundqvist had a bad outing. The Rangers were down by three goals late in the second period and had to mount a furious comeback to beat the European champions 4–3.[10]

The Rangers then headed to Prague for the start of the season against the Tampa Bay Lightning. Czech fans were so excited to see NHL players that thousands of them crowded into the arena to watch the teams practice. It was an exciting time for the Rangers too; they won back-to-back games against the Lightning, both by a score of 2–1.

Valiquette, who played for the Rangers for five seasons, said that when the team arrived at the arena in Prague, all the players except one were wearing their Reebok tracksuits. Lundqvist was in a three-piece suit. He helped the Rangers win both games.

"Everything had to be perfect on game day. Even for the morning skates, he showed up looking like a million bucks. He would show up for a game in a double-breasted suit with a pocket square, and his hair was perfect," says Valiquette today. "I felt that he wanted everything to be perfect on game day so he could play his best."

Valiquette also remembers getting a fashion tip from Lundqvist. "Once, when he was wearing a suit, he leaned forward and stretched his arms in front of him, so his jacket was pulled tight across his back. He said to me, 'Vally, you shouldn't be able to get even a pinch of fabric between your fingers. If you're going to spend money on a good suit, you need to feel it.'"

LUNDQVIST'S FASHION sense made a big impression during his time with the Rangers. "Page Six," a gossip column in the *New*

York Post, named him as one of the most stylish men around. *Vanity Fair* and GQ magazines did the same.

"The Rangers goalkeep knows his way around a trim-tailored suit and skinny sports jacket, always finished off with a skinny tie, and brings the same sleekness to his downtime rigs," GQ wrote when introducing him as one of the 25 most stylish men of 2013. "What seals it all together is a consistently well-groomed head of hair that obviously hasn't succumbed to the perils of spending most of its time under a helmet." (Not behind a mask but *under a helmet*.)[11]

Lundqvist says he has always had a creative side, and developed a casual interest in fashion in high school. He finds New York is an easy place to be fashion-forward. "There are so many different styles, backgrounds and opinions on fashion in the city. It's a great place to explore and to find out what you really like," he says. "In New York, it's easy to be who you want to be."

THE RANGERS continued their winning ways when they returned to New York. By the end of October, they had won 10 of their first 13 games, the best start in franchise history. Lundqvist was in fine form and attributed his success to a minor change in technique. He started standing more and crouching less in the crease. He found he had faster reflexes from that position and was able to see the game better. In March, he became the first NHL goalie to win at least 30 games in each of his first four seasons.

But the good times didn't last. The second half of the season wasn't kind to Lundqvist or his teammates. Between Christmas and the end of the regular season, the Rangers tumbled from the top of the conference standings to seventh place with 95 points.

They opened the playoffs against the Washington Capitals (108 points). Lundqvist was stellar in the first four games but stumbled badly after that. He was pulled in the fifth and sixth games after allowing a handful of goals in each. The Rangers fought hard and pushed the series to seven games, but resistance proved futile. Alexander Semin and Alex Ovechkin, who had finished second in scoring in the regular season (110 points), led the Capitals to victory.

2009-11

The Rangers' fortunes went from bad to worse in the next two years. Despite the addition of high-scoring forward Marián Gáborik, the team failed to make the playoffs in 2010. The next season, the Capitals eliminated the Rangers in the first round again. That series wrapped up in five games. Lundqvist won more than 30 games in each of those two seasons and notched a league-leading 11 shutouts in the second one, but he also navigated some choppy waters.

He donned the *Tre Kronor* for Sweden at the 2010 Winter Olympics but there was no magic this time. His team bowed out in the quarterfinals. Four days after the closing ceremony in Vancouver, Lundqvist had an altercation with the man who had scored the goal that clinched the gold medal for Canada. During a home game against the Penguins, Lundqvist left his crease to shout at Crosby, accusing him of embellishing a fall after being cross-checked by a Rangers defenseman. Crosby shoved Lundqvist—and then paid the price. Rangers forward Brandon Dubinsky pummeled the Canadian star while fans in Madison Square Garden, still stinging from their national team's overtime loss in the Olympic final, chanted "USA! USA!" Dubinsky just shrugged when asked about the incident. "Hank is our best player, and we've got to make sure we protect him and take care of him."[12]

Crosby wasn't the only target of Lundqvist's wrath. Less than a year later, the goalie jumped on Habs forward Max Pacioretty after the two collided and landed a series of blows. Lundqvist later admitted he "lost it there a little bit," but John Tortorella, who was the Rangers' head coach at the time, didn't mind. He said he wished the goalie had landed more punches.

Lundqvist's life was eventful off the ice during those two years. He sold his Manhattan condo, which had a bathroom with one-way glass that allowed occupants to watch the sun set while taking a bath. The listing agent described it as "sexy." But really, what other kind of bathroom could Lundqvist have had? Answer: none. After all, *People* magazine had included him on its list of the world's most beautiful people, and *Vogue* magazine would soon take notice of his mane, describing him as "a hair god." When Lundqvist married Therese in August 2011, a collective sigh of disappointment could be heard from eligible women across Manhattan.

2011-12

Less than four months after the wedding, the Rangers played the Philadelphia Flyers in the 2012 Winter Classic at Citizens Bank Park, which is home to the Philadelphia Phillies. The temperature was below freezing but must have felt balmy to Lundqvist, who had grown up just a short sleigh ride from Santa's workshop. He was so hot that afternoon, the Flyers begged for mercy. Microphones installed by the producers of 24/7, a documentary series on HBO, caught Flyers forward Claude Giroux's plea: "Henrik, let me score one tonight. Just one." He ended up scoring one goal but it wasn't enough. New York won the game 3–2, thanks mostly to Lundqvist. He made 34 saves, including one on a penalty shot in the last seconds of the game.

The following month, he attended a casino night at Gotham Hall, an event space in Midtown Manhattan, and auctioned off a signed jersey. It sold for almost $10,000. The proceeds went to the Garden of Dreams Foundation, a nonprofit organization that works mostly with Madison Square Garden and its tenants to host charitable events and grants wishes to kids facing health or financial challenges. Lundqvist became a spokesperson for the foundation in 2009. He also launched a clothing line, Crown Collection, and donated a percentage of sales to the foundation.

IT WAS one of many charitable initiatives with which Lundqvist was involved during his time with the Rangers. His band, the Noise Upstairs, performed at a bar in Lower Manhattan in 2012, raising tens of thousands of dollars for charity. Lundqvist had formed the band with John McEnroe. Yes, *that* John McEnroe. Turns out, the tennis legend makes almost as much noise off the court as he did on it.

"That event was a lot of fun," Lundqvist says. "We had to make time to rehearse before the show, but it was worth it. It was a nice turnout and we raised a lot of money."

Two years later, he and Therese established the Henrik Lundqvist Foundation, a nonprofit organization that creates positive change in people's lives through education and health services. It hosted its first fundraising event at a Manhattan bar. The event included a silent auction and an acoustic performance by Lundqvist and McEnroe.

Lundqvist also once interviewed McEnroe as part of a television series in which the goalie and celebrity guests chatted while designing goalie masks to be auctioned off for charity. Actor Michael J. Fox and NASCAR champion Jeff Gordon also appeared on the show, called *The Mask with Henrik Lundqvist*.

The goalie attended many events in New York to help raise money for charity, and he once worked with teammate Mats Zuccarello, a Norwegian, to organize an outdoor charity hockey game in Oslo.

AT THE time of the event at Gotham Hall, the Rangers were sitting atop the conference standings. They finished the season there with 109 points. Lundqvist, who finished third in the NHL in shutouts (8) and overall wins (39), was key to his team's success.

The Rangers started the playoffs by taking on the Senators (92 points). The series turned out to be a pitched battle that went the distance. Lundqvist made 26 saves in Game 7 including several in the final few minutes as the Rangers clung to a 2–1 lead. The Rangers survived the onslaught. "It was a tough final seven minutes," Gáborik said. "Hank stood on his head. He made unbelievable saves there." Daniel Alfredsson, Lundqvist's compatriot and summer workout buddy, scored the Senators' lone goal.[13]

Two days later, the Rangers took on Washington once again. The Capitals (92 points) were in tough against the Rangers. Bruce Boudreau, who had been fired as the Capitals' coach five months earlier, once made it clear why the Capitals viewed the Rangers as a formidable foe. Before the teams met in the 2011 postseason, a sportswriter asked him if there was anything about the Rangers that concerned him. He said, "Their goalie." He repeated the answer when he was asked if there was anything else about the team that concerned him. Boudreau proved to be a wise man. Two weeks after the Senators fell to the Rangers in seven games, the Capitals suffered the same fate. Lundqvist played in every game in that series, allowing just 13 goals.[14]

Despite his best efforts, the Rangers' luck ran out in the conference finals. Lundqvist posted two shutouts, but the Devils (102 points), led by sniper Ilya Kovalchuk, who had finished fifth in league scoring (83 points), eliminated the Rangers in a six-game series.

A few weeks later, Lundqvist attended the NHL Awards show at a Las Vegas hotel. He was a finalist for two awards. Malkin ended up winning the first one, the Hart Trophy, but Lundqvist won the Vezina Trophy. When actor Ray Liotta, looking only a little less menacing than he did on the silver screen, made the announcement, Lundqvist stood up, fastened the top button of his suit jacket and walked to the stage to accept his award. "It feels amazing to be on the same list as Patrick Roy, Dominik Hašek, Martin Brodeur," he said before thanking his teammates, family members and goalie coach Benoit Allaire, who had tweaked the goalie's technique by instructing him to maintain a higher stance and line up deeper in the crease to reduce his movements and give him more time to react. Lundqvist hailed Allaire as "the best goalie coach in the world."

2012-13

A labor dispute delayed the start of the next season, but when it began in January 2013, it was clear the three-month delay hadn't rattled Lundqvist. He notched a league-leading 24 wins that season. Lundqvist was also a Vezina finalist again.

The Rangers, who finished sixth in the conference with 56 points, opened the playoffs by defeating the Capitals (57 points) in a seven-game series. Lundqvist had much to do with that. He allowed just 12 goals and held Ovechkin to two points. The goalie also posted shutouts in the final two games.

Rangers fans had high hopes heading into the conference semifinals against the Boston Bruins (62 points) but were soon disappointed. The Bruins won the series in five games and forward Brad Marchand, such a pest on the ice that his many nicknames were selected from an assemblage of rodents, led the charge by scoring two goals and four assists. Rangers management responded to the loss by firing head coach John Tortorella and replacing him with veteran Alain Vigneault.

Around that time, Lundqvist flew to Milan and marked the 10th anniversary of Jim Nelson's tenure as editor of GQ. Lundqvist attended a party at a villa, hobnobbing with fashion-world luminaries such as Giorgio Armani, who lived in sartorial splendor with his beloved black cat. As always, the goalie's coiffed hair made an impression. "Look at that sh*t! It exudes virility," a GQ writer remarked. "I love the sweep. Godlike. You can tell the man is of Viking stock."[15]

2013-14

The Rangers weren't an offensive powerhouse the following season. In fact, they finished in the bottom half of the conference in goals scored. But they allowed fewer goals (193) than all teams in the conference except the Bruins, and Lundqvist deserved much of the credit.

He stumbled early on—he allowed close to three goals a game on average—and sat on the sidelines for a few games while Cam Talbot, a great rookie, strutted his stuff. But Rangers executives viewed Lundqvist as indispensable and signed him to a seven-year $59.5 million contract extension, making him the highest-paid goalie in the NHL. His play improved after that.

In February, the best NHL players headed to Sochi, Russia, for the Winter Olympics. The Swedes won each of their first five games and Lundqvist posted two shutouts. But they fell short in the gold-medal game, losing to Canada 3–0. Crosby put a backhand shot past Lundqvist on a breakaway in the second period—sweet revenge for the beating he took after his tussle with Lundqvist in 2010. Lundqvist ended the tournament in Sochi with a 1.50 goals-against average, second only to Canadian Carey Price. The Habs goaltender recorded a 0.59 goals-against average.

In the weeks following the Olympics, Lundqvist set two franchise records: 302 wins and 50 shutouts. The Rangers honored him in a ceremony before a home game. He stood at one end of the rink with his parents, Therese and the couple's one-year-old daughter, Charlise—whose name ended up as a tattoo on her father's forearm—while highlights were shown on the scoreboard screen. Also in attendance were the men whose records he had broken: Mike Richter (wins) and Ed Giacomin (shutouts).

The Rangers finished fifth in the conference with 96 points and met the Flyers (94 points) in the first round of the playoffs. The series went the distance and Lundqvist was in net for all of it except the third period of Game 5. (He got the hook after allowing four goals on 23 shots in two periods.) Claude Giroux, who had finished third in NHL scoring that season (86 points), scored two goals and notched four assists for the Flyers in the series, but his team came up short. The Rangers sealed the deal in Game 7, then squared off against the Penguins (109 points) in Pittsburgh.

Crosby was the NHL's top scorer that season (104 points), but Malkin led the team in this series, notching three goals and four assists. The Rangers had trouble generating offense and Marc-André Fleury was solid in the Penguins net, keeping the Rangers off the board in two games. They were on the brink of elimination heading into Game 5 but managed to win that game and the next two. While the Penguins cleaned out their dressing room stalls, the Rangers headed to Montreal to meet the Canadiens (100 points) in the conference final.

The series was a heated battle that included two games decided in overtime. Lundqvist was in net for all but 27 minutes of the series. He held Pacioretty, one of the NHL's most prolific goal scorers, to just four points. He also made two spectacular saves in Game 6. There was no score late in the second period, when Habs forward Thomas Vanek took a backhand shot. The puck seemed destined for the back of the net, but Lundqvist released his stick, swung his right arm in the air like the blade of a windmill and batted the puck away with his blocker.

Talbot still remembers that save vividly. "I'd never seen anyone stop a puck like that before," he said years later. "You can think of him helping the Rangers come back from 3–1 down against the Caps a couple times, against Pittsburgh. He was at his best when it mattered most."[16]

But that wasn't Lundqvist's only party trick of the night. He also used his head, literally, to direct the puck out of play late in the third period and preserve the Rangers' 1–0 lead. (Lundqvist relied on that soccer-style move quite often. John Tortorella hated it, but the fans loved it.) When the game ended, the crowd erupted. Lundqvist's shutout had sent the Rangers to the Stanley Cup final for the first time in 20 years. It was the goalie's 42nd playoff win, a franchise record. To this day, he views that victory as one of the high points of his career.

The Rangers headed west to start their series against the Los Angeles Kings, who had finished sixth in the Western Conference with 100 points.

In both of the first two games, the Rangers gave up two-goal leads, and they lost in overtime and double overtime, respectively. Few people blamed Lundqvist for those losses. He allowed just eight of 87 shots to get past him—and one of those goals should have been overturned.

It came in the second game, when the Rangers were leading 4–2. A pileup in the crease ended with the puck in the net. Lundqvist slammed his hands on the ice and shouted at the officials, claiming goalie interference, but they weren't receptive. They more or less clasped their hands over their ears and exclaimed,

"Nah, nah, nah. We can't hear you!" Five months later, the NHL reviewed some playoff games and decided the goal shouldn't have been allowed because Kings forward Dwight King had fallen on top of Lundqvist, preventing him from making a save. *Ooops.*

The Kings won the third game 3–0 in Madison Square Garden. Jonathan Quick notched the shutout for Los Angeles. The Kings outshot the Rangers in the next game 41 to 19 but Lundqvist held the fort and the Rangers managed to stave off elimination with a 2–1 victory.

The Rangers had a one-goal lead heading into the third period of Game 5 but couldn't hang on. Gáborik, whom the Rangers had traded away in 2013, tied the game for Los Angeles and sent the contest into overtime. With little more than five minutes left in the second overtime period, Kings defenseman Alec Martinez scored to give the Kings a 3–2 win. The horn blared, Kings players jumped into each other's arms and fans at the Staples Center sprang to their feet, whooping with joy over the team's second Cup victory in three seasons. Lundqvist had made a spectacular 48 saves in that game (20 more than Quick), but it barely mattered to him as he lay face down on the ice. "It kills you, but you just have to get up and try and do it again," he said three days later. "It's definitely tough when you are that close."[17]

In September, some of the world's most stylish people descended on New York for Fashion Week, an annual event at which designers and companies that specialize in high-fashion clothing display their latest collections on the runway. Lundqvist, who had been named the "most stylish athlete" at the event two years before, was sporting formal wear for another occasion that week—the NHL's Player Media Tour, a two-day media blitz that brought together a few dozen NHL stars for interviews, photo shoots and promotional videos.

Sportswriter Eric Duhatschek covered the event. "Fashion week is underway in New York and no one enjoys the event more than the New York Rangers' stylish GQ icon, Henrik Lundqvist, a man born to wear Zegna," he wrote when the event started.

"For the next two days, Lundqvist will be in his element, making more wardrobe changes than a runway model. He will be in uniform, in sweats, in Rangers' branded gear, along with a variety of different suits—casual for print interviews, a more elegant grey, three-piece number for an evening appearance on the David Letterman show."[18]

When Lundqvist appeared on the *Late Show with David Letterman*, he conceded that he was probably more limber than the host, who confessed to watching the previous postseason wearing only his underwear. While entertaining, the goalie's appearance on that show was less memorable than a 2013 cameo on *The Tonight Show Starring Jimmy Fallon*, when he played "Sweet Child o' Mine" by Guns N' Roses on a glowing, multicolored guitar.

2014-15

Buoyed by their success in the playoffs, the Rangers had their eyes on the prize when the season started. But they didn't reach the Stanley Cup final and they played much of the season without their star goalie. Lundqvist took a shot to the neck in a game against the Carolina Hurricanes on January 31. He stayed in net and made 31 saves in a 4–1 Rangers victory. Two days later, he made 33 saves in a 6–3 victory over the Florida Panthers. But at that point, he was having trouble breathing and was suffering from headaches and light-headedness. Doctors discovered that a blood vessel in his neck had been damaged in the game against Carolina and he was sent to the sidelines to recover.

Talbot took over and made the most of his time in net. By the time Lundqvist returned on March 28, Talbot had won 16 of the 23 games he had started, and the Rangers were sitting at the top of the conference standings. There was some faint rumbling about a possible changing of the guard in the Rangers net, but it didn't last long. The Rangers won six of their last nine games and Lundqvist was in net for all but one of those victories. The team held on to their position as the top seed in the conference, finishing the season with 113 points. The team's goaltenders got much of the credit.

The Rangers advanced through the first two rounds of the playoffs, beating the Penguins (98 points) and the Capitals (101 points), but they fell short in the conference final against the Tampa Bay Lightning (108 points). Steve Stamkos, Nikita Kucherov and Tyler Johnson led the attack as Tampa beat New York in a seven-game series. Lundqvist allowed 21 goals on 215 shots and posted a .902 save percentage in the series. One of the internet memes that surfaced after the series featured an image of Lundqvist's face superimposed on Queen Elizabeth's head—implying either that "King Henrik" was a girlie man or that the British monarch had a beard.

2015-20

In the next five seasons, the Rangers made it past the first round of the playoffs only once—they lost to the Senators in the second round of the 2017 postseason—and they missed the playoffs twice. In February 2018, the front office decided to rebuild and issued a letter to fans warning that they would soon have to bid farewell to some familiar faces. The club traded Rick Nash, Ryan McDonagh, who had been the team's captain since October 2014, and J.T. Miller before the end of the month.

Lundqvist had flashes of greatness during that span. For example, he was strong at the 2016 World Cup of Hockey, where Sweden won the bronze medal. The team's goalie coach, Stefan Lahde, was pleased to see fame and fortune had not changed Lundqvist. "He was still a happy guy who always had a smile on his face. He clearly enjoyed his time with the national team, and he always had time for fans who would ask him for his autograph or to pose for photos," Lahde says today. "I didn't see him turn down a single request."

Seven months later, Lundqvist was exceptional in the final game of a first-round playoff series over the Canadiens, preserving his team's 3–1 lead while the Habs buzzed around the net.

He also played a pivotal role in Sweden's gold-medal victory at the 2017 world championship, stopping three Canadian players in the best-of-five shootout. (His brother, Joel, was Sweden's captain in the tournament.)

But Lundqvist also suffered injuries to his knee and hip during those five seasons and was no longer a force of nature in the Rangers net. He managed just 26 wins in the 2017–18 season—his lowest total in a full season to that point.

In July 2018, *Sports Illustrated* included Lundqvist on its list of the 50 most stylish athletes for the third year in a row, crediting him with being "one of the first to introduce fashion to the NHL" and with bringing his "suave European style throughout his years in the league." But it couldn't have been much consolation for the ultra-competitive goalie.

The next two seasons saw a pair of young Rangers goaltenders, Igor Shesterkin and Alexandar Georgiev, emerge as possible successors to King Henrik. As he inched closer to 40, Lundqvist found himself watching more games from the bench. It became clear that he would soon be the odd man out.

His future with the Rangers was uncertain, but he still loomed large in the team's dressing room. In August, teammate Chris Kreider sang Lundqvist's praises. "I've seen him go about his business on a daily basis, and I have the ultimate respect for Hank as an individual and as a player," the forward told sports journalist Dave Caldwell, who noted that Lundqvist had recently been a finalist for the King Clancy Memorial Trophy, which is awarded annually to a player with outstanding humanitarian and community efforts.[19]

The next month, the Rangers bought out the final year of Lundqvist's contract, ending his days as face of the franchise. He sent out a series of tweets expressing gratitude for his time in the Big Apple. He was sorry to be leaving his teammates. "We all spent so much time in the locker room getting ready for those games," he says today. "My memories of those times are as strong as my memories of the games themselves."

New York hockey fans and fashionistas had little time to wipe their tears and say goodbye. Nine days later, he signed a one-year contract with the Capitals.

BUT THE next season didn't go according to plan. After Lundqvist signed with the Capitals, tests revealed a long-standing heart condition had worsened. In December 2020, he announced he would miss the entire season. The next month, he underwent open-heart surgery (ascending aortic replacement) in Cleveland.

In late February, Lundqvist returned to the ice to gauge his fitness. Former teammate Kevin Weekes joined him for a session. "He's going through all his moves, and the only thing was he couldn't go above a certain heart rate. He was wearing a monitor he had to check every so often," Weekes recalled. "It's the single most impressive thing I've ever seen in hockey. We finish up after an hour and 20 minutes or so, and my jaw's still on the floor."[20]

His former teammates weren't surprised; Lundqvist had always played with unsurpassed intensity. Valiquette remembers a practice early in Lundqvist's career. "It was the morning after a game, so I expected Hank to be a bit relaxed, but he approached the practice like it was a game," says Valiquette. "I was ready to leave the ice after an hour or so, but the backup goalie can't leave before the starter, so I had to stay while Hank took one breakaway after another with no letup. I had never played with anyone that intense. Sure, he was one of *People* magazine's most beautiful people, but under those nice clothes and nice cars, Hank was an animal."

Despite his dedication, Lundqvist wasn't ready to join the Capitals' lineup in 2021. In April, tests revealed more inflammation in his heart. Four months later, he announced his retirement. "It's time," he wrote in a social media post. "For the last 30 years, I have devoted my life to the game of hockey and now it's time to walk away from the game I love and begin a new chapter."

RETIREMENT

That month, he became a commentator for MSG Networks, which broadcasts Rangers games. In October, the day of the Rangers' home opener against the Dallas Stars, Lundqvist tweeted a photo of himself standing outside Madison Square Garden wearing a dark suit and sunglasses and holding an attaché case, looking much like an international man of mystery.

"Back to work. Feels good to be back on 32nd street," he wrote before adding "#rookie."

In January 2022, less than five weeks before his 40th birthday, Lundqvist once again stepped onto the ice at Madison Square Garden, where he was joined by teammates, friends and many family members, including Therese and their two young daughters, Charlise and Juli. The crowd roared as his jersey was raised to the rafters. In an emotional moment, Rangers equipment manager Cass Marques, who had been undergoing treatment for lung cancer, presented Lundqvist with a gift—a frame containing the pucks from all of his shutouts.

Lundqvist rode into the sunset—or drove in his customized Lamborghini—with many franchise goaltending records to his credit, including regular-season games (887), wins (459) and shutouts (64). He had more wins than any other European goalie in NHL history.

When his career ended, he had more time to enjoy the finer things in life—like James Bond movies. "I really enjoy watching them," he told a sportswriter. "Not only because they are really great movies, but they always bring in the latest technology, cars and fashion. It's just fun to see. Last movie, he had some great looks. And I'm a big fan of cars. So it all ties in. And of course he's a badass too, saving the world."[21]

||||||||||||||||||||||||||||||||||||||||||||||||||||||||||||||||||||||||||||||||||||||||||||||||||||||||||||||||||

HENRIK LUNDQVIST • ALL-TIME RANKING

REGULAR SEASON			PLAYOFFS		
GAMES + RANK	WINS + RANK	SO + RANK	GAMES + RANK	WINS + RANK	SO + RANK
887 [9TH]	459 [6TH]	64 [17TH]	130 [10TH]	61 [15TH]	10 [11TH]

+ NHL ALL-ROOKIE TEAM (1ST) 2005–06

+ NHL ALL-STAR TEAM (1ST) 2011–12

+ NHL ALL-STAR TEAM (2ND) 2012–13

THE STOIC
CAREY PRICE

IIIIIIIIIIIIIIIIIIIIIIIIIII

THOUSANDS OF MONTREAL Canadiens fans settled into their seats at the Bell Centre for a game in December 2016 expecting to see Carey Price do what he had been doing for the better part of 10 seasons—stop pucks with a lot of skill and little emotion. But they were in for a surprise. He allowed four goals on 18 shots against the San Jose Sharks, leading coach Michel Therrien to pull him from the game early in the second period. On his way to the dressing room, Price turned and glared at his coach.

Habs fans held their breath, recalling a dark moment in the team's history. When superstar goalie Patrick Roy was pulled from a game in 1995, he quit the team in a fit of pique. But there was no cause for alarm this time. Price defused the situation after the game, telling reporters he was "just pissed" when he was pulled and had since smoothed things over with his coach.

Nothing to see here, fellas.

Price is one of the best goalies in NHL history—the only one to win four individual awards in a single season—and one of the most poised. He has suffered major setbacks in his career but has never lost his composure in public. In fact, a sportswriter once speculated that "Price may be one of the few people on the planet who could use a prescription to increase his blood pressure."[1]

Price was phenomenal at the 2007 world junior championship in Sweden and was named the tournament's MVP. Just another day at the office for the future NHL star. **MIKAEL FRITZON/INTERNATIONAL ICE HOCKEY FEDERATION**

ALMOST TWO decades before Price first donned the *bleu, blanc et rouge* of the Montreal Canadiens, his family moved from Vancouver to Anahim Lake, in northern BC. His parents wanted him to be connected to his Indigenous roots and the tiny community is home to the head office of Ulkatcho First Nation. His mother, Lynda, would be named chief more than once.

In the years after the family settled into their home, a log cabin with a tin roof near the shore of the lake, young Carey grew to love the outdoors. He spent much of his time fishing for trout, riding horses and hunting. He once spent hours perched in a tree with a bow and arrow made of willow branches, waiting for a deer to wander into sight.

Price, who was born in August 1987, took his first tentative steps an outdoor rink his father had built on the family's 35-acre property. Jerry Price, an administrator of an adult learning center, was delighted to slip a homemade mask over his son's face and teach him the finer points of goaltending. Jerry had been a professional goalie in the 1970s, and while he never played in the NHL, he was good enough to be drafted by the Philadelphia Flyers in 1978.

The younger Price and his friends played on that patch of ice for hours, trying to keep the puck away from each other and from the chicken wire that surrounded the makeshift rink, even when the temperature dropped so low they lost feeling in their fingers and toes.

Price's younger sister sometimes joined them. "I remember spending time out there pretending that I played for the Anaheim Mighty Ducks and Carey would take shots on me," Kayla Price recounted on the Montreal Canadiens website. "One time he shot the puck and it [deflected off] the blade of the stick and hit me in the nose. I don't think I went in net again."

When Price was 10 years old, he was ready to play on a rink that didn't have boards designed to keep poultry from running amok. Because there were no leagues nearby, he joined one in Williams Lake, a small community nestled in a valley in the Central Interior of BC. It was 185 miles away, so Jerry and Carey spent long hours in the car driving to and from games and practices. Carey used much of that time to do homework or sleep—sometimes both at the same time.

The round trips became exhausting, so Jerry sought an alternative. He bought a Piper Cherokee, a small airplane commonly used as an air taxi. He later described the aircraft as "a lawn mower with wings." He regularly loaded Carey and his equipment into the winged grass cutter, and took to the open skies.

Carey and his father eventually moved to Williams Lake, where the family kept a car and a condominium. (Lynda and Kayla remained in Anahim Lake.) Carey attended high school, and in his last season in the Williams Lake Minor Hockey Association, he led his triple-A team to the 2003 provincial title.

THE PREVIOUS year, the Tri-City Americans had chosen him in the first round of the WHL bantam draft. Heading into the draft, general manager Bob Tory was dismissive of Price publicly to ensure he wouldn't be scooped up by another team. "For me, it was an obvious decision. When I saw Carey in bantam, you could see the natural ability was there—the quickness, the size, the concentration," Tory said later. "I wanted to keep that quiet because I didn't want other teams to know what I was thinking. I was really excited about the possibility of drafting him."[2]

Price ended up spending four full seasons (2003–07) with the team, which was based in Kennewick, Washington, a small city about 225 miles southeast of Seattle. He was a standout for the Americans as he developed into an elite goaltender. Fans still remember him leading the team to an upset win over the Portland Winter Hawks in the first round of the 2004 playoffs. He was exceptional at positioning, controlling rebounds and puck-handling. He rarely looked chaotic in net and was patient enough to allow shooters to make the first move.

Tory says the goalie's best attribute on the ice was his mental toughness. "He really focused on the present and didn't get too caught up in overanalyzing what had already occurred or what might have occurred in the future," he says.

Olaf Kölzig, who won the Vezina Trophy in 2000, agrees. During the 2004–05 NHL labor dispute, Kölzig headed to Kennewick to train and took Price under his wing. "Carey's demeanor and approach to the game are his biggest assets," says Kölzig, who played for the Americans in the 1980s. "He doesn't get flustered or panicky. He has a way of calming down his teammates. If something is bothering him, you'll never know. If there is one person who is perfect for the job of being a goalie in Montreal, it's him."

At the end of one of their on-ice sessions, Price made a special request of the veteran goalie. "He said, 'Do you want to have a play fight to see how you stack up against me?'" Kölzig recalls. They dropped their gloves and grappled like two sumo wrestlers on skates. "He didn't understand the meaning of old-man strength at the time. I think I got the better of him," says Kölzig, who became part owner of the Americans that season. "We still talk about that day."

Price attracted the attention of the Montreal Canadiens, and he impressed them further at the 2005 NHL combine—three days of physical tests and personal interviews held in Toronto. "I think it was the maturity level at the time that really came across with Price," Trevor Timmins, who was then the Habs director of amateur scouting, said years later. "He was calm, patient, poised. Those were the things that stood out."[3]

The Habs selected Price fifth overall in the 2005 NHL Entry Draft—the first time the franchise had picked a goalie in the first round since 1972, when they chose Michel "Bunny" Larocque sixth overall.

Price attended the draft at the Westin Hotel in Ottawa and watched the proceedings in a room with family members. When Timmins called out his name, Price headed to the main ballroom. His dreams had come true, but he was stone-faced when he stepped onto the dais and donned the iconic Habs jersey for the first time.

The Canadiens' decision surprised many people. At the time, the team's roster included goalie José Théodore, who had won the Hart and Vezina Trophies in the 2001–02 season. TSN sportscaster Pierre McGuire expressed his shock during a live broadcast of the draft. "Oh man, this is off the books. This is right off the reservation!" Many people thought the remark was in poor taste given Price's Indigenous heritage. But the goalie was unfazed. "He called me the next day and apologized. I knew he meant nothing by it," Price said. "All good."[4]

A few months later, Price returned to Kennewick to work on his game. In the 2006–07 season, he was so good he was more popular in the community than the juiciest berry at the annual grape festival. He was named the top goalie in the WHL and in the Canadian Hockey League, which encompasses the WHL as well as two other major junior leagues.

He was also a standout at the 2007 world junior championship in Sweden during the holiday season. He posted six wins including two shutouts, a 1.14 goals-against average and a .961 save percentage. In a semifinal game still regarded as one of the most exciting in the history of the tournament, Price made 35 saves in a 2–1 shootout victory over the US. Canada won the gold medal and Price was named the tournament's MVP.

The Tri-City Americans were eliminated in the first round of the WHL playoffs despite their goalie's heroics that season, but Price wasn't done. He joined the Hamilton Bulldogs of the AHL and led the team to its first title. He was also named the playoffs MVP.

NHL

2007-08

In April 2007, the Canadiens signed Price to a three-year entry-level contract. When the team's rookie camp started five months later, all eyes were on him and brash defenseman P.K. Subban. Price, who then spent much of his downtime playing video games and strumming Johnny Cash songs on his acoustic guitar, didn't seem the least bit nervous. He appeared relaxed on the opening day, telling media he had gained some valuable experience. "I'll do what [the Canadiens] want me to do," he said.

In October, he made his NHL debut in a road game against the Pittsburgh Penguins and rising superstar Sidney Crosby. The goalie turned aside 26 shots in a 3–2 victory. After the game, he said the significance of the moment hadn't yet sunk in. "But it's pretty exciting," he said with as much enthusiasm as a man who had just spent two hours watching paint dry.

The Habs soon sent him back to the Bulldogs for seasoning, but he didn't have enough time to get settled in Steeltown. The Canadiens called him back in early February and traded Cristobal Huet to the Washington Capitals a few weeks later. It was a risky move because Huet was a top-notch goalie and a fan favorite.

Price played well in subsequent weeks, giving him license to be a little cheeky. At one point in a game against New Jersey, the Devils were swarming around the Montreal net. A time-out was called and the Habs gathered in front of their bench for a confab. A few minutes in, the rookie goalie piped up with an idea. "Why don't we go play in their end for a bit?" he said, grinning. Teammate Josh Gorges later recalled that incident, telling media Price was always relaxed and calm. "He doesn't change his attitude or perspective no matter what the score is," said Gorges.[5]

Gorges, who retired in 2019, remembers Price as the consummate team player. "Sometimes, a puck would get by him because he was screened. But he never made a show of it not being his fault," the former defenseman recalls. He would just look at me and shrug as if to say, 'What are you going to do?' He never expressed frustration or tried to blame you."

The Habs finished at the top of the Eastern Conference (104 points) that season for the first time since 1993, and Price finished with a 24-12-3 record. He impressed fans and players alike. "It's just his attitude, just his demeanor on the ice," Canadiens forward Chris Higgins said in 2008. "He hates to lose, he hates to give up even one goal, he wants to get a shutout every game."[6]

Higgins still laughs when commentators praise Price's composure and wonder aloud if he even has a pulse. "Oh, he has a pulse, but it may not go above 60 beats per minute," Higgins says. "When we were teammates, he never looked like he was worked up or tired. He was never *not* in control."

Price notched a shutout in Game 4 of the opening round against the Boston Bruins (94 points), becoming the first Canadiens rookie to post a playoff shutout since Patrick Roy in 1986. When he posted another one in Game 7, visions of a Stanley Cup parade started dancing in the heads of Habs fans.

After the first game of the conference semifinals against the Flyers (95 points), a 4-3 overtime win, Price acknowledged the mounting pressure. "Every round it gets worse," he said. "But it doesn't bother me one bit." The series went sideways after that. Montreal lost the next four games and Price was in net for three of them.[7]

2008-09

Price's fortunes went from bad to worse the following season. He suffered an ankle injury and started in just 49 games during the regular season. He also made headlines for his off-ice exploits. Fans were treated to photos of him and two teammates at play. In one image that spread across the internet like a bad smell, Price is seen hauling on a cigarette. He insisted the photo was taken the previous summer, but didn't deny he had been out on the town recently. "I'm a young kid. It sucks when you try … [to] have a good time, and things come up and bite you," he said. What did he learn from the experience? "In the end my dad always said your sins will sort you out," he said, "and evidently they did."[8]

Higgins was one of the players whom former coach and hockey commentator Jean Perron identified as one of Price's partners in crime. "We were a young team. We got along really well," Higgins says, looking back. "There were seven or eight of us who hung out a lot. We had a fun time away from the rink. We were goofy and we acted stupid like normal twenty-somethings. We needed that because there was so much pressure playing in Montreal. That can be overwhelming for kids.

"You often hear retired players say they wish they had appreciated the experience of playing in the NHL more at the time. Well, we appreciated it. We were young and living our dream. I don't think we should apologize for that."

Higgins, who was traded to the New York Rangers in 2009, remembers his former teammate as being good-natured. "We were competitive guys who wanted to win badly. Carey would sometimes break the tension with a funny comment during the game. He was a very easy guy to like."

But not an easy guy to dress, apparently. "In his rookie year he was a terrible dresser," Higgins recalls. "He wore a lot of plaid, a lot of hoodies. It was farm-boy stuff. That didn't really work in Montreal, which is a bit more chic. It wasn't my style, but I loved it. Carey always stayed true to himself and I'm sure he still does." Higgins hastens to add that Price's fashion sense improved after a few seasons.

Perhaps the only positive development in Price's sophomore season was receiving an autographed photo of Garth Brooks from the country music star himself. "I was trying to remember if I had ordered anything through eBay," Price said at the time. "But it turned out to be an autographed picture. That was pretty cool."[9]

Captain Saku Koivu, Alex Kovalev and Alex Tanguay were the cornerstone of the Canadiens' offense as the team finished eighth in the conference (93 points). General manager Bob Gainey, who had taken over as head coach late in the season, put Price between the pipes for four games in the first round of the playoffs against the Bruins (116 points). The Habs lost every one.

In his final outing that season, Price let in four goals in two periods. Fans cheered sarcastically when he made a routine save and he responded by raising his arms in a sarcastic salute. In the end, Price kept calm and carried on. He knew that, contrary to popular belief in Canada, hockey was "just a game."[10]

2009-10

Price's performance continued to tank the following season. He won just 13 games in the regular season and lost his starting job to Jaroslav Halák.

The Habs finished eighth in the conference (88 points) but surprised everyone—maybe even themselves—by advancing deep into the playoffs. Halák was instrumental in their success. He made 53 saves in a 4-1 win over league-leading Washington (121 points) in Game 6 of the opening round, leaving Capitals sniper Alexander Ovechkin shaking his head in disbelief.

The Habs beat the Capitals and the Penguins (101 points) before taking on Philadelphia (88 points) in the conference final. The Flyers won the five-game series, but Halák remained the toast of the town. He became a restricted free agent that spring along with Price, who had started in just one postseason game. Many fans assumed the team would hold on to Halák, but the Habs rolled the dice, signing Price to a two-year contract and sending Halák to the St. Louis Blues for two prospects. The Habs' new general manager, Pierre Gauthier, said the team was "looking into the future" but his words were drowned out by howls of outrage from Laval to the South Shore.[11]

2010-11

Fans were still livid when the Habs started their preseason three months later. Price allowed four goals on 10 shots in an exhibition game against the Bruins and was treated to a chorus of boos at the Bell Centre. But he was unfazed. He described the game as just "another day on the job" and said he was "pretty numb" to the booing. He even scolded fans, saying that shouting obscenities at him wasn't "the correct way to go about" voicing their displeasure with management's decision to keep him.[12]

Price had a rocky start to the season but regained his footing. He played in 72 games, a franchise record, posted a league-high 38 wins and placed third in shutouts (8). He helped the Habs finish sixth in the conference (96 points). He played well in the postseason too, recording a .934 save percentage, but the injury-plagued Habs came nowhere close to the Stanley Cup. The Bruins (103 points) beat them in a seven-game opening round.

2011-12

The Canadiens' fortunes didn't improve the next season. Au contraire. They had sunk low enough by January to elicit a public thrashing from high-scoring forward Mike Cammalleri. "We prepare for our games like losers," he said. "We play like losers so it's no wonder we lose." Management responded to his musings by yanking him off the ice mid-game and sending him to the Calgary Flames with his equipment, sticks and a bruised ego.

Price didn't suffer the same fate but may have wished he had. The Habs finished third from the bottom of the league standings with 78 points, 11 spots behind the Flames, and missed the playoffs for the first time since 2007. Price finished with a bang, in the literal sense, when teammate David Desharnais fell on his head in a practice.

Despite the dismal season, most Habs fans stood by Price. When he visited a pet food store in the Montreal neighborhood of Pointe-Claire that spring, the starstruck clerk forgot to hand the goalie's credit card back after he purchased a shedding blade to groom his dogs. She finally returned the card with a smile and words of encouragement. "I told Carey, 'I really feel bad for you. You can stand on your head and give 500 per cent and it's never enough. You don't deserve that,'" she recalled. "He just said, 'Thank you. It's a good thing I love hockey.'"[13]

When the season ended, Price retreated to his new home in Kelowna, BC, where he replaced his air mattress with a real bed and "failed miserably" at taking care of his spacious yard. Price, who owned three horses at the time, also participated in a steer-roping event at a rodeo in nearby Vernon. He earned a share of the $600 prize, but as it turned out, he didn't need the money. He soon signed a lucrative six-year deal with the Canadiens.[14]

2012-13

The following season was cut almost in half because of another labor dispute. During the four months the season was on hold, some Habs gathered for informal practices. Gorges spent much of that time giving Price the gears, insisting that goalies had it easier than other players because they weren't expected to play in every game. Price rolled his eyes and suggested the two men switch equipment. "I put on his equipment and could barely make it through the warm-up. I was out of breath and felt like I was going to puke. It was hard to breathe through the mask," Gorges recalls. "But he was fine in my equipment. He took a lot of shots on net, and even picked the corner a few times."

The season finally started in January and two rookies, Brendan Gallagher and Alex Galchenyuk, gave the Habs a much-needed boost. The team finished second in the conference (63 points). Fans were enthusiastic about the team's prospects, but their hopes were dashed in the first round of the playoffs. The team managed just one win against the Ottawa Senators (56 points).

Price struggled late in the regular season and then suffered a groin injury in the fourth game of the playoffs. When the series ended, he broke new ground by displaying—wait for it—*emotion*.

He spoke about the strain of tending net before fans who scrutinized his every move with as much intensity as preschoolers examining a moth trapped in a mason jar. "That's the one thing I miss, being anonymous," he told reporters while cleaning out his locker. "I don't even go to the grocery store anymore. I hardly do anything anymore. I'm like a hobbit in a hole."[15]

"It's normal in a market like Montreal or Toronto or Vancouver, or even Chicago or Philadelphia," new general manager Marc Bergevin said. "Goaltending's a difficult position, very demanding. So it's normal that a young player feels pressure. We'll do everything we can to make sure he gets through this stage. Maybe I can do his groceries for him."[16]

2013-14

The Canadiens rebounded the next season, thanks to the contributions of forward Max Pacioretty, who was one of the NHL's top goal scorers (39), Subban, one of the league's best defensemen, and their top goalie.

Price finished with 34 wins and the best goals-against average (2.32) and save percentage (.927) of his career to that point. He also had the second-most shutouts (6) in the NHL.

The Habs gained momentum late in the season and finished fourth in the conference (100 points). They also swept the Tampa Bay Lightning (101 points) in the first round of the playoffs. Price was in net for all four games.

He was in fine form when the Habs stepped onto the ice in Boston to start a series against the Bruins (117 points). Boston had finished at the top of the NHL standings, but Price was not the least bit intimidated. He shut out the Bruins in the sixth game, and stopped 29 shots in a 3–1 victory in Game 7. During the second intermission of that game, he promised his teammates he wouldn't allow any more goals, and he kept his word. "To say he's going to shut the door, I don't think there are too many goalies who are confident enough to make that call," said forward Dale Weise. "He doesn't say a lot, but when he does, guys take it seriously."[17]

Price was flying high when the Habs started the conference final against the Rangers (96 points) but he soon made a crash landing. In the second period of Game 1, hard-charging Rangers forward Chris Kreider bowled over the goalie. The net spun off its moorings, and Price crumpled to the ice clutching his knee. He ended up leaving the game and being replaced by Peter Budaj. Price watched from the sidelines as New York won the game (7–2) and the series (4–2). He later revealed he had suffered a medial collateral ligament (MCL) injury.

Habs fans still shudder when they recall that collision, wondering what might have been if Price had been fighting fit for the entire series. Dale Weise, who was on the ice at the time, was still shaking his head about the incident seven years later. "Price is a big strong guy and a serious competitor," he said on a podcast. "I never thought it was serious until we heard the actual diagnosis. It pains me to this day."[18]

BUT PRICE'S memories of that season aren't all bad. Just before it started, he and his girlfriend, Angela, tied the knot in Washington State. The next day, the groom and a wedding guest, Subban, boarded a plane headed north. Canadian officials were assembling a team to compete at the 2014 Winter Olympics in Sochi, Russia, in February, and had asked some NHL players to attend an evaluation camp.

Price and Subban both made the team, and coaches named Price the starting goalie over his NHL rival, Roberto Luongo. Price rewarded them for their confidence, allowing just three goals in five games and posting incredible statistics—a 0.59 goals-against average and a .972 save percentage. Team Canada shut out the US in the semifinals (1–0) and Sweden (3–0) in the gold-medal game. Price was named the top goalie of the tournament.

He impressed everyone who watched him play in Sochi, including his teammates in Russia. "He's so calm and composed back there," Patrick Marleau said after the game against the US. "It's nice to have. He was big the whole night for us."[19]

No Canadians were more enthusiastic about Price's accomplishments in Russia than residents of his hometown. They packed a school gym that summer when he visited to promote his role as First Nations ambassador for the Breakfast Club of Canada. Residents learned that the organization, in partnership with a major airline, the Ulkatcho First Nation and the local school district, would provide a breakfast program for schools there.

Price, who has the Ulkatcho First Nation logo tattooed on one arm, has since attended breakfast programs across the country with Angela, and has been involved with several charities over the years. In 2014, Price was awarded the Jean Béliveau Trophy for his extensive contributions to the Montreal community. The following year, he teamed up with sports-equipment manufacturer CCM to donate $10,000 worth of equipment to a minor hockey league in Williams Lake.

"He is not looking for applause or credit for his charity work," says Bob Tory, who is still with the Tri-City Americans. "It's just something he does out of the kindness of his heart."

Tory still sees Price most summers when the goalie returns to Kennewick with Angela and their three young children. "For me, it is almost like he never left. When he walks through that door with that smile on his face, I still see that 17-year-old kid."

2014-15

Price was back in the Canadiens net the next season, and it turned out to be one for the ages. The team wasn't an offensive powerhouse—they finished in the bottom third of the NHL in number of goals scored (214)—but their goalie was exceptional. With Price between the pipes, the team finished second (110 points) behind the Rangers (113 points) in league standings.

Price finished at the top of the standings in goals-against average (1.96), save percentage (.933) and wins (44), which was a franchise record. He also placed second in shutouts with nine.

Price was the toast of the town by mid-March, when the Canadiens traveled to Long Island, New York, for a game against the Islanders. During a break in action, the Habs gathered around their bench. A young fan nearby turned his back to the team, extended his arm and snapped a photo of himself standing in front of Price. The selfie showed Price leaning in and smiling for the camera. It was the faintest of smiles but it was enough to thrill the boy, who marveled at the image while Price sipped some water and chatted with teammates. Price had reason to smile that day. He stopped 35 out of 36 shots and the Habs won 3-1.

A month later, they opened the playoffs at home against the Ottawa Senators (99 points). Price was stellar for most of that series. His crowning achievement was a 2-0 shutout in the sixth and deciding game. He made 43 saves in that outing, leaving fans, players and coaches bowing before him, chanting, "We're not worthy."

"He's the best player every night. He's the best player on our team," Pacioretty exclaimed. "It's always the last worry on our minds, how Carey Price is going to play. He's the best competitor I've ever seen."[20]

Perhaps the highest praise of all came from another netminder—a Hall of Famer. Ken Dryden, who won six championships in eight seasons with Montreal in the 1970s, said he had been a good goalie on great teams, while Price was a great goalie on a good team.[21]

Montreal took on the Tampa Bay Lightning (108 points) next. The Habs lost the first three games but fought back to win the next two. Their battle ended there, however. They were running on empty when the teams clashed in Game 6 in Tampa. The Lightning, led by Nikita Kucherov and Steve Stamkos, won the game (4-1) and the series.

Price was done for the season, but he had made an indelible mark. He won a handful of awards—the Hart Trophy, the Vezina Trophy and the William M. Jennings Trophy. He added one more item to his shopping cart before proceeding to checkout—the Ted Lindsay Award, given to the most outstanding player in the regular season as selected by the NHL Players' Association.

"Everything has fallen into place for some reason," he said at the awards ceremony at the MGM Hotel in Las Vegas. "The team has been playing well. Things are just awesome at home. My family is doing great. It's just been such a blessing." Price remains the only goalie to win all four individual awards in the same season.

In December 2015, he won the Lou Marsh Award as Canada's top athlete, as chosen by a panel of sports journalists. He said he hoped Indigenous people would draw inspiration from his accomplishments and believe that success is attainable for their children. "All it takes is a lot of dedication and hard work and luck," he said.

2015-16

Montreal won nine of their first 10 games of the season—their best start in franchise history—and Price was in net for seven of those victories. The Habs had already won eight straight games when they prepared to take on the Toronto Maple Leafs. The day before the game at the Bell Centre, reporters asked Leafs forward Michael Grabner about Price. "He's very calm," said Grabner, who had played against Price in the WHL. "He doesn't let anything bother him." Price remained composed against the Leafs, making 49 saves in a 5–3 Montreal victory.[22]

He seemed destined to get a whole lotta love during NHL Awards season, but he suffered a lower-body injury during a game in Edmonton in late October and missed the next nine games. He returned to take on the Islanders on November 20, but his homecoming was short-lived. He suffered another injury five days later—and this one was serious. He sat out the rest of the season with a sprained MCL in his right knee.

Without their star goalie in net, the Habs floundered and missed the playoffs.

2016-17

Price returned to the ice late that summer to prepare for the World Cup of Hockey in Toronto. He looked lean when he stepped onto the ice, having lost almost 10 pounds thanks to a workout routine that incorporated yoga. He was the starting goalie for Team Canada, which proved to be unstoppable.

Sidney Crosby joined forces with Brad Marchand and Patrice Bergeron of the Boston Bruins to form a line that dominated the 12-day competition. The Penguins captain led the tournament with 10 points in six games, but he wasn't the only outstanding player on the roster. Price was undefeated in the tournament and stopped 33 shots in a 2–1 win over Team Europe in the final. A spectacular save on Slovak forward Marián Hossa late in the game brought fans to their feet in the packed Air Canada Centre. Coach Mike Babcock later described the save as "unbelievable." With unsurpassed insight and exceptional eloquence, the veteran coach concluded that Price "just does what he does."[23]

During a raucous celebration in the dressing room after the game, reporters asked the goalie if he was aware he had gone 16 international games without a loss. *Duh.* "Everybody's brought it up, yeah," said Price, who had a pair of goggles on hand to prevent rivulets of booze from dripping into his eyes. "I thought it might be over tonight, but we willed our way through it."[24]

The NHL season started less than two weeks later. Pacioretty led the Habs' charge once again, while Price held the fort.

In a game at the Verizon Center in December, Price made 20 saves as the Canadiens notched a 2–1 victory over the Capitals. That made Price the fourth goalie in franchise history to record 250 wins, joining Jacques Plante, Dryden and Roy in the pantheon of great Habs goaltenders. "It's just another win for me," he said after the game. "I don't really care a whole bunch about milestones that much."[25]

The Habs finished fourth in the conference that season (103 points) but bowed out in the first round of the postseason, losing to the Rangers (102 points) in a six-games series.

Despite the early exit, Canadiens management had unwavering faith in their starting goalie, who was a Vezina Trophy finalist that season. In July, they signed Price to an eight-year contract extension worth $84 million (US). That made him the highest-paid goalie in the NHL. "I never thought about playing anywhere else," Price said, speaking to media from his summer home in Kelowna. "It's hard at times, but other times the most fun you're going to have in the entire NHL is playing well in Montreal. There's nothing that compares to it."

2017-18

The good times ended just a few months later. The Canadiens had the worst 10-game start in franchise history, losing all but two games. Price was mediocre during that span. He suffered another lower-body injury in early November and sat out for three weeks.

Demanding Montreal fans started baying for blood. One columnist noted that the Habs had not won anything since Price joined the team, and there was speculation that he was having problems at home—that his wife wanted to leave Montreal and was separating from her husband. Angela Price squelched the rumors in a social media post that ended with "#chilloutpeople."

But Price was back in the good graces of fickle fans in short order. He returned to the ice in late November and shut out the Buffalo Sabres in a 3–0 win. He then notched four straight wins, allowing just six goals in that span.

But the roller-coaster ride continued, and fans soon plummeted to Earth, screaming in terror. Price suffered a concussion after taking a shot to the head in a game against the Flyers on February 20 and was out for a month. The Canadiens missed the playoffs.

It was Price's worst NHL season statistically to that point—he ranked near the bottom of the league in goals-against average and save percentage among starters—but not everyone abandoned him. Three fans started a GoFundMe page to raise $1,500 for a billboard showing their support.

"After a terrible season for all of the Montréal Canadians [sic], Carey Price, the centerpiece of this team got a lot of criticism from the media and the fans, leaving him and his coach to believe fans didn't like him anymore," one of the fans wrote, adding that the perception couldn't be further from the truth.[26]

The fans exceeded their fundraising goal but fell far short of the $22,000 needed to buy a billboard. Moved by their devotion, the Canadiens' franchise footed the bill, and the money the trio had raised went to charity. A billboard soon went up near the Habs' practice rink in Brossard, across the St. Lawrence River from Montreal.

It featured Price's jersey number and a giant heart set against a *bleu, blanc et rouge* backdrop. Price described the gesture as "heartwarming," and he met the three teenagers after a preseason game at the Bell Centre. "It was kind of nice to put a face to a person who was willing to reach out and be proactive," he said.[27]

2018-19

Fan support for Price was tested again early in the next season, when he had another rough start. One of the lowest points was a loss in Buffalo in early November. He gave up six goals on 31 shots as the Sabres posted a 6–5 overtime win. Reporters gathered around Price after the game. "Let's cut to the chase," he told them. "I wasn't very good." But the wolf pack was hungry for more. What was wrong with him? they wanted to know. Was it a recent change in the color of his goalie pads, from red to white? "No, it's upstairs," he said, pointing at his noggin. "Gotta figure it out."[28]

Price got his groove back in the new year. He was great in a 3–2 overtime win against the Boston Bruins in mid-January, turning aside 41 shots and standing his ground as Boston forwards swarmed his net. "Price was the hero regardless of who potted the game-winning goal," the *Hockey News* reported. "He was calm, cool, collected. He looked like the Price we had grown accustomed to seeing, the one who had seemingly gone missing through the 2017–18 campaign and into the first two months of this season."[29]

Price gained momentum from there. In a home game against the Detroit Red Wings two months later, he notched his 315th victory, breaking a franchise record set by Plante in 1963. He was spectacular in the third period, when he made a kick save on Tyler Bertuzzi on a breakaway and then scooped up the puck on a rebound. "He's the best in the world for a reason, he has been for a long time and he will be for an even longer time," said Habs forward Max Domi, who scored twice in the 3–1 win. "It's honestly insane to put into words what he's accomplished. It's just another level."[30]

The Canadiens finished 10th in the conference (96 points) and missed the playoffs again, but it was an eventful spring for one young Habs fan. Three months after his mother died of cancer, 11-year-old Anderson Whitehead met his hero—just as his mother had promised he would. After a morning skate in Toronto in late February, Price stopped to talk to Whitehead, who was in the stands. When the overwhelmed boy burst into tears, Price removed his goalie mask and gloves, reached out and gave him a warm hug. Price then autographed Whitehead's Habs jersey and gave him two autographed sticks. He also signed a mini-stick that Whitehead had brought with him. "It was very cool," the Brantford, Ontario, boy said about meeting Price. "It's the happiest I've ever been in my life. I always hoped it was going to happen. My mom always said it could happen."[31]

Three months later, Whitehead was surprised again at the NHL Awards in Las Vegas. He appeared onstage for the presentation of a $100,000 check from an insurance company to Hockey Fights Cancer, a charity that raises money for cancer research. He beamed as he watched a video greeting from Price. When the goalie stopped mid-sentence and walked onstage a moment later holding a Habs jersey, Whitehead looked on in disbelief, then started crying. Audience members gave the pair a standing ovation as Price leaned down, put an arm around the boy and comforted him. "Everything is okay," he whispered as Whitehead sobbed. "Everything is great." Price then presented him with the jersey and invited him to the following season's all-star game. There wasn't a dry eye in the house.

2019-20

Price struggled through the next regular season. He started in more games (58) than any other goalie in the league, but he also led the league in the number of goals allowed (160).

In March, the season was suspended due to the COVID-19 pandemic. A week later, the NHL Players' Association released the results of its annual players' poll. It was clear that, despite his lackluster performance in the shortened regular season, Price was still a Goliath in the minds of his peers.

When 588 players were asked to name the league's top goalie, 42 percent of them chose Price. Andrei Vasilevskiy, who led the league in wins (35) that season, finished a distant second with 17 percent of the votes. He was followed by Marc-André Fleury of the Vegas Golden Knights and Sergei Bobrovsky of the Florida Panthers.

"You just don't understand as a shooter how difficult it is to score on him, how much you have to be on your game and how prepared you have to be when you face a goaltender like him," Leafs captain John Tavares said. "Even if he's not having a year like he did when he won the Hart Trophy and Vezina, he's still one of the best goalies in the world."[32]

Legendary NHL goalie Martin Brodeur said the perception of Price was probably influenced by his cool demeanor and the fact that he was playing for a team whose fans were more demanding than most. "Guys are like, 'Man, he's able to do that well while everybody's all over him all the time,'" said Brodeur.[33]

The modified postseason started in August. The top 12 teams in each conference based on points percentage took to the ice in two hub cities—Toronto and Edmonton. The Habs, who had finished near the bottom of the conference standings (71 points), squeaked into the playoffs for the first time in three years and squared off against the Penguins (86 points) in the qualifying round.

Price returned to top form and, like the Ghost of Christmas Past, reminded everyone of better times. Thanks in part to his exceptional rebound control and puck-handling, Price led the Habs to a victory (3–1) over the Penguins in the opening round. He posted a 1.67 goals-against average and a .947 save percentage, the highest by a Habs goalie in a playoff series since Dryden in 1976. He also shut out the Penguins in a 2–0 win in Game 4.

Price stymied the Flyers (89 points) in the second game of the next round. After the Habs' 5–0 win at Scotiabank Arena, Canadiens coach Kirk Muller made it clear he was also impressed by Price's temperament. "If you're a player, there's nothing better than walking into a room and your No. 1 goalie is a very calm type of guy and, you know, very relaxed," he said, "and that is his demeanor as a person."[34]

Unfortunately for Canadiens fans, the Zen Master couldn't lead his team to victory this time. The Flyers beat the Habs four games to two.

2020-21

The pandemic led to dramatic changes in the next NHL season. It didn't start until January, so each team played just 56 regular-season games. They were also divided into four divisions. The Canadian teams played only each other in the North Division.

It was a challenging season for the league and for the Habs' starting goalie. In fact, it proved to be one of the toughest campaigns of his career. Price spent much of it sidelined by injuries and he was mediocre in most of the 25 games in which he appeared. By February many fans had given up on him. Sports journalist Ken Campbell concluded that Price was no longer an elite goaltender and, with the exception of the previous playoffs, hadn't been in a long time. "The Canadiens have a myriad of woes right now, among them a Carey Price problem that needs attention," Campbell wrote. "Because if it isn't solved, this team could be in for a world of hurt for a long time."[35]

In March, the Canadiens sent goalie coach Stéphane Waite packing during the second intermission of a game and replaced him with former NHL goalie Sean Burke. Price regained his form and was working his way into Montreal fans' good books when he suffered another setback. He sustained a concussion in mid-April and ended up watching from the sidelines yet again.

Despite the contributions of Tyler Toffoli, one of the league's top goal scorers, the Habs finished fourth in their seven-team division and had fewer points (59) than any other team that advanced to the postseason.

A few days before the start of their opening-round series against the division-leading Leafs (77 points), Habs management sent Price and Brendan Gallagher, who had missed almost two months with a broken thumb, to the Laval Rocket of the AHL for that team's final game of the season. Fans were still settling into their seats when Price gave up two goals in four minutes against the Toronto Marlies. He didn't appear troubled, though. "It was nice to get some game time," he said afterwards, "to diversify my hockey game portfolio."[36]

Price silenced his critics again, returning to form in the opening game against Leafs snipers Auston Matthews and Mitch Marner, two of the NHL's top scorers. With the Habs ahead 2–1 in the final minutes, the Leafs buzzed around Price but couldn't beat him.

No sooner had the game ended than the hand-wringing began in Toronto. Long-suffering Leafs fans asked themselves and each other what had gone wrong. Some insisted the deciding factor in the outcome was the loss of captain John Tavares, who was carried off the ice on a stretcher in the first period after being struck in the head by Corey Perry's knee. Others pointed to Price as the Leafs' main problem. Many sports journalists did, too.

"He sees the puck so damn well, almost mystifyingly well," wrote *Toronto Star* columnist Rosie DiManno. "If his most recent stats don't particularly send shivers up Toronto's spine, there's still the Price who, while a man of few words off the ice, evinces both elegance and swagger in the cage. Even his body language can demoralize shooters." Pouring a shaker of salt into her readers' wounds, DiManno noted the Leafs had not beaten Montreal in a playoff game since 1967. To do it this time, she said, they "will have to go through Carey Price."[37]

The Leafs fought hard, pushing the series to seven games, but Price and his teammates proved too hot to handle. Matthews, who had a league-leading 41 goals in the regular season, managed just one goal in the series. The Habs won the final game 3–1. The players were still shaking hands when scores of Leafs fans dropped to their knees and looked heavenward, pleading for an explanation from the hockey gods. Others kept their composure but initiated divorce proceedings against the team. The Habs headed to Winnipeg (63 points) for their next series.

The Jets had high scorers in Mark Scheifele and Kyle Connor, but they were no match for the surging Habs. Montreal defenseman Joel Edmundson notched two assists in the opening game, leading his team to a 5–3 win. When forward Jake Evans scored an empty-net goal against the Jets in the last minute of regulation time, Scheifele rewarded him by flattening him and sending him off the ice on a stretcher. The NHL grounded the Jet for four games. The Habs responded with a four-game sweep. Price was excellent, posting a shutout in the second game and allowing just six goals overall.

During some downtime in Winnipeg, he spent a few hours greeting residential school survivors. "He's one of the busiest athletes in the world, but he took the time to make a detour, on foot, right before a game to be close to his community, it's remarkable," said Indigenous hockey player Mikisiw Awashish. The 20-year-old also commented on Price's famous cool. "Indigenous people, we're calm in general, but above all very resilient," he said. "Resilience is a quality that develops with obstacles, and maybe his calm comes from there."[38]

Montreal then took on the Vegas Golden Knights, who had finished second in the West Division (82 points). The series pitted Price against Fleury, one of the best goalies in the game.

He helped lead his team to a 4–1 victory in Game 1 but the Habs staged another upset, clinching the series in six games. When they notched a 3–2 overtime win in the final game, Habs fans poured onto the streets to celebrate, and the team prepared to play in their first Stanley Cup final in 28 years.

With an outstretched arm and much facial hair, Patrick Roy had led the Habs out of the wilderness and into the Promised Land in 1993, but Price couldn't match that. He started the final series against Tampa Bay, which had finished third in the Central Division with 75 points, but soon faltered.

On the first night of the final, a convoy of trucks adorned with Canadiens flags drove through Anahim Lake and the surrounding area, stopping in Indigenous communities along the way. The show of support in Price's hometown was inspiring but not enough to secure a Habs victory.

Price allowed 16 goals in five games and was outshone by Lightning goalie Vasilevskiy, who had finished first in wins (31) in the regular season. He allowed just eight goals in the series and posted a shutout in Game 5. The Lightning won that game 1–0 and won the Cup for the second straight season.

Tampa sports fans were ecstatic. In the previous 12 months, their Major League Baseball franchise had played in the World Series and football deity Tom Brady had descended from the heavens—New England—to lead their NFL franchise to a Super Bowl victory. Montreal fans could only console each other, praise their team for surpassing expectations and get their Habs jerseys dry-cleaned.

2021-23

The next two seasons were eventful for Price but not in a way that made him or his fans happy. Just a few weeks after bowing out of the 2021 playoffs, the 33-year-old goaltender agreed to waive a no-movement clause in his contract so that Montreal could protect backup goaltender Jake Allen instead of him in the expansion draft. But the new franchise, the Seattle Kraken, passed on Price. Hockey pundits attributed the decision to the goalie's age and the fact that he had five years remaining on a lucrative contract. His health might have been a factor, too.

Just days later, Price underwent surgery to repair a torn meniscus. The Canadiens said he would be out for as long as three months but expected him to be back for the start of the following season. That didn't happen.

The week before the start of the season, he entered the league's player-assistance program, which helps players with mental-health issues, substance abuse and other matters. "Over the last few years I have let myself get to a very dark place and I didn't have the tools to cope with that struggle," Price said in November. "Things had reached a point that I realized I needed to prioritize my health for both myself and for my family. Asking for help when you need it is what we encourage our kids to do. And it was what I needed to do."[39]

With their team floundering in his absence, Habs fans hoped Price would return after finishing the 30-day program. But their hopes were dashed when, in January, he announced that all was not tickety-boo with his injured knee. He said it wasn't game ready but added that he hoped to be back before the end of the season. "Being a goaltender for the Montreal Canadiens has been my life for over a decade," he said. "Ending the season on such a disappointing note last year, I just want to be able to get back in there, continue playing and to be able to put that sweater on again," he said. "It's something that's keeping me motivated at this point."[40]

He played his first game of the 2021–22 season in mid-April, allowing two goals on 19 shots in a 3–0 loss to the New York Islanders. It wasn't the most spectacular outing of his career—far from it—but fans were tickled pink to see him back between the pipes. They cheered for him from the moment he stepped onto the ice until the moment he left.

Fifteen days later, a reporter asked Price if his knee would be well enough for him to play 50 to 60 games the following season. "My honest opinion is, 'No,'" the goalie said impassively.[41]

Later that spring, Price won the Bill Masterton Memorial Trophy as the player that best exemplifies the qualities of perseverance and sportsmanship.

That summer, Price was a topic of conversation in and around Montreal. At restaurant tables, at grocery store checkouts and on the docks of cottages in the Laurentians, fans wondered aloud if he would be in net for the start of the 2022–23 season.

The Canadiens answered that question in September, when they put Price on the long-term injured reserve list. That led to a bittersweet moment during player introductions before the first game of the season in October. Spectators at the Bell Centre were disappointed he wasn't dressed for the game, but were happy just to see him. They gave him a standing ovation as he stood before them in a black suit and matching cowboy hat.

Hawkeyed observers noticed the trace of a smile on his face as he tipped his hat to fans as if to say, "Thank y'all kindly."

The love-in ended for some fans in December, when Price took to social media to express his opposition to the federal government's new firearms bill. He posted a photo of himself wearing camouflage and holding a firearm. In the caption, he expressed support for the Canadian Coalition for Firearm Rights, a gun-rights organization that used the promo code POLY to sell merchandise—an apparent reference to a mass shooting that claimed the lives of 14 women at École Polytechnique, a Montreal university, in 1989. Politicians and others lashed out at Price, who then apologized. He said he hadn't intended to cause pain to those affected by gun violence.

The furor died down in subsequent weeks, but Price was a topic of conversation again in January, when his wife announced the family would be moving to Kelowna, BC, at the end of the 2022–23 season. That led many fans to see his retirement as a *fait accompli.*

Price had spent many summers in Kelowna—and it was where he had gathered with current and former teammates at the end of the Canadiens' remarkable playoff run in 2021. "It was a really big group, but Carey was the center of attention," Josh Gorges recalls. "People in the restaurant gawked at him and approached him, asking him to sign autographs and pose for photos. Carey doesn't like that kind of commotion. He prefers to be outdoors on his own or with his kids. But the clatter didn't appear to faze him," says Gorges. "Not much does."

‖‖‖

CAREY PRICE • ALL-TIME RANKING

REGULAR SEASON			PLAYOFFS		
GAMES + RANK	WINS + RANK	SO + RANK	GAMES + RANK	WINS + RANK	SO + RANK
712 [28TH]	361 [22ND]	49 [33RD]	92 [25TH]	43 [28TH]	8 [16TH]

+ NHL ALL-ROOKIE TEAM (1ST) 2007–08

+ NHL ALL-STAR TEAM (1ST) 2014–15

NOTES

||||||||||||||||||||||||||||

CHAPTER 1

The Nervous Wreck: Roger Crozier

1. Norman MacLean, "Itchy Fidgety Crozier Can Still Stop Pucks," *Hockey World*, 1969.
2. Dave Makichuk, "Legendary Wings' Goalie Crozier Deserves to Be in the Hall," *Western Standard*, May 20, 2022.
3. Rex Lardner, "Wispy and Worrying, but He Wins," *Sports Illustrated*, November 23, 1964.
4. Ron Cantera, "Hot-Shot on Hot Spot," *Red Wing Magazine*, March 21, 1965.
5. Roger Crozier, as told to George Vass, "The Game I'll Never Forget," *Hockey Digest*, January 1983.
6. Lardner, "Wispy."
7. Dick Beddoes, "Singer Midget Hits High C," *Globe and Mail*, November 13, 1964.
8. Lardner, "Wispy."
9. Ibid.
10. Roger Crozier, "On the Wings of Victory," *Hockey Illustrated*, November 1965.
11. Cantera, "Hot-Shot."
12. Martin Kane, "Habs Hold a Torch Bien Haut," *Sports Illustrated*, May 16, 1966.
13. "Crozier May Be Ready to Play," *Globe and Mail*, May 3, 1966.
14. MacLean, "Itchy."
15. "Roger Crozier Decides to Call It Quits," *Red Wing Magazine*, November 9, 1967.
16. Stan Fischler, "Fear!," *True's Hockey Yearbook*, 1970.
17. Glen MacNow, "Remembering When Crozier Ruled the Ice at the Aud," *Buffalo News*, January 15, 1986.
18. Dick Johnston, "Buffalo Hopes Roger Crozier Will Become the Sharpest Sabre of All!," *Hockey Pictorial*, December 1971.

19. MacNow, "Remembering."

20. Ibid.

21. Ibid.

22. Associated Press, "Ageless Crozier Blanks Colorado," March 19, 1977.

CHAPTER 2
The Castaway: Rogie Vachon

 1. John Hall, "Around Town," *Los Angeles Times*, May 24, 1976.

 2. Dan Rosenburg, "Vachon Earns His Stripes," *Hockey World*, April 1968.

 3. Gil Smith, "Pressure Keeps Rogatien Vachon Going," *Hockey World*, December 1969.

 4. Stan Fischler, "The Best No. 2 Goalie in the Business—Rogatien Vachon," *Hockey Illustrated*, February 1970.

 5. Ibid.

 6. Ibid.

 7. Ibid.

 8. Rex MacLeod, "Gump Has Confidence in Rogatien," *Globe and Mail*, April 24, 1969.

 9. Joe Resnick, "Rogie Vachon Speaks Out!," *Action Sports Hockey*, December 1975.

10. MacLeod, "Gump."

11. Jim Page, "Rogatien Vachon: The Darling of Canada Cup '76," *Hockey Illustrated*, January 1977.

12. John Hall, "Around Town," *Los Angeles Times*, January 10, 1975.

13. Resnick, "Rogie Vachon."

14. Kevin Allen and Bob Duff, *Without Fear: Hockey's 50 Greatest Goaltenders* (Chicago: Triumph Books, 2002), 254.

15. Page, "Rogatien Vachon."

16. Frank Orr, "The Party's Over—But It Was Great," *Toronto Star*, September 16, 1976.

17. Bill Libby, "At Peace Between the Pipes," *Goal Magazine*, vol. 4, issue 7, 1977.

18. Ibid.

19. "What Has Red Wings but Won't Fly?," *Sports Illustrated*, December 4, 1978.

20. "Tending Goal for Fourth Team Vachon Starting Over After Failing as Moses," *Globe and Mail*, December 29, 1980.

21. Ibid.

22. Dave Stubbs, "Rogie Vachon Finally Gets Hall of Fame Call," NHL.com, November 9, 2016.

23. Dave Stubbs, "Vachon Enjoying Farm Living, Reflects on Trade to Kings 50 Years Later," NHL.com, November 4, 2021.

24. Ken Campbell, "Top 100 Goalies of All Time," *Hockey News*, December 31, 2018.

CHAPTER 3

The Character: Gerry Cheevers

1. Trent Frayne, "Hockey's Happy Scapegoat," *Maclean's*, February 1, 1951.
2. Tom Monahan, *Hockey Pictorial*, January 1967, 15.
3. Ben Olan, *Hockey Illustrated*, May 1972, 59.
4. Leo Monahan, *Hockey Illustrated* 1980–81, 56.
5. Larry Milson, "Cheevers a Two-Way Pro: No Horsing Around, at Rink or Racetrack," *Globe and Mail*, December 23, 1978.
6. Pete Axthelm, "You Gotta Have Sock," *Sports Illustrated*, December 11, 1967.
7. Norman MacLean, *Hockey World*, March 1969.
8. Olan, 59.
9. Lance Hornby, "50 Years Later: Pat Quinn's Hit on Bobby Orr Set Stage for Leafs-Bruins Rivalry," *Toronto Sun*, April 2, 2019.
10. Gary Ronberg, "Grand Jean a Mighty Man Is He," *Sports Illustrated*, May 5, 1969.
11. Dan Proudfoot, "Suffolk Wagers Balm to Gerry Cheevers," *Globe and Mail*, April 8, 1970.
12. Larry Felser, "Goalie Cheevers a Hit With Race Track Fans," *Sporting News*, August 15, 1970.
13. "Gerry Cheevers," *Hockey Illustrated*, February 1971, 22.
14. Gerry Cheevers, *Goaltender* (Toronto: McClelland & Stewart, 1971), 188.
15. Ibid., 201.
16. Ben Olan, "Cheevers and Johnston, Hellzapoppin'," *Hockey Illustrated*, May 1972.
17. Mark Mulvoy, "Violence Is the Goal," *Sports Illustrated*, May 9, 1972.
18. Dan Proudfoot, "Cheevers Fears Garden Missiles as Cup Final Moves to New York," *Globe and Mail*, May 4, 1972.
19. Mark Mulvoy, "An Iceman Too Hot to Handle," *Sports Illustrated*, May 22, 1972.
20. Dan Proudfoot, "Bobby Most Valuable: Cashman, Orr Score, Cheevers Unbeatable; Bruins Win Cup," *Globe and Mail*, May 12, 1972.
21. "Cheevers Signs With WHA Crusaders for $1 Million," *Globe and Mail*, July 28, 1972.
22. Milson, "Cheevers."
23. Jerry Kirshenbaum, "He Was a Two-Time Loser," *Sports Illustrated*, May 16, 1977.
24. Ibid.

25. Peter Gammons, "They Ruined the Bruins," *Sports Illustrated*, May 23, 1977.

26. Allen Abel, "There's No Justice for This Goaltender," *Globe and Mail*, May 17, 1978.

27. Kirshenbaum, "Loser."

28. "Say What?!?," *Hockey News*, December 23, 2009.

29. Associated Press, "Cheevers Accepts Bruins Coaching Job," July 8, 1980.

30. James Christie, "Mother Cheevers Busy Preparing for a Future Without Goaltending," *Globe and Mail*, July 12, 1980.

31. "Bruins' Gerry Cheevers Remembering 1970 Stanley Cup & Bobby Orr Magic," Dailymotion, 2020, www.dailymotion.com/video/x7tsx0g.

32. William Houston, "Five Ex-NHLers Enter Hall of Fame," *Globe and Mail*, September 13, 1985.

CHAPTER 4
The Working-Class Hero: Ed Giacomin

1. Tad Richard, *Great Goalies: Giacomin, Vachon, Parent, Esposito* (New York: Tempo, 1975), 16–17.

2. Joe Sexton, "A Permanent Home for No. 1," *New York Times*, March 14, 1989.

3. Richard, *Great Goalies*, 20.

4. Norman MacLean, "Go-go Giacomin Came Long Way," *Hockey World*, February 1969.

5. Louis Cauz, "Maple Leafs Gain 3–3 Tie, 3–1 Win Against N.Y. Rangers: Giacomin's Error Lets Keon Score Equalizing Goal," *Globe and Mail*, November 7, 1966.

6. MacLean, "Long Way."

7. Louis Cauz, "Cured of Wanderlust, Giacomin Plays Angles," *Globe and Mail*, February 7, 1967.

8. Norman MacLean, "'Go Go' Giacomin May Be Answer to Long Suffering Net Problem," *Hockey World*, November 1966.

9. Dick Beddoes, "By Dick Beddoes," *Globe and Mail*, June 5, 1970.

10. Stan Fischler, "Four Goalies in Tag Team Battle," *Toronto Star*, April 7, 1969.

11. Ben Olan, "Ed Giacomin: Revenge Could Be Sweet," *Sports Review*, 1969–70.

12. Mark Mulvoy, "It Takes Two to Win the Cup," *Sports Illustrated*, January 11, 1971.

13. Ibid.

14. Canadian Press, "NHL President Fines Leafs, Rangers $16,950 for Playoff Brawls," *Globe and Mail*, April 14, 1971.

15. Hugh Delano, "Fast Eddie," *National Hockey League Magazine*, 1974.

16. Ibid.

17. Hugh Delano, "Hazards of Being a Goalie," *New York Times*, May 2, 1976.
18. Gerald Eskenazi, "Giacomin Excels as Rangers Down Black Hawks, 4–1," *New York Times*, February 10, 1972.
19. Red Burnett, "Bruins Demolish a Hockey Myth," *Toronto Star*, May 12, 1972.
20. Rex MacLeod, "Rangers Eliminated Bruins in Five Games," *Globe and Mail*, April 11, 1973.
21. Dan Proudfoot, "Dennis Hull, No Longer No. 2, Leads Chicago's Bid for Cup," *Globe and Mail*, April 25, 1973.
22. Dick Irvin, *In the Crease* (Toronto: McClelland & Stewart, 1995), 80.
23. Norm MacLean, "Ed Giacomin: New Yorkers Poured Out Their Hearts," *Hockey Pictorial World*, 1977.
24. Irvin, *In the Crease*, 84.
25. "Eddie Giacomin Returns," *The 50 Greatest Moments at Madison Square Garden* (TV documentary series, 2006–07).
26. Norm MacLean, "Idol in Exile," *Hockey World*, January 1976.
27. Stan Fischler, "Top 100 Goalies: No. 30—Ed Giacomin," *Hockey News*, November 9, 2018.
28. MacLean, "New Yorkers."
29. Associated Press, "Giacomin a Bitter 'Outcast,'" *Toronto Star*, November 7, 1984.

CHAPTER 5
The Kid Brother: Tony Esposito

1. Jack Olsen, "Oh, Brother! A Pair to Watch," *Sports Illustrated*, March 29, 1971.
2. Alan Walker, "I Didn't Raise My Boy to Be a Hockey Player...," *Toronto Daily Star*, February 13, 1971.
3. Olsen, "Brother."
4. Ibid.
5. Brian Kelly, "Tony Esposito Was 'the Ultimate Competitor,'" *Sault Star*, August 11, 2021.
6. Dick Beddoes, "By Dick Beddoes," *Globe and Mail*, April 30, 1973.
7. Bob Verdi, "The Verdict: On Ice and Off, Tony Esposito Brought Excellence," *Blackhawks.com*, August 12, 2021.
8. Dave Stubbs, "Phil Esposito, Tony Esposito Share Stories, Laughs," *NHL.com*, March 5, 2017.
9. Gary Ronberg, "Montreal Less Two Goalies Is Still No. 1: In the Town Where You Dare Not Lose, the Canadiens Have Stayed on Top Despite Heavy Attrition," *Sports Illustrated*, January 6, 1969.
10. Dan Moulton, "Esposito Passed Credit on to Hawk Teammates After Winning Vezina," *Hockey News*, January 30, 1970.
11. Gary Ronberg, "Hunker Down and Fly Right: By Curbing Their Free-Ranging Stars and Signing Some Talented Rookies, the Chicago Black

Hawks Have Spiraled up Into the Heat of the NHL Race," *Sports Illustrated*, March 16, 1970.

12. Lance Hornby, "Remembering Goalie Great Tony Esposito," *Sault Star*, August 11, 2021.

13. Ronberg, "Hunker Down."

14. Olsen, "Brother."

15. Ibid.

16. Ibid.

17. Ben Olan, "It's No Fun Playing Goal," *Hockey Illustrated*, December 1970.

18. Gerald Eskenazi, "Hawks Win by 4–2, Oust Rangers," *New York Times*, May 3, 1971.

19. Olsen, "Brother."

20. Kelly, "Competitor."

21. "The West: Hawk Roost Chicago Is Teaching the Game to the New Kids on the Block, Who Would Probably Find It Fun If They Could Just Play It All by Themselves," *Sports Illustrated*, October 18, 1971.

22. Bill Libby, "Tony O Won't Be the One to Go," *Hockey News*, April 14, 1972.

23. Dave Zarum, "Tony Esposito," *Canadian Encyclopedia*, August 13, 2021.

24. Dick Beddoes, "Tony Esposito Spikes Red Guns," *Globe and Mail*, September 5, 1972.

25. "A Delirious Scene of Singing and Dancing," *Toronto Star*, September 29, 1972.

26. Lance Hornby, "Remembering Blackhawks Goalie Great Tony Esposito," *Toronto Sun*, August 10, 2021.

27. Dan Proudfoot, "Eagleson Sees No Aftereffects in NHL: Team Canada Players Would Go Another Round," *Globe and Mail*, April 28, 1973.

28. Dick Beddoes, "By Dick Beddoes," *Globe and Mail*, April 30, 1973.

29. Al Strachan, "A Big Switch for Tony O," *Globe and Mail*, August 26, 1981.

30. UPI, "Chicago Black Hawks Goalie Tony Esposito Found It Nearly…," April 19, 1984.

31. Canadian Press, "Four Named to Hockey Hall," *Ottawa Citizen*, June 14, 1988.

32. Verdi, "Excellence."

CHAPTER 6
The Stranger: Vladislav Tretiak

1. Vladislav Tretiak, "Cowards Do Not Play Hockey," *Hockey Magazine*, October 1977. Reprinted in Vladislav Tretiak, *The Hockey I Love* (Lawrence Hill & Company, 1977).

2. Ibid.

3. Ibid.

4. Ibid.

5. Jim Proudfoot, "Summit Series Game 5: Canadian Collapse in Moscow Makes Clear the Soviets Are 'the Better Team,'" *Toronto Star*, September 22, 1972.

6. Jay Greenberg, "The Goal Interview: Vladislav Tretiak," *Goal Magazine*, May/June 1983.

7. Tretiak, "Cowards."

8. Bob Neumeier, "Nobody Noticed the Hot Goaling," *Hockey World*, May 1975.

9. Doug Gilbert, "Fans in Orbit Over a Star Struck Vladislav," *Gazette*, January 2, 1976.

10. Reggie Leach, *The Riverton Rifle: My Story—Straight Shooting on Hockey and on Life* (Vancouver: Greystone Books, 2015), 95.

11. "Tretiak Was Sensational," *Lowell Sun*, January 12, 1976.

12. Walt Burrows, "Soviets Rip NHL Stars," *Courier-Post*, February 12, 1979.

13. Greenberg, "Goal Interview."

14. Ibid.

15. Red Fisher, "Pressure Too Much for Team Canada?," *Gazette*, September 14, 1981.

16. Karl S. Samuelson, "Vladislav Tretyak: A Fanatic in the Net," *Hockey Digest*, April 1984.

CHAPTER 7
The Shooting Star: Mike Palmateer

1. Kristina Rutherford, "With One Save, Palmateer Steals Show at Centennial Classic Alumni Game," *Sportsnet*, December 31, 2016.

2. Warren Gerard, "The Famous Confidence of Mike Palmateer," *Toronto Star*, March 19, 1978.

3. Scott Radley, "Small Goalie Delivered Big Memories," *Spectator*, January 19, 2019.

4. Gerard, "Famous."

5. Eaton Howitt, "Palmateer Won't Settle for Anything but an NHL Job," *Toronto Sun*, May 9, 1973.

6. Jeff Goodman, "Mike Palmateer Foils Late Rush by 67s, Marlboros Hang On to Salvage a 5–5 Tie," *Globe and Mail*, January 16, 1974.

7. Ryan Kennedy, "Top 100 Goalies: No. 90—Mike Palmateer," *Hockey News*, November 9, 2018.

8. Ibid.

9. Earl McRae, "The Power of Popcorn," *Toronto Star*, December 15, 1979.

10. Frank Orr, "Mike Palmateer Too Nervous to Be Tired," *Toronto Star*, October 29, 1976.

11. Jim Kernaghan, "Leafs Blank Hotshot Habs," *Toronto Star*, November 18, 1976.

12. Allen Abel, "What, No Bleeps in Mike Palmateer Broadcasting?," *Globe and Mail*, December 17, 1977.

13. Frank Orr, "Leaf Goalie Mike Palmateer Sidelined 10 Days With Eye Injury," *Toronto Star*, December 13, 1976.

14. Frank Orr, "Thomas Says He's Ready for the Flyers," *Toronto Star*, April 21, 1977.

15. Peter Gammons, "The Away Advantage," *Sports Illustrated*, April 25, 1977.

16. *Toronto Star*, March 19, 1978.

17. Gerard, "Famous."

18. Ibid.

19. Mark Mulvoy, "Battered Into Submission," *Sports Illustrated*, May 8, 1978.

20. Frank Orr, "Maple Leafs off to Montreal Thanks to Lanny McDonald," *Toronto Star*, April 30, 1978.

21. Frank Orr and Jim Kernaghan, "Islander Attitude Angered Leafs," *Toronto Star*, April 30, 1978.

22. McRae, "Power."

23. Ibid.

24. Hal Quinn, "The Falling Leaves," *Maclean's*, January 28, 1980.

25. Ibid.

26. Michael McAteer, "Girls Sad to See Mike Leave," *Toronto Star*, June 12, 1980.

27. Rutherford, "One Save."

28. Ibid.

CHAPTER 8
The Survivor: Grant Fuhr

1. Ralph Wiley, "The Puck Stops Here," *Sports Illustrated*, January 11, 1988.

2. Ibid.

3. Kevin Shea, "One on One With Grant Fuhr," Hockey Hall of Fame, May 11, 2007.

4. Jim Matheson, "1982 All-Star Game," *Edmonton Journal*, February 9, 1982.

5. Shea, "One on One."

6. Wiley, "Puck."

7. Jim Matheson, "And the Heroes Came Marching Home," *Edmonton Journal*, April 13, 1982.

8. Sam McManis, "Kings' Brass OKs 'O Canada,'" *Los Angeles Times*, January 26, 1983.

9. "For the Fans, the Thrill of Victory," *Edmonton Journal*, May 20, 1984.

10. Jim Matheson, "Fuhr Reason Oilers Are in Driver's Seat," *Edmonton Journal*, April 13, 1985.

11. Wiley, "Puck."

12. Armen Keteyian, "The Joyless End of a Joyride," *Sports Illustrated*, May 12, 1986.

13. Wiley, "Puck."

14. Jim Matheson, "Oilers Close Canuck Coffin," *Edmonton Journal*, April 13, 1986.

15. *Goal*, December 1988.

16. Canadian Press, "Fuhr the Difference in Oiler Win," May 12, 1987.

17. Norm Cowley, "Oilers Ran Red on Playoff Trail," *Edmonton Journal*, May 31, 1987.

18. Jim Matheson, "Oilers Rest in Cup Afterglow," *Edmonton Journal*, June 2, 1987.

19. Canadian Press, "Firemen Hose Down Oiler Fans," June 1, 1987.

20. Gary Loewen, "Bubbly Efforts by Fuhr," *Globe and Mail*, September 16, 1987.

21. Jim Matheson, "Thanks for the Memories—No. 7," *Edmonton Journal*, November 25, 1987.

22. Wiley, "Puck."

23. Cam Cole, "Oilers Simply NHL's Best," *Edmonton Journal*, May 27, 1988.

24. Jim Matheson, "Oilers Among Best Ever Says Sinden," *Edmonton Journal*, May 28, 1988.

25. Jeff Bradley, "Canadians Shed '99 Tears' After Loss of 'The Great One,'" Associated Press, August 11, 1988.

26. Jim Matheson, "Leaving Oilers Tough on Fuhr," *Edmonton Journal*, September 20, 1991.

27. Ibid.

28. Canadian Press, "Leafs Trade Fuhr for Andreychuk," February 3, 1993.

29. James Christie, "Fuhr Simply Stymies Bruins," *Globe and Mail*, April 23, 1993.

30. Associated Press, "Fuhr Accepts Club's Apology," June 1, 1993.

31. Eric Duhatschek, "NHL99: Grant Fuhr Teed It Up—Often—to Mentally Prepare for 4 Stanley Cup Runs," *The Athletic*, November 14, 2022.

32. Austin Murphy, "Old Faithful at Age 33, Goalie Turned Iron Man Grant Fuhr Has Saved His Career and the St. Louis Blues," *Sports Illustrated*, February 19, 1996.

33. Duhatschek, "NHL99."

34. Murphy, "Old Faithful."

35. Duhatschek, "NHL99."

36. Dave Luecking, "Fuhr 'Stones' Kypreos, Leafs," *St. Louis Post-Dispatch*, April 20, 1996.

37. Alan Adams, "Fuhr Retires After 19 Seasons as Goalie in NHL," *National Post*, September 7, 2000.

38. George Johnson, "Athletes Can Pay Dear Price for Clinging to Glory Days," *Calgary Herald*, September 7, 2000.

39. Jim Matheson, "Fuhr Granted Well-Deserved Kudos," *Edmonton Journal*, October 9, 2003.

40. Luke DeCock, "Net Asset: Fuhr Finally Getting Respect for His Work in Goal," *News and Observer*, November 9, 2003.

41. Duhatschek, "NHL99."

42. Ibid.

CHAPTER 9
The Crowd-Pleaser: Roberto Luongo

1. Thomas Drance, "Roberto Luongo Q&A: On Being Named to Hall of Fame Alongside the Sedins and More," *The Athletic*, June 27, 2022.

2. Nicholas J. Cotsonika, "Luongo's Competitiveness, Longevity Earned Him Place in Hall of Fame," *NHL.com*, November 10, 2022.

3. Canadian Press, "Roberto Luongo Joins Martin Brodeur After Arena Named in His Honour," *NHL.com*, August 22, 2009.

4. David Ebner, "The Yin and Yang of Roberto Luongo (or Why He Just Can't Seem to Get It Right All the Time)," *Globe and Mail*, April 7, 2012.

5. Ibid.

6. Ryan Kennedy, "Snapshots of Louie," *Hockey News Yearbook*, 2007–08.

7. Anthony McCarron, "Isles' Luongo Hoping to Stop Milbury's Shots," *Daily News*, January 14, 2000.

8. Canadian Press, "Horcoff's Line Called Upon to Stop Forsberg in Gold Medal Game," May 9, 2004.

9. Iain MacIntyre, "The Star Patient," *Vancouver Sun*, January 17, 2007.

10. Iain MacIntyre, "In Luongo, the Canucks Trust," *Vancouver Sun*, April 13, 2007.

11. Ibid.

12. Alex Prewitt, "When Nature Calls a Goalie," *Sports Illustrated*, February 9, 2016.

13. "Captain Luongo," *Globe and Mail*, October 2, 2008.

14. Gary Mason, "The Difference Maker," *Globe and Mail*, April 24, 2009.

15. "Gameover," *Province*, March 1, 2010.

16. Cotsonika, "Competitiveness."

17. Ben Kuzma, "Luongo Steps Up, Fulfils the Hopes," *Province*, April 26, 2010.

18. Cam Cole, "Burr-fect Time to Play the Legend Card," *Vancouver Sun,* April 27, 2011.

19. Cam Cole, "What Has Happened to Roberto Luongo?," *Calgary Herald,* June 9, 2011.

20. James Murphy, "Roberto Luongo Regrets Comments," ESPNBoston.com, August 17, 2011.

21. Ibid.

22. Cam Cole, "Canucks' Big Guns Went Silent as Bruins' Thomas Shut Door on Stanley Cup Dream," *Vancouver Sun,* June 16, 2011.

23. Eric Duhatschek, "Appreciating Luongo's Funniest Videos and 5 NHL Surprises So Far," *The Athletic,* November 11, 2022. Video is available on *The Athletic* website.

24. Ebner, "Yin and Yang."

25. Lynn Zinser, "Luongo on Luongo (on Twitter)," *New York Times,* February 18, 2013.

26. Matt Larkin, "Roberto Luongo Says Goodbye—but Strombone Lives On," *Hockey News,* July 11, 2019.

27. Erin Brown, "Five Games That Defined Roberto Luongo's Career in Florida," *The Athletic,* March 7, 2020.

28. Ibid.

29. Ben Kuzma, "Canucks Hockey Hall of Fame Induction Live: Glitzy Gala Cherry on Top for Sedins, Luongo," *Province,* November 15, 2022.

CHAPTER 10
Mister Congeniality: Marc-André Fleury

1. Jesse Granger, "Golden Knights Sign Marc-Andre Fleury to 3-Year, $21 Million Extension," *Las Vegas Sun,* July 13, 2018.

2. Jesse Granger, "Vegas Goalie Marc-Andre Fleury Is 'Just a Guy From a Small Town," *The Athletic,* August 2, 2020.

3. Ibid.

4. Stu Cowan, "A Special Bell Centre Celebration for Marc-André Fleury," *Montreal Gazette,* December 10, 2021.

5. Philip Croucher, "Marc-Andre Fleury's Nova Scotia Roots Still Showing," *Star Metro Halifax,* May 26, 2018.

6. Ibid.

7. Associated Press, "Fleury Makes 46 Saves, but Can't Save Pens," October 10, 2003.

8. Tim Wharnsby, "Look Back at 2004 WJC Final Between U.S., Canada," NHL.com, December 20, 2015.

9. Pittsburgh Penguins website.

10. "All in the Family: Fleury's Dad Takes Part in Penguins Camp," NHL.com, March 8, 2006.

11. "Penguins Goalies Benefiting From Meloche's Direction," NHL.com, March 13, 2007.

12. "Marc-Andre Fleury Back, but Penguins Undecided When He Will Play," NHL.com, February 28, 2008.

13. Dan Rosen, "Pens' Fleury Becoming a Big-Game Hunter," NHL.com, April 25, 2008.

14. "Game 5 Postgame Quotes: Malone, Fleury, Crosby, Therrien," NHL.com, May 18, 2008.

15. Bill Roose, "Game 1 Notebook, Rough Start for Fleury," NHL.com, May 24, 2008.

16. "Fleury's Misplay Becomes Red Wings' Winner," NHL.com, June 5, 2008.

17. "Penguins Win Stanley Cup," Aljazeera.net, June 13, 2009.

18. Jason Mackey, "Fleury's Many Admirers Include the Backups He's Kept Laughing Over the Years," Pittsburgh Post-Gazette, December 14, 2016.

19. Kevin Allen, "Reason to Smile Again," USA Today, December 30, 2010.

20. Kevin Allen, "Goalie Fleury's Role Looms as Offseason Focus for Pens," USA Today, June 7, 2013.

21. Allan Kreda, "Once Shaky in Post-Season, Fleury Continues Steady Play in Goal," New York Times, May 7, 2014.

22. Kevin McGran, "Goaltending Top of Mind in Pittsburgh and Beyond," Toronto Star, April 25, 2014.

23. Kevin Allen, "Marc-Andre Fleury the Linchpin Holding Penguins Together," USA Today, February 12, 2015.

24. Jenn Menendez, "Fleury Deserved Better for Strong Effort," Pittsburgh Post-Gazette, April 25, 2015.

25. Jason Mackey, "Fleury's Demeanor Helps Keep Penguins Loose, Him Playing His Best," Pittsburgh Tribune-Review, October 7, 2015.

26. Ibid.

27. Ron Cook, "Penguins Goalie Marc-Andre Fleury a Team Man, Family Man," Pittsburgh Post-Gazette, April 2, 2016.

28. Jenn Menendez and Sam Werner, "Penguins Goalie Fleury Plans to 'Stay Ready' in Backup Role," Pittsburgh Post-Gazette, May 3, 2016.

29. Jonathan Bombulie, "Unselfish Fleury Ponders What's Ahead for Himself, Penguins," Pittsburgh Tribune-Review, June 13, 2016.

30. Jason Mackey, "Murray Thrilled Fleury Still a Teammate; Penguins Beat Lightning, 5–2," Pittsburgh Post-Gazette, March 3, 2017.

31. Mackey, "Fleury's Many Admirers."

32. Ibid.

33. Bill West, "Fleury Amusing Penguins Amid Flurry of Shots," Pittsburgh Tribune-Review, April 20, 2017.

34. Jason Mackey, "Marc-Andre Fleury, 'a Special Human Being,' Surprises Matt Murray With Cup Gesture," *Pittsburgh Post-Gazette*, June 12, 2017.
35. Greg Wyshynski, "Marchessault: Penalty on Vegas Stole Game 7," ESPN.com, April 24, 2019.
36. Justin Emerson, "Fleury's Stunning Save Caps Golden Knights' Win Over Maple Leafs," *Las Vegas Sun*, November 20, 2019.
37. Nicholas J. Cotsonika, "Fleury Embraces Change to Blackhawks After Trade From Golden Knights," NHL.com, September 16, 2021.
38. Joe Smith, "Behind the Marc-Andre Fleury-Jordan Binnington Fight That Almost Happened," *The Athletic*, March 16, 2023.

CHAPTER 11
The Class Act: Henrik Lundqvist

1. Dave Caldwell, "Dilapidated Distinction for the Rangers' Best," *New York Times*, January 17, 2012.
2. Allan Kreda, "Lundqvist Welcomes a Rangers Rebuild," *New York Times*, June 23, 2018.
3. Ben Shpigel, "Lundqvist, Longtime Rangers Goalie and Icon, Retires," *New York Times*, August 21, 2021.
4. Ben Shpigel, "Focused on the Cup," *New York Times*, April 8, 2012.
5. Lee Jenkins, "Sweden's Lundqvist Still Playing to the Crowd," *New York Times*, February 26, 2006.
6. Associated Press, "Rangers' Lundqvist Has Career Night Against Twin, Stars," December 15, 2006.
7. Greg Logan, "NHL: Ice Girls Flap Done," *Newsday*, April 6, 2007.
8. Lynn Zinser, "Lundqvist Is on a List He Never Expected," *New York Times*, April 22, 2008.
9. Michael Farber, "A Tale of Three Goalies," *Sports Illustrated*, January 14, 2008.
10. Arthur Staple, "Untold Stories of Henrik Lundqvist From His 7 Rangers Backups: 'Beneath the Suit, the Hair, the Look, There's an Assassin,'" *The Athletic*, January 27, 2022.
11. Matthew Sebra and Jian DeLeon, "The 25 Most Stylish Men of 2013," GQ, December 16, 2013.
12. Jeff Z. Klein, "Few Signs of Olympic Warmth but Lots of Fire at Garden," *New York Times*, March 5, 2010.
13. Steve Zipay, "Lundqvist the Difference in Game 7," *Newsday*, April 27, 2012.
14. Brian Cazeneuve, "The King of New York," *Sports Illustrated*, April 16, 2012.

15. E.J. Samson, "Milan Fashion Week MVP: Henrik Lundqvist's Hair," GQ, June 23, 2013.
16. Staple, "Untold."
17. Barbara Barker, "Lundqvist Reflects on Rangers' Run," *Newsday*, June 16, 2014.
18. Eric Duhatschek, "'It's 48 Hours of Craziness'; Two Days, Dozens of Outfit Changes, Countless Interviews, 32 Athletes Just Trying to Keep Up Welcome to the Player Media Tour," *Globe and Mail*, September 13, 2014.
19. Dave Caldwell, "He's a Key to the Rangers' Past. Is He a Part of Their Future?," *New York Times*, August 17, 2020.
20. Staple, "Untold."
21. Jamie Lisanti, "Henrik Lundqvist Brings His Classic Style—and a Bit of European Flair—to the NHL," *Sports Illustrated*, July 13, 2017.

CHAPTER 12
The Stoic: Carey Price

1. Sean Gordon, "Cool, Calm, Carey," *Globe and Mail*, December 27, 2008.
2. Matt Cudzinowski, "Tory: Drafting Price 'an Obvious Decision,'" NHL.com, August 16, 2018.
3. Eric Engels, "The Unclear Choice," *Sportsnet.ca*.
4. Ibid.
5. Bill Beacon, "Price's Confidence Grows in Montreal Crease," Canadian Press, March 13, 2008.
6. Steve Milton, "Carey Price's Meteoric Rise Has Made Believers in Montreal," *Hamilton Spectator*, April 8, 2008.
7. Roy MacGregor, "The Puck Stops Here," *Globe and Mail*, April 26, 2008.
8. Michael Farber, "Party Interrupted," *Sports Illustrated*, March 9, 2009.
9. Gordon, "Cool."
10. Roy MacGregor, "Price's New Life," *Globe and Mail*, April 15, 2009.
11. Damien Cox, "Canadiens Make the Toughest Choice, Trade Halak," *Toronto Star*, June 17, 2010.
12. Pat Hickey, "Price Tells Fans to 'Chill Out,'" *Gazette*, September 24, 2010.
13. Dave Stubbs, "So Carey Price Walks Into a Pet Food Store," *Montreal Gazette*, March 21, 2012.
14. Dave Stubbs, "Carey Price Waits for Answers," *Montreal Gazette*, September 16, 2012.
15. Michael Farber, "Keep Calm and Carey On," *Sports Illustrated*, May 4, 2015.
16. "Bergevin Says Price Still Maturing, Pledges Full Support to Struggling Goalie," Canadian Press, May 13, 2013.

17. Sean Gordon, "How the Canadiens' Price Became a Hart-Vezina Candidate," *Globe and Mail*, April 12, 2015.
18. *Habs Tonight*, March 16, 2021, wwwyoutube.com/watch?v=–m5TORVyEg.
19. Grant Robertson, "Carey Price Shines in Shutout Win Against U.S.," *Globe and Mail*, February 22, 2014.
20. Bill Beacon, "Canadiens Confident in Any Series With League-Leader Price in Goal," Canadian Press, April 28, 2015.
21. Farber, "Calm."
22. Mark Zwolinski, "Leafs Will Try to Lower Price, Canadiens in Montreal," *Toronto Star*, October 23, 2015.
23. Michael Farber, "Carey Price Just Can't Lose in Canada Jersey," *Sports Illustrated*, September 30, 2016.
24. Ibid.
25. Dave Stubbs, "Carey Price Joins Elite Company in Montreal," NHL.com, December 17, 2016.
26. Stu Cowan, "Habs Fan Starts GoFundMe Page to Pay for Billboard Tribute to Price," *Montreal Gazette*, June 16, 2018.
27. Stu Cowan, "Carey Price Touched as Fans Show Their Support in Biggest Way Possible," *Montreal Gazette*, October 2, 2018.
28. Pat Hickey, "In the Habs' Room: 'Let's Cut to the Chase; I Wasn't Very Good': Price," *Montreal Gazette*, November 9, 2018.
29. Jared Clinton, "Carey Price Looks Like He's Back and That's Bad News for the Eastern Conference," *Hockey News*, January 15, 2019.
30. Associated Press, "Price Becomes Winningest Goaltender in Canadiens History," March 13, 2019.
31. Stu Cowan, "Canadiens' Carey Price Helps Mend a Boy's Broken Heart," *Montreal Gazette*, March 2, 2019.
32. Matt Larkin, "Carey Price: The Man vs. the Myth," *Hockey News*, August 18, 2020.
33. Ibid.
34. Stu Cowan, "Canadiens Game Day: Calmness and Confidence Are Keys for Carey Price," *Montreal Gazette*, August 16, 2020.
35. Ken Campbell, "Carey Price Isn't the Habs' Only Problem, but He's Their Biggest One," *Hockey News*, February 26, 2021.
36. Rosie DiManno, "Carey Price: The Man, the Myth and the Mystery the Maple Leafs Will Have to Solve," *Toronto Star*, May 5, 2021.
37. Ibid.
38. Canadian Press, "'He Never Forgot Us': Price's Hometown Rallies Behind Canadiens Goalie," July 1, 2021.
39. Canadian Press, "Habs Goalie Carey Price Says 'Substance Use' Led Him to NHL's Assistance Program," November 9, 2021.

40. Canadian Press, "Canadiens Goalie Carey Price Hopes to Play This Season Despite Setbacks," January 30, 2022.
41. Pat Hickey, "Carey Price Looking for Answers as He Ponders His Future," *Montreal Gazette*, April 30, 2022.

GLOSSARY

|||||||||||||||||||||||||||||

LEAGUES

Ontario Hockey Association (OHA)

American Hockey League (AHL)

Eastern Professional Hockey League (EPHL)

Central Professional Hockey League (CPHL)

Ontario Minor Hockey Association (OMHA)

Eastern Hockey League (EHL)

Northern Ontario Junior Hockey League (NOJHL)

Western Hockey League (WHL)

Quebec Major Junior Hockey League (QMJHL)

TROPHIES

All are NHL *Awards unless otherwise indicated*

ART ROSS TROPHY—top point scorer

CALDER MEMORIAL TROPHY—best rookie as selected by members of the Professional Hockey Writers Association

CONN SMYTHE TROPHY—most valuable player in the postseason as selected by members of the Professional Hockey Writers Association

HAP HOLMES MEMORIAL AWARD—goaltender(s) who have played at least 25 games for the AHL team allowing the fewest goals
Before 1972, it went to the goalie with the lowest goals-against average who appeared in at least half his team's games.

HART MEMORIAL TROPHY—most valuable player as selected by members of the Professional Hockey Writers Association

JAMES NORRIS MEMORIAL TROPHY—best defenseman as selected by members of the Professional Hockey Writers Association

KING CLANCY MEMORIAL TROPHY—player who best demonstrates leadership and humanitarian contribution as selected by members of the Professional Hockey Writers Association and the NHL Broadcasters Association

TED LINDSAY AWARD—most outstanding player as selected by the NHL Players' Association

VEZINA TROPHY—best goalie as selected by NHL general managers
From 1946 to 1981, it went to the goaltender(s) who appeared in at least 25 games for the team allowing the fewest goals.

WILLIAM M. JENNINGS TROPHY—the goaltender(s) who appeared in at least 25 games for the team allowing the fewest goals

ACKNOWLEDGMENTS

||||||||||||||||||||||||||||||

IF I named every person who played a part in producing *Behind the Mask*, this section would be longer than the NHL *Official Guide & Record Book*. I owe a debt of gratitude to dozens of people. I will name some of them here:

Tom Sandford helped me with research on a handful of goalies and fact-checked many statistics. Paul Patskou provided me with dozens of old hockey publications and contact information for former players and coaches, while Alex Braverman connected me to Vladislav Tretiak. He also helped with that interview by translating my questions into Russian, then translating the former goalie's answers into English.

Todd Denault took time away from researching his fifth book to read my manuscript and share his thoughts as a hockey writer, historian and fan. He also provided research material and free psychological counseling over Buffalo chicken wraps—and he did so despite his misgivings about my lack of devotion to his beloved Montreal Canadiens. Keep blowin' smoke, Todd!

The team at Greystone was top-notch, from founding publisher and CEO Rob Sanders to editorial director Jennifer Croll and creative director Jess Sullivan. Two editors, Brian Lynch and Derek Fairbridge, were incredibly thorough and saved me from certain embarrassment.

Hilary McMahon at Westwood Creative Artists was supportive through the entire process just as she has been for more than a decade. I couldn't have a better cutman in my corner.

I'm thankful to the many current and former NHL players and coaches as well as other hockey insiders who took the time to talk to me. Finally, I tip my hat to the goalies featured in this book. I spoke to many of them and enjoyed every conversation—including the one with Marc-André Fleury, who had to repeat every sentence twice because the cell phone reception was so poor. All these men's accomplishments on and off the ice are truly inspirational.

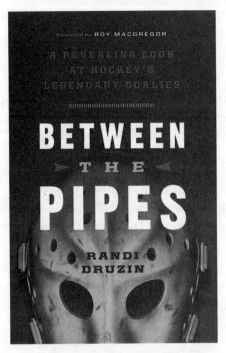

Between the Pipes:
A Revealing Look at Hockey's Legendary Goalies
By Randi Druzin
Foreword by Roy MacGregor
ISBN 978-177100-014-7

"Druzin details each net-minder's origin and career, and
in so doing reveals the changing face of professional hockey
in the last half century... Those unfamiliar with these grand figures
will find this an engrossing read." ***PUBLISHERS WEEKLY***

"This is a storyteller's book, and as such it is also a reader's book.
You don't have to be a goaltender to enjoy it; you just have to be a reader
who loves words, loves sports and appreciates the sorts of insights that
will never be found in 140 characters or less." **ROY MACGREGOR**

SOME GOALIES ARE great while others are intriguing. But only a handful
are both. In *Between the Pipes*—the companion to *Behind the Mask*—Randi
Druzin profiles a dozen of these legendary netminders, homing in on the
personality trait that makes each one unique.

GOALIES PROFILED INCLUDE: TERRY SAWCHUK •
GLENN HALL • JACQUES PLANTE • GUMP WORSLEY • JOHNNY BOWER •
BERNIE PARENT • KEN DRYDEN • RON HEXTALL • PATRICK ROY •
ED BELFOUR • DOMINIK HASEK • MARTIN BRODEUR

RANDI DRUZIN is an author and journalist based in Toronto. She has worked at several major media outlets including the *National Post* and the Canadian Broadcasting Corporation, and has written for dozens of publications, from the *New York Times* and *Time* magazine to the *Globe and Mail* and the *Toronto Star*. She's a lifelong Toronto Maple Leafs fan, and has the psychological scars to prove it. She has written the bestselling *Between the Pipes* and two other books.